Copyright © 2023 by Glen Pavlovich, All rights reserved.

No portion of this book may be reproduced in any form without written permission from the publisher or author, except as permitted by U.S. copyright law.

This publication is designed to provide accurate and authoritative information in regard to the subject matter covered. It is sold with the understanding that neither the author nor the publisher is engaged in rendering legal, investment, accounting or other professional services. While the publisher and author have used their best efforts in preparing this book, they make no representations or warranties with respect to the accuracy or completeness of the contents of this book and specifically disclaim any implied warranties of merchantability or fitness for a particular purpose. No warranty may be created or extended by sales representatives or written sales materials. The advice and strategies contained herein may not be suitable for your situation. You should consult with a professional when appropriate. Neither the publisher nor the author shall be liable for any loss of profit or any other commercial damages, including but not limited to special, incidental, consequential, personal, or other damages.

ISBN: 979-8-9889217-3-8 (Paperback)
ISBN: 979-8-9889217-4-5 (Hardcover)
ISBN: 979-8-9889217-2-1 (Ebook)
ISBN: 979-8-9889217-5-2 (Audio Book)

Library of Congress Control Number: 2023917886

www.closerclasses.com
www.glenpavlovich.com

Contents

Foreword	V
Title Page	VII
1. The Making of the Master Salesman	1
2. Beyond Transactions	13

The Triad Of Belief

3. The "Triad of Belief" and the "Triune God"	17
4. Belief in Your Industry	19
5. Belief in Your Product or Service	23
6. Belief in Yourself	29
7. Transferring Your Belief to the Customer	35

The IDEAS Sales System

8. The Foundations of the IDEAS Sales System	41
9. INTRODUCING	55
Your Master List	67
Powerbase	73

Sold Customers	83
Unsold Customers	113
Orphans	141
Customers of Your Competitors	151
10. DISCOVERING	185
11. EVALUATION	227
12. ADAPTING	267
13. SERVING	285
14. Navigating Ethical Crossroads	303
15. Embracing the IDEAS Sales System	319
The Timeless Sales Model	
More about Service	
16. Embracing Change	332
Afterword	335
About the Author	339

Foreword

Sales is often perceived as a profession driven by numbers, targets, and personal gain. But what if we were to look at sales through a different lens? What if we were to see it as a calling to serve others, guided by principles that transcend time and culture?

"The Master Salesman: Jesus and the Art of Service" invites you to embark on a journey that explores the profound connection between the teachings of Jesus of Nazareth and the world of sales. This book is not just for sales professionals; it's for anyone seeking to understand the transformative power of service in all aspects of life.

The author, a seasoned sales coach and trainer, presents the IDEAS Sales System, a unique framework that aligns with the principles Jesus lived by. Through this system, you will discover how to approach sales with empathy, integrity, and a genuine desire to help others.

But this book goes beyond mere techniques and strategies. It delves into the heart of what it means to live a life of service, drawing parallels between Jesus' teachings and modern sales practices. It challenges conventional thinking and encourages you to see sales not just as a job but as a mission to enrich the lives of others.

Whether you are a seasoned sales professional, a business leader, or simply someone interested in personal growth, "The Master

Salesman" offers insights that can transform your approach to sales and life itself. It's a call to action, a call to serve, and a call to embrace a higher purpose.

Join us on this enlightening journey, and discover the Master Salesman within you.

> **"Do nothing out of selfish ambition or vain conceit. Rather, in humility value others above yourselves, not looking to your own interests but each of you to the interests of the others."**
>
> (Philippians 2:3-4 (NIV)

THE MASTER SALESMAN

JESUS AND THE ART OF SERVICE

GLEN PAVLOVICH

INDUSTRY IGNITORS PUBLISHING

INDUSTRY IGNITORS PUBLISHING

Chapter One

The Making of the Master Salesman

Jesus' Early Life and Society

When you think of sales, images of sleek suits, polished shoes, and smooth presentations might come to mind. You may envision handshakes, negotiations, and the exhilaration of closing a deal. But sales is about more than just these surface elements. At its core, sales is a journey of belief.

Being in sales is akin to embarking on an adventure, filled with highs and lows. While some might perceive it as merely showcasing a product and persuading someone to buy, those who have walked the path of sales know it's a more intricate dance. Salespeople meet new faces, travel far and wide, and sometimes even cross international borders, all in pursuit of that next agreement. But it's not just about the physical miles covered; it's about the emotional journey of transforming doubt into belief. Every trip, every late night, every presentation is a step leading to that magical moment when a customer's uncertainty turns into conviction.

At its essence, sales is about belief. It's about believing in the product or service you're offering, believing in your industry, and most importantly, believing in yourself and your ability to connect with others. This Triad Of Belief is the foundation of success in sales. Without it, the road can be arduous. But with belief, every rejection becomes a stepping stone to the next triumph.

Now, imagine a salesperson unlike any other. Someone who wasn't merely selling a product but offering a whole new way of thinking and living. He faced skepticism and doubt but never wavered in His conviction. His name? Jesus of Nazareth.

Comparing Jesus to a salesperson might seem unconventional, even startling. But in this book, we'll delve into stories from the Bible that reveal how Jesus was, in many ways, the ultimate salesperson. Using the IDEAS Sales System, from INTRODUCING to SERVING, we'll uncover a new perspective on sales.

So, come along on this journey with us. Let's explore the intersection of the world of sales with ancient wisdom and discover how belief is the key to every successful pitch. We'll see how the principles that guided Jesus' teachings can illuminate our understanding of sales today.

Sales is belief. Believe in your industry, your product, and yourself. Believe in the transformative power of service. Believe in the path laid out in the IDEAS Sales System. And most of all, believe in the possibility of aligning your professional life with values that transcend time and context.

Welcome to "The Master Salesman: Jesus and the Art of Service." Your journey begins here.

Israel Before the Advent of Jesus: A Tapestry of Faith, Politics, and Society

The historical context into which Jesus was born was marked by a fragile balance of hope and despair. The Israelites had endured a harsh history filled with oppression, invasion, and exile. Their collective experience was a complex blend of triumphs, like the exodus from Egypt, and tragedies, such as the invasions that dismantled their unity.

In Deuteronomy 6:21-23, this dramatic journey is recounted: "We were slaves of Pharaoh in Egypt, but the Lord brought us out of Egypt with a mighty hand. Before our eyes, the Lord sent signs and wonders—great and terrible—on Egypt and Pharaoh and his whole household. But he brought us out from there to bring us in and give us the land he promised on oath to our ancestors."

Amidst turmoil, the Israelites were nourished by the voices of prophets like Isaiah, Jeremiah, and Micah, who foretold a coming Messiah, an anointed leader sent by God. Jeremiah 23:5-6 proclaims a hopeful future: "The days are coming," declares the Lord, "when I will raise up for David a righteous Branch, a King who will reign wisely and do what is just and right in the land. In his days Judah will be saved and Israel will live in safety. This is the name by which he will be called: The Lord Our Righteous Savior."

This promise, however, was not without complexities. The Israelites interpreted these prophecies in diverse ways. Some expected a political liberator who would free them from Roman rule, like the Maccabees had over the Greeks. Others hoped for a spiritual savior to redefine their bond with God, as reflected in Psalms 89:20-21: "I have found David my servant; with my sacred oil I have anointed him. My hand will sustain him; surely my arm will strengthen him."

Enter Jesus, a figure who began teaching and performing miracles, casting a new vision that challenged expectations. Rather than assembling an army against the Romans, Jesus spoke of love, forgiveness, and a heavenly kingdom. Mark 1:15 captures his profound message: "The time has come. The kingdom of God has come near. Repent and believe the good news!"

In this complex setting, Jesus found himself in a salesperson's role, having to convince a skeptical and divided audience of his divine mission. The Messiah that the Israelites had awaited for centuries was before them, but his teachings were unexpected and transcendent, promising eternal life and a deep spiritual connection with God. The Israelites were prospective buyers in the grandest sale of all time, and Jesus, through his teachings, was offering them the most valuable product imaginable: salvation and eternal life.

Through his words and actions, Jesus adapted the presentation of his message to his audience, resonating with their needs and yearnings yet challenging their preconceptions. His sales pitch wasn't about earthly conquest but spiritual fulfillment, a theme that would redefine the Israelites' understanding of salvation. Here, the IDEAS Sales System is manifest, as Jesus Introduced his message, Discovered the needs of the people, Evaluated their expectations, Adapted his Presentation to those needs, and aimed to Serve them with love, forgiveness, and eternal hope.

Political Structures: The Roman Influence and Jewish Identity

During Jesus' era, the Israelites were struggling under the heavy hand of Rome, a political colossus that had absorbed Israel as a mere fragment in its vast empire. For the Israelites, centuries of struggle had been devoted to preserving their autonomy and religious heritage against successive empires, including the Babylonians, Persians, Greeks, and now the Romans. Each dominion had inflicted its unique political structures and cultural ideologies on the Israelites.

The Roman Empire's complex governance was characterized by its multifaceted bureaucracy and formidable military strength. Although the Pax Romana, or "Roman Peace," marked this epoch, it was a peace maintained by the relentless crushing of dissent and revolts. Rome's sprawling road systems, vital for trade, doubled as swift passages for their legions to quash insurrections. Roman laws and taxation, while establishing order, also spawned resentment among those burdened by heavy fiscal demands.

In this turbulent landscape was King Herod the Great, ruling Judea from 37 BCE to 4 BCE. His alignment with Rome, despite being a practicing Jew, made him a polarizing figure. His grand building projects, although aspiring for a lasting legacy, were financed through oppressive taxation and forced labor, further straining his subjects.

Herod's rule was additionally tainted by brutal paranoia. His ruthless elimination of perceived threats, even within his family, demonstrated a reign governed by fear. The Massacre of the Innocents, recounted in the Gospel of Matthew, epitomizes the extent of his desperate terror.

Amidst this political turbulence, various Jewish factions arose, each with differing visions for Israel's future. This multifaceted socio-political atmosphere provided the context for Jesus to commence his ministry.

Parallel to this political turmoil, daily life in Israel was defined by religious traditions, agrarian rhythms, and social roles. Homes were built to accommodate the needs of farming communities. Agriculture dictated the tempo of existence, intertwining with religious festivals like Passover and Pentecost.

Despite the hardships of life, which limited life expectancy and presented various health challenges, faith and family remained central. The Sabbath allowed a universal pause, emphasizing the sacredness of worship and family bonds.

Fashion was utilitarian and modest, with fabric choices even governed by religious edicts, such as those found in Deuteronomy 22:11. The economy, shaped by Roman occupation, used Roman and regional currencies, and bartering remained widespread.

A Society of Classes: Priests, Peasants, and Procurators

In the intricate social fabric preceding Jesus' ministry, Israel was marked by a mosaic of varied classes, each with distinct roles and challenges. The priests, spiritual linchpins, served as the bridge between the people and God. Their lives were rhythmically punctuated by rituals, teachings, and community involvement, and their revered roles required dedication to spiritual excellence.

In stark contrast to the priests, peasants made up the majority of Israelites, leading lives anchored in the soil. Their existence was intertwined with agricultural cycles, labor, and family, finding comfort in the rhythm of the land and spiritual nourishment through faith. Above these foundational classes were the Roman-appointed rulers, Herodian dynasty, and local nobility. Their lives, rich with Hellenistic influences, were a blend of administrative tasks and leisurely indulgences. Despite their comfort, they faced the daily challenges of maintaining power, political negotiation, and territory management.

Into this diverse landscape emerged Jesus, recognizing and addressing the unique needs, values, and struggles of each class. To the priests, He presented a higher understanding of the Law, challenging ritualistic practices and calling for a deeper spiritual connection. To the peasants, He offered words of hope, healing, and love, recognizing their daily hardships and providing a message of redemption. To the elite, He engaged in questions of morality, justice, and leadership, confronting their political and intellectual concerns.

Through His teaching, healing, and dialogue with figures across the social spectrum, Jesus tailored His message to resonate with every layer of society. Whether speaking in synagogues, dining with commoners, or grappling with rulers, He found ways to bridge social divides and present a unified vision of the Kingdom of Heaven. In a world segmented by classes and overshadowed by the Roman Empire's might and Herod's ambiguous rule, Jesus offered a profound alternative: a spiritual Kingdom that transcended earthly limitations. His approach was not about worldly freedom alone but about eternal salvation. He navigated the complex landscape of ancient Israel with a message that spoke to every heart, transcending barriers of class, culture, and creed. It was a timeless call that still resonates today, offering not merely a temporal solution but a pathway to everlasting life.

Israel Before Jesus - Politics, Homes, Class, and Affluence

The Israel into which Jesus was born was a land of contrasts, marked by political turbulence, economic disparities, and a rich tapestry of social classes. Understanding this historical context is essential to grasp the revolutionary nature of Jesus' teachings and their timeless relevance to belief, authenticity, and the art of sales. Let's embark on a journey through ancient Israel, exploring the political landscape, housing, class system, economy, and the profound message that Jesus brought to this diverse society.

The Political Landscape: A Rollercoaster of Change The years leading up to Jesus' arrival were characterized by political upheavals.

From the united kingdom under David and Solomon to divisions, conquests, and exiles, Israel's history was a complex blend of triumphs and tragedies. The region's transition from Egyptian, Assyrian, and Babylonian rule to Greek and Roman dominion set the stage for Herod the Great, a king aligned with Rome yet deeply rooted in Jewish tradition.

Housing: A Reflection of Social Standing Housing in ancient Israel was a mirror of social status. The average Israelite lived in modest mud-brick or stone houses, while the wealthy resided in grand estates influenced by Greek and Roman architecture. These homes were not just shelters but symbols of identity and societal roles.

The Class System: A Mosaic of Roles and Challenges Within the intricate social fabric of Israelite society, distinct social classes emerged, from royalty, priests, and the upper class to commoners, laborers, and slaves. This class system was not merely a division of wealth but a complex hierarchy that influenced power, influence, and daily life.

A Farming Economy: The Heartbeat of Society Israel's economy was anchored in farming. Land ownership signified wealth and status, while those without land faced hardships. Trade existed, but most people lived modestly, focusing on daily needs. This agrarian lifestyle shaped the rhythm of existence, intertwining with religious festivals and family bonds.

Wealth and Poverty: A Land of Contrasts The stark economic disparities between the rich and the poor were more than mere financial differences. They were signs of a deeper divide that affected people's opportunities and life chances. This gap was woven into the fabric of daily life, setting the backdrop for Jesus' revolutionary teachings on money, fairness, and kindness.

Waiting for Hope: The Messiah's Promise Amid struggles and inequalities, the Israelites were waiting for something better. The prophets' promises of a Messiah resonated with their deepest hopes, creating a real and present expectation. This longing for a brighter future laid the groundwork for Jesus' ministry, offering a message of hope that transcended earthly limitations.

Jesus' Message: A Timeless Call Jesus' teachings challenged the social norms of his time, emphasizing faith and inner richness over worldly wealth and status. He spoke to everyone, rich or poor, offering a new way to think about life. His message was not confined to ancient Israel; it still speaks to us today, offering a deeper sense of purpose and happiness.

Conclusion: A Pathway to Everlasting Life In the midst of a society segmented by classes and overshadowed by political might, Jesus offered a profound alternative: a spiritual Kingdom that transcended earthly limitations. His approach was not about worldly freedom alone but about eternal salvation. He navigated the complex landscape of ancient Israel with a message that spoke to every heart, transcending barriers of class, culture, and creed. It was a timeless call that still resonates today, offering not merely a temporal solution but a pathway to everlasting life. His teachings, emphasizing belief, love, and social justice, resonate with universal themes that echo into our modern understanding of belief and sales, reflecting the transformative power of genuine conviction.

Walking in Jesus' Sandals: Life in 1st Century Israel

Nestled in the region of Galilee, Nazareth, where Jesus spent his childhood, was a modest farming village. Surrounded by fields and orchards, the community's simple homes housed hardworking people engaged in farming, carpentry, and various crafts. This unassuming lifestyle likely influenced Jesus' teachings and provided a backdrop for his humble upbringing.

The family of Jesus lived a straightforward, working-class life. Joseph, Jesus' earthly father, was a carpenter, a trade typically passed down from father to son. Jesus probably spent many years learning this skilled craft, absorbing lessons in patience, precision, and humility. Their Jewish faith was central, shaping their daily lives through Sabbath observance, dietary laws, and community connections.

Jewish education during Jesus' time centered on the Torah and Jewish law. Boys began studying under local rabbis at a young age, memorizing scriptures and engaging in religious debates. Jesus' wisdom, evident at age 12 in the Temple, suggests he excelled in his studies, preparing him for his future role as a teacher and leader.

The years between Jesus' childhood and the onset of his public ministry around age 30 are often referred to as the "silent years." This period can be seen as one of spiritual and practical preparation. Jesus likely experienced profound spiritual growth during these formative years. The manual labor of carpentry, coupled with family and faith, may have shaped his character, fostering empathy, patience, and an understanding of human suffering. Growing up in Nazareth, Jesus gained insights into the lives of everyday people. He would have understood their struggles and joys, and the contrasting world of the wealthy. This understanding would later influence his teachings and approach to ministry.

A glimpse into a typical day for young Jesus reveals a life filled with work, learning, spiritual growth, and community engagement. His days began with traditional Jewish prayers, followed by carpentry work with Joseph, simple lunches, and ended with sunset reflections and evening prayers.

Raised by devout parents, Jesus' early years were steeped in faith. Regular synagogue visits, Jewish holiday celebrations, and commitment to Torah teachings shaped his spiritual life. His earthly life was marked by simplicity, from basic clothing to plain meals.

Despite being the Son of God, his lifestyle was unadorned, reflecting his humble origins.

In Nazareth's close-knit community, Jesus interacted with various people, from farmers to possibly Roman soldiers. These interactions formed his understanding of society, influencing his later ministry.

Jesus' early life in Nazareth paints a picture of a young man maturing in a modest environment. His days were filled with work, learning, spiritual growth, and societal engagement. The skills and wisdom he gained during these formative years played a vital role in shaping his ministry and message. His humble upbringing and compassionate outlook continue to resonate, providing insight into the life and teachings of someone whose impact is still felt around the world.

> **"For we walk by faith, not by sight."**
> 2 Corinthians 5:7 (NKJV)

CHAPTER TWO

BEYOND TRANSACTIONS

THE SPIRITUAL ESSENCE OF SALES

Sales is not merely a transaction; it's a profound connection between the seller and the buyer, grounded in trust, understanding, and belief. This concept transcends the boundaries of commerce and finds resonance in spiritual history. At the core of Jesus' teachings and the Gospel is the transformative power of belief.

As we embark on this exploration, we will uncover three fundamental beliefs that form the bedrock of successful sales. These beliefs mirror the essence of Jesus' life and teachings. Let's first examine these principles within the context of contemporary sales:

Belief in the Industry: Every industry is a manifestation of human ingenuity, fulfilling desires, needs, and aspirations. Whether it's the technological advancements that revolutionize our lives or healthcare innovations that enhance well-being, every industry serves a noble purpose. To excel in sales, you must not only understand but also passionately believe in this overarching mission. Investigate your industry's evolution, its challenges, and its future potential. A robust belief in these facets fortifies your determination and enables you to convey this vision to prospective clients.

Belief in Your Product, Service, or Company: Your conviction in the specific product, service, or company you represent can be your most potent tool. Embrace its story, recognize its uniqueness, and comprehend the genuine problems it addresses. This belief is not about unthinking loyalty but about informed trust in what you're promoting. When you are convinced of its value, your authenticity resonates with others, attracting them to what you offer.

Belief in Yourself: The path of sales is strewn with obstacles. Rejection, rivalry, and demanding targets can be daunting. However, every triumph in sales springs from an unshakable belief in oneself. Envisioning yourself as competent and tenacious is vital. The annals of history are filled with tales of individuals who transcended doubts through unwavering self-belief.

As we traverse this enlightening path, the parallels between these three pillars of sales and Jesus' teachings will become evident. Jesus embodies these principles, shedding light not only on spiritual truths but also on a world of sales fueled by conviction. Join us in bridging these seemingly disparate realms, uncovering profound connections between the art of selling and the sharing of the Gospel.

> **"Whatever you do, work at it with all your heart, as working for the Lord, not for human masters."**
> Colossians 3:23 (NIV)

THE TRIAD OF BELIEF

THE CORNERSTONE OF CONVICTION: BELIEF

INDUSTRY IGNITORS PUBLISHING

Chapter Three

The "Triad of Belief" and the "Triune God"

Understanding the Difference in Belief and Divinity

At first glance, the terms "Triad of Belief" and "Triune God" might appear to share a connection. Both encompass the number three and imply a unified relationship among their components. However, despite their structural resemblance and phonetic similarity, they represent entirely different concepts.

Recognizing the Sacred: Intent and Reverence

Before we delve into the deeper meanings of belief and conviction, it's essential to pause for reflection. While the "Triad of Belief" in sales and the "Triune God" in Christianity share the commonality of the number three, we must emphasize their profound distinctions and understand the rationale behind their comparison.

A Coincidental Similarity, Not an Equation

The framework I created for achieving success in sales is founded on three principles: belief in the industry, product, and oneself.

The resemblance between this triad and the Triune God was not intentional but emerged as an intriguing parallel. I did not seek to equate the divine Trinity—a fundamental doctrine in Christian theology—with the three beliefs essential to sales.

Respecting the Profound

The Triune God—the Father, Son, and Holy Spirit—is a profound mystery and a central Christian tenet. It transcends human comprehension and embodies the magnificence of God's essence. In contrast, the "Triad of Belief" in sales is a pragmatic guide for achieving success. While it offers valuable insights into the field of sales, it remains a concept firmly rooted in the earthly realm of commerce.

For Understanding, Not Disparagement

In drawing this comparison, my primary concern is maintaining the Triune God's sanctity and honor. It's crucial to clarify that this analogy is not about diminishing or commodifying the divine. Instead, it's an exploration of the multifaceted nature of belief, utilizing familiar concepts to investigate new perspectives.

As we delve further into the "Triad of Belief" and its implications for success in sales, let's proceed with a clear understanding of the purpose guiding this discourse. I trust that readers will derive insights from both the spiritual and the practical realms, recognizing the consideration and respect that inform this work.

> **"For God is not a God of confusion but of peace."**
> 1 Corinthians 14:33 (ESV)

CHAPTER FOUR

BELIEF IN YOUR INDUSTRY

EMBRACING YOUR INDUSTRY WITH CONVICTION

"AND JESUS WENT THROUGHOUT all the cities and villages, teaching in their synagogues and proclaiming the gospel of the kingdom and healing every disease and every affliction." - (ESV, Matthew 9:35)

In sales, a genuine belief in one's industry consistently emerges as a unifying force, serving as the bedrock of influential and successful salesmanship. This belief goes beyond mere endorsement of a particular product or service; it embodies an unwavering faith in the broader context of the market and its potential for growth and transformation.

The Impact of Authentic Commitment

In the world of fashion, think of a salesperson who endorses a brand of eco-friendly clothing, yet is frequently spotted wearing fast fashion brands known for unsustainable practices. The disparity between their personal choices and their professional endorsements can lead potential customers to question the authenticity of their commitment to sustainable fashion.

Similarly, in the automotive industry, a salesperson who extols the virtues of electric vehicles but drives a gas-guzzling SUV to work every day might find it challenging to convince potential buyers of the benefits of going green. Such a discrepancy can make customers wonder if the salesperson truly believes in the environmental benefits of electric vehicles or is merely reciting a sales script.

In the health and wellness sector, a salesperson promoting organic, healthy foods but is often seen indulging in junk food during breaks can raise eyebrows. Their personal choices might make clients skeptical about the genuine health benefits of the products they're selling.

These examples underscore the importance of alignment between personal beliefs and professional commitments. Authenticity in one's actions and words is paramount in establishing trust and credibility with clients.

The Core of Genuine Salesmanship

These scenarios underscore that true salesmanship arises from a harmonious relationship between personal conviction and professional duty. When a salesperson's actions mirror their words, their message resonates more deeply with prospective customers.

This congruence between belief and conduct mirrors the teachings and actions of Jesus, as highlighted in the opening quote. It emphasizes the importance of living one's beliefs, not merely professing them.

Belief in one's industry is not a fleeting or superficial posture; it's a profound understanding and trust in the overarching vision and objectives. It acknowledges the potential contributions and the vital role that an industry may play in enriching the lives of individuals and the broader community.

Such belief fuels passion, enhances credibility, and ultimately, paves the way for success in sales. By adopting a comprehensive view of their industry, sales professionals can craft compelling narratives, cultivate significant relationships, and engender trust with their audience. In the end, a sincere belief in the industry transcends mere transactions, transforming them into meaningful connections and shared aspirations.

In the context of the Triad of Belief, this chapter illustrates the importance of belief in your industry. Just as Jesus of Nazareth was unwavering in his belief in his industry, the Kingdom of God, so too must salespeople be steadfast in their belief in their industry. This belief, coupled with the IDEAS Sales System, forms a comprehensive approach to sales that emphasizes not only the practical aspects but also the ethical and human connections that make sales a truly fulfilling profession.

Jesus and His Industry: The Kingdom of God

In drawing a connection to the spiritual world, Jesus' industry was without question the advancement of the Kingdom of God. His actions were more than isolated events; they were part of an intricate tapestry, woven with faith and conviction. Every healing, every miracle, and every word taught were affirmations of this kingdom. The relief and joy He brought were not the end but rather an invitation to a more profound, all-encompassing narrative.

Jesus unrelentingly highlighted the critical need for salvation, his product. Through His teachings, He exposed the intrinsic human failing and the urgent call to seek repentance and a relationship with the divine. The Kingdom of God, as depicted by Jesus, was not merely a vague, heavenly concept but a tangible reality. It was a place where love, peace, and justice were not ideals but daily experiences.

However, Jesus' advocacy for the Kingdom was not solely a distant promise. He stressed its immediate presence, encouraging people to tap into its grace and strength in their current lives. For Jesus, the Kingdom of God was both a grounding reality and an eternal aspiration.

The concept of belief in one's industry, whether in a commercial industry like sales or in Jesus' spiritual outreach, is a compelling blend of personal faith and public endorsement. It transcends mere words, manifesting in aligned actions, resonating stories, and an inspiring vision. Whether it's marketing a product, promoting a service, or inviting souls to connect with a divine purpose, belief stands firm as the unwavering foundation. It's a shared commitment to a cause, fueled by authenticity, that can transform ordinary encounters into meaningful connections and a shared pursuit of higher goals.

> **"Let your light shine before others, so that they may see your good works and give glory to your Father who is in heaven."**
>
> Matthew 5:16 (ESV)

CHAPTER FIVE

BELIEF IN YOUR PRODUCT OR SERVICE

AN AUTHENTIC COMMITMENT

"If you believed, really believed, what Moses said, you would believe me." - Jesus (The Message, John 5:45-47)

In the demanding field of sales, authenticity is paramount. Success often comes to those who are not only knowledgeable about their product's features but also deeply aligned with the fundamental value that their products or services provide. This heartfelt conviction serves as a compelling guide that not only attracts potential customers but also validates their choices and fosters lasting relationships.

The Power of Authentic Endorsement

A salesperson's enthusiasm carries more than emotional weight; it stands as evidence of their faith in what they are selling. This zeal can spark curiosity, encourage trust, and pave the way for enduring connections with customers.

Conversely, insincerity is easily detected. The disconnect between a personal trainer's advocacy for well-being and their personal lifestyle can erode credibility. Likewise, trust can falter when an insurance agent promotes a plan they don't themselves rely on, or a builder lives in a house apart from their own creation. These contradictions may lead to doubts about their confidence and integrity.

However, when genuine belief and the product align, remarkable connections can occur.

From Tragedy to Trust: A Transformative Journey

Life's unexpected twists and turns can lead to profound transformations, and I've had the privilege of witnessing one such transformation in someone I've come to know. A bartender, once shaken by personal loss, evolved into a passionate financial advisor. Her transition was not merely a shift in career but a profound embodiment of authentic belief in a service.

I met her after this transformation had occurred, and her story has been a source of inspiration for me. Once a keeper of a bustling bar, an unforeseen tragedy altered her path. The sudden loss of her spouse plunged her into a world of grief and uncertainty. During this tumultuous time, the support of her life insurance provider, Northwestern Mutual, emerged as more than just a financial transaction; it was a lifeline during her darkest hour.

Her experience with Northwestern Mutual transcended customer satisfaction; it became a revelation of the essential role that financial preparedness can play in life. She transformed from a policyholder into a believer, embracing a new mission to offer financial assurance to others facing unpredictable challenges.

In her newfound role, she found a connection with blue-collar workers, a group often neglected by the financial industry. Her story, rich with empathy and understanding, resonated with her clients, establishing a bond of trust that went beyond a mere sales pitch. Her engagement was more than a business interaction; it was a heartfelt desire to protect others from financial devastation.

Her journey illustrates the profound influence of a genuine connection to a product or service. It's about more than just promoting a product; it's about experiencing its benefits and understanding its vital role in life's complex fabric. Her metamorphosis from bartender to financial advisor wasn't just a change in profession; it was a vocation driven by real belief and deep personal insight.

In the final analysis, her story exemplifies the authenticity factor in sales, transcending mere knowledge of a product's features. It's about alignment with the underlying values and an ability to convey that belief convincingly to potential clients. This is not mere salesmanship; it is a connection that resonates on a human level, transforming ordinary transactions into meaningful engagements.

Her story is a living testament to the principles I often emphasize in my coaching, especially the Triad of Belief. Her belief in the industry, her company, and herself allowed her to transfer that belief to her clients. Her transformation from tragedy to trust is a powerful example of how genuine belief can shape not only a career but a life. Her journey continues to inspire me, and I believe it will inspire others who recognize the power of belief in their own lives and careers.

Jesus' Profound Offering: The Gift of Salvation

In the vast tapestry of human history, Jesus of Nazareth occupies a unique role, not as a traditional salesperson, but as the best salesperson ever, offering an intangible yet profound promise: salvation. His industry, far from a commercial endeavor, was divinely inspired, and His approach was rooted in unconditional love, unflinching faith, and unparalleled self-sacrifice.

Jesus' message was filled with sincerity and authenticity. He wasn't merely advocating abstract or theoretical ideas; He was living them.

His entire existence, characterized by His teachings and actions, manifested an intimate and unbreakable connection with God, the Father. This connection transcended mere belief; it became His identity. As the Son of God, and true God Himself, His belief in Himself was unwavering.

His life, marked by prayer, miracles, and sermons, was anchored in a profound conviction. When Jesus confronted the agonizing reality of the cross, it was His unwavering faith in God's plan that sustained Him. His belief was not an external strategy or a carefully crafted message; it was the very core of His being.

This authentic commitment did not merely resonate with His immediate followers. It created ripples that cascaded through time and space, touching the lives of billions. In the context of human interaction and influence, Jesus' genuine endorsement of salvation stands unmatched and continues to inspire and guide.

In the realm of sales, as I often emphasize in my coaching, the Triad of Belief is paramount: belief in your industry, belief in your company, product, or service, and belief in yourself. Then, transferring that belief to your prospect. Jesus' life and industry exemplify this Triad in the spiritual realm. His belief in the Kingdom of God as His industry, His product or service as salvation, and His unwavering belief in Himself form a perfect parallel to the principles that guide successful salesmanship.

Whether in the secular realm of sales or the spiritual journey embodied by Jesus, a consistent theme emerges: Genuine belief is not just a useful tool or asset. It forms the very heart of influence and leaves a lasting impact that transcends generations.

This profound lesson, drawn from the life and teachings of Jesus, invites reflection on the importance of authenticity and conviction, not only in our professional pursuits but also in our personal lives and spiritual explorations. It underscores the universal power of belief to inspire, guide, and transform, aligning perfectly with the principles I teach and practice in my coaching. It's a timeless example that continues to resonate, offering insights that are as relevant to the world of sales as they are to the spiritual journey of each individual.

> **"Whatever you do, work heartily, as for the Lord and not for men."**
>
> Colossians 3:23 (ESV)

Chapter Six

Belief in Yourself

The Journey from Self-Doubt to Unwavering Confidence

"I AM THE WAY and the truth and the life. No one comes to the Father except through me." - Jesus (ESV, John 14:6)

These powerful words from Jesus of Nazareth, the best salesperson ever, are more than mere declarations; they stand as a profound testament to self-belief. In His earthly life, Jesus did not only assert His divinity but fully embodied it, even in the face of relentless adversity.

Understanding Jesus' Steadfast Self-Belief

In the Gospel of John, statements like "I and the Father are one." (John 10:30) and, "If you have seen me, you have seen the Father." (John 14:9) highlight the unwavering confidence Jesus had in Himself and His divine mission. Yet it's essential to recognize that Jesus' life was not devoid of human complexities that are rife with challenges and doubts.

What distinguishes Jesus from others is not the absence of struggle but rather His unshakeable faith in His purpose and capabilities. He did not allow external circumstances to deter Him from His mission.

As the Son of God, and true God Himself, His belief in Himself was unwavering.

The dichotomy of the world's response, fluctuating between adoration and outright denial, provided a complex backdrop to Jesus' ministry. The scorn, ridicule, and doubt directed at Him would have the power to shake the resolve of most individuals. But not Jesus; His self-belief remained resolute and unbroken.

Application to Our Lives

The story of Jesus' unwavering self-confidence offers a powerful lesson for our personal and professional lives. It teaches us that genuine belief in ourselves and our mission is not about the absence of challenges, skepticism, or even failure. It is about our ability to remain steadfast and true to our convictions, regardless of external circumstances.

We, too, can cultivate this unwavering self-belief by aligning ourselves with a clear purpose, nurturing our inner conviction, and not allowing external criticism or failure to deter us from our path. By doing so, we can transform self-doubt into a wellspring of strength and motivation.

Jesus' unwavering self-belief provides a timeless example of how conviction in oneself can be a beacon of strength and a catalyst for transformative action. It invites us to reflect on our beliefs, values, and purpose, and to cultivate a sense of self-confidence that can endure even the most challenging trials.

In a world where self-doubt often prevails, the lesson drawn from Jesus' life serves as a guiding light, inspiring us to believe in ourselves and our ability to make a meaningful difference. It is a reminder that our belief in ourselves is not just a personal attribute; it's the cornerstone of our ability to influence, inspire, and lead.

The journey from self-doubt to unwavering confidence is a path that many of us walk in our lives. Jesus' example shows us that it's possible to cultivate a belief in ourselves that is as strong and unwavering as His belief in His divine mission. It's a lesson that resonates with the principles of belief that are vital in sales and life. By embracing these principles, we can find inspiration in Jesus' example and apply it to our own lives, whether in our personal growth or professional endeavors, without losing sight of the spiritual significance of His teachings.

Our Battle with Self-Doubt: A Road to Confidence

Much like the challenges Jesus faced, individuals often grapple with doubts regarding their capabilities, particularly in their professional lives. These doubts, if unchecked, can become significant roadblocks, preventing us from realizing our full potential. Whether it's avoiding risks out of fear of failure or sabotaging success with unrealistic expectations, self-doubt can be a debilitating factor.

For professionals, especially salespeople, self-confidence is more than a personal trait; it's a vital asset. A confident salesperson becomes assertive, persuasive, and resilient against rejection. But how can this confidence be cultivated? The answer lies in understanding the Triad Of Belief: belief in your industry, belief in your company, product, or service, and belief in yourself.

Building Confidence: A Journey from Knowledge to Authenticity

The bedrock of confidence lies in a profound understanding of one's product, industry, and, crucially, oneself. The journey begins by acquiring the knowledge necessary for the field. This aligns with the first part of the Triad Of Belief, where belief in your industry is foundational.

Developing a personalized sales process is essential for any salesperson who wishes to stand out from the crowd. Simply emulating the techniques of others can often lead to discomfort, insincerity, and self-doubt, ultimately hindering your success. By taking the time to understand your own strengths and weaknesses, and leveraging them to build an authentic and effective sales approach, you can set yourself apart and achieve greater success in your sales career.

Jesus' unconventional journey illustrates this point. Although referred to as the "Lord of lords and King of kings" (NIV, Revelation 17:14), He led a life that defied conventional kingship. His humble beginnings, association with marginalized individuals, and distinctive teaching methods made Him stand out. As the Son of God, and true God himself, His belief in Himself was unwavering.

Sales professionals can draw inspiration from this example. Carving out a unique selling style, one that resonates with their individuality, can distinguish them in a competitive market. This aligns with the second and third parts of the Triad Of Belief, where belief in your company, product or service, and belief in yourself are essential.

The battle with self-doubt is a common struggle, but it's one that can be overcome by following a path to confidence. By understanding the importance of belief in oneself, one's industry, and one's product, and by drawing inspiration from Jesus' example, sales professionals can cultivate the confidence needed to succeed. It's a journey that requires authenticity, individuality, and a deep connection to one's values and mission. By embracing these principles, we can transform self-doubt into a wellspring of strength and motivation, not only in our professional pursuits but also in our personal lives.

Crafting Confidence: An Attainable Skill

Unlike what many believe, confidence is not merely an inborn trait; it can be cultivated and refined. By dissecting the elements of selling into teachable, repeatable, and measurable components, salespeople can refine and perfect their approach. As they become more adept at these elements, their self-belief grows.

The journey from self-doubt to belief in oneself, as illustrated by Jesus' life, involves recognizing one's value, embracing individuality, and engaging in continuous learning and growth. For salespeople and professionals in other fields, this journey lays the foundation for success.

In a world where imposter syndrome and self-doubt often hinder progress, the path to self-assurance is not merely about personal growth. It's a vital aspect of professional development, equipping individuals with the tools and mindset needed to excel in their careers and contribute positively to their industries. This journey is a universal one, connecting the wisdom of spiritual teachings with the practicalities of modern professional life.

> "For we are his workmanship, created in Christ Jesus for good works, which God prepared beforehand, that we should walk in them."
>
> Ephesians 2:10 (ESV)

CHAPTER SEVEN

TRANSFERRING YOUR BELIEF TO THE CUSTOMER

THE FINAL STEP

IN THE NUANCED WORLD of sales, simply believing in what you're selling doesn't always suffice. The real triumph lies in your ability to transfer that belief to your potential customers. This process is an art that goes beyond mere conviction, requiring an understanding of human emotions and behaviors that must be honed and mastered.

The Power of Genuine Conviction

Your belief in your product, your industry, and yourself creates the foundation of your sales process. When your conviction is genuine, it radiates an energy that others can sense, sometimes without understanding why they feel drawn to what you're offering. This palpable aura can lead people to buy into what you're selling.

A simple yet powerful example can be found in a child's fervent desire to visit a theme park. While parents may initially hesitate due to financial considerations, the child's unbridled enthusiasm and conviction often win them over. This successful transference of belief from child to parent enables them to overcome their reservations and make the investment.

Jesus: Master of Belief Transference

The life and teachings of Jesus offer an enlightening example of this profound art of belief transference. Jesus did more than preach about the Kingdom of God, salvation, or His divinity; He embodied these principles with unwavering certainty, attracting followers to Him.

A striking transformation in the Bible is that of Saul, who became Paul. Once a vehement persecutor of Christians, Saul's direct encounter with the resurrected Christ altered him entirely. The conviction and belief he experienced were so profound that he promptly began to spread the word of Jesus as the Son of God (Acts 9:20).

Similarly, on the day of Pentecost, Peter, filled with the Holy Spirit, spoke fervently about Jesus and His resurrection. His words were infused with such belief and passion that around three thousand people were moved to join the faith that day (Acts 2:41).

The ability to transfer one's belief to others is an intricate skill that plays a vital role not only in sales but in various aspects of life. It's a blend of sincere conviction, empathy, and understanding of human psychology.

Whether in the realm of business, personal relationships, or spiritual pursuits, the art of belief transference can forge connections, inspire change, and lead to success. It's about moving beyond surface-level transactions and creating meaningful interactions, where beliefs are shared, understood, and embraced.

The lessons drawn from both everyday experiences and profound spiritual teachings highlight the universal application of this principle. By studying and applying these insights, individuals across different fields can enhance their ability to connect, influence, and achieve their goals.

My Mustardseed Of Faith

In my journey as a salesperson and sales trainer, I constantly strive to grow, improve, and create a system that would align with my Christian faith, introverted personality, strengths, and even weaknesses. The path was not always smooth; sometimes, my faith wavered, feeling as fragile and small as a mustard seed.

Jesus Himself spoke of faith in terms of a mustard seed, saying, "For truly, I say to you, if you have faith like a grain of mustard seed, you will say to this mountain, 'Move from here to there,' and it will move, and nothing will be impossible for you." (Matthew 17:20, ESV). This metaphor resonated with me, as there were moments when my faith felt insignificant and incapable of moving even the smallest obstacles in my path.

The mustard seed, though tiny, is known for its potential to grow into a large tree. It's a symbol of something small that can have a significant impact. This realization became a profound metaphor for my own faith journey. Though my faith sometimes felt as small as a mustard seed, I came to understand that it had the potential to grow and flourish.

In a surprising moment of clarity, I had an epiphany. I realized that my faith was not separate from my career but was, in fact, the driving force behind it. My desire to sell to help, to genuinely serve others, was a reflection of my Christian beliefs. This realization was like a seed taking root, and it began to grow, transforming not only my approach to sales but also my understanding of myself and my relationship with God.

This epiphany was a turning point, a moment when the wavering mustard seed of faith began to sprout into something more substantial. Just as a mustard seed grows into a large tree, my faith began to expand, reaching into every aspect of my life. It was a reminder that faith is not a static entity but a dynamic, growing relationship with God. It can be challenged, tested, and even falter, but it can also grow, strengthen, and transform us in ways we never thought possible.

The mustard seed analogy became more than just a metaphor; it became a living reality in my life. It was a symbol of hope, growth, and transformation, a reminder that even the smallest seed of faith can take root and grow into something beautiful and life-changing. It was a lesson in the power of faith, the potential for growth, and the profound connection between my beliefs.

> **"Let your light shine before others, so that they may see your good works and give glory to your Father who is in heaven."**
>
> Matthew 5:16 (ESV)

THE IDEAS SALES SYSTEM

IDEAS In Action

INDUSTRY IGNITORS PUBLISHING

CHAPTER EIGHT

THE FOUNDATIONS OF THE IDEAS SALES SYSTEM

A TIMELESS APPROACH

THE IDEAS SALES SYSTEM connects with a timeless method, resonant with how Jesus communicated His teachings about the Kingdom of God, Salvation, and His divine nature. In a similar vein, salespeople utilizing this system are trained to share not just facts but beliefs about their industry, the unique benefits of their products, and their personal commitment to what they're selling.

When executed with skill and authenticity, the IDEAS Sales System enables the transference of belief, transforming potential clients into committed believers, and believers into loyal customers. It's not a mere step-by-step process; it's an art that requires empathy, sincerity, and an in-depth understanding of human behavior.

The Components of the IDEAS Sales System

The IDEAS Sales System is an acronym that represents the five essential stages of the sales process:

INTRODUCING: Identifying a customer and making an intentional introduction.

DISCOVERING: Engaging in extreme active listening.

EVALUATING: Taking time to really understand what the customer is saying.

ADAPTING: Tailoring the presentation so it is most valuable to the person.

SERVING: Recognizing that selling is serving, and that we sell to help the customer.

These components form a cohesive framework that guides sales professionals in their interactions, aligning with the principles of belief and service.

To encapsulate, the act of transferring belief extends beyond a strategic technique. It's an art form and a skill that, when cultivated and refined, can generate unparalleled outcomes. This goes beyond personal or financial gains for the salesperson. When belief becomes contagious, it emanates a ripple effect that reaches further, positively impacting not just individuals but the community at large.

In the modern era, we often marvel at the ubiquity of certain products and brands. However, when we shift our perspective and look at the influence of Jesus Christ, the reach of modern products pales in comparison. Jesus' success in spreading His message was rooted in His unwavering belief in His industry, His product, and Himself.

Comparing the reach of Jesus' message to modern-day products offers a perspective shift. It challenges us to look beyond the surface-level metrics of success and recognize the profound impact that belief, conviction, and authenticity can have.

Whenever we interact with others, there is a delicate balance between trust and skepticism that must be maintained. This is especially true in the field of sales, where salespeople are often viewed in a negative light. However, what if we change our perspective and view sales as a way to genuinely help others? What if every sales transaction is driven by a sincere desire to serve? Imagine a world where salespeople are not just trying to make a quick buck, but are genuinely interested in helping their customers find the best product or service. This shift in mindset could revolutionize the way we view sales and the people who work in this field. It could lead to more positive interactions between customers and salespeople, and ultimately, a more satisfying buying experience for everyone involved. So let's strive to approach sales with empathy and a desire to truly help others, and see what positive changes we can bring about in our interactions with each other.

However, the narrative doesn't end with admiration for Jesus' profound impact. Instead, it serves as a prelude, a tantalizing glimpse into the masterclass that follows. How did Jesus, with humble beginnings, revolutionize the world? How did he craft his message, resonate with varied audiences, and navigate the challenges of his time?

In the vast tapestry of sales and persuasion, the story of a carpenter from Nazareth stands out as a beacon of unmatched prowess. As we delve deeper into his techniques and approach, prepare to be enlightened, inspired, and perhaps even transformed. Join us in discovering the secrets behind the world's most influential 'salesman' and how you too can learn from His timeless wisdom.

Selling to Serve: Redefining the Sales Paradigm

In every interaction, there exists a delicate dance between trust and skepticism. The world of sales is no exception. Traditional perspectives often paint salespeople in a somewhat unfavorable light: aggressive, dishonest, or simply trying to make a quick buck. But what if we shift this paradigm? What if the genuine intention to serve is at the heart of every sales transaction?

The Service Mindset and the IDEAS Sales System

If you begin with a service-first mindset, everything changes. The core of your interactions becomes centered on the customer's genuine needs. This authentic intention is felt, not just in words but in nuances, gestures, and the very energy that permeates the conversation. When a customer senses this shift, defenses drop and meaningful dialogues begin.

A sale isn't a one-time transaction. When you approach with genuine care, you're laying the foundation for a lasting relationship. A satisfied customer, treated with respect and understanding, will likely become a loyal advocate for your product or service, and, more importantly, for you as a trusted advisor.

At its core, the IDEAS Sales System champions this fresh approach. Our training emphasizes the importance of active listening, adapting to individual customer needs, and fostering a post-sale relationship that provides ongoing value. It's not just about making a sale; it's about making a difference. When you sell to serve, you're not just offering a product or service; you're offering a solution, a better future, a helping hand. This perspective transforms the sales process from a chore or challenge into a fulfilling, rewarding journey of genuine human connection.

Jesus: The Quintessential "Sell to Help" Proponent

In the vast panorama of human history, Jesus stands out as a figure whose mission was deeply rooted in service. His approach to spreading the message of salvation was not about selling a product but about offering a transformative solution to humanity's deepest needs. This perspective aligns perfectly with the "sell to help" philosophy, a concept that transcends mere transactions and focuses on genuinely helping others.

Jesus' ability to recognize the profound spiritual needs of those around Him set the stage for His mission. He saw beyond surface-level wants and tapped into the spiritual yearnings within the human soul. His invitation, "Come to me, all you who are weary and burdened, and I will give you rest" (Matthew 11:28 NIV), resonated because it addressed these deep-seated desires.

Jesus' offer of salvation was not presented as a commodity to be consumed. Instead, He framed it as the answer to humanity's age-old problem of sin and estrangement from God. His words, "For the Son of Man came to seek and to save the lost" (Luke 19:10 NIV), remind us that the core of sales should be centered on providing transformative solutions, not just promoting product features.

His approach to building connections was marked by authenticity, empathy, and compassion. His interactions were not transactional but relational, as evidenced by His command, "A new command I give you: Love one another. As I have loved you, so you must love one another" (John 13:34 NIV). This genuine engagement built unparalleled trust, a lesson that modern salespeople can embrace.

A New Sales Paradigm

Describing Jesus as the epitome of salesmanship is not an attempt to diminish His divine essence. Instead, it's a recognition of the unparalleled effectiveness of His method and message. His proclamation, "I am the way and the truth and the life. No one comes to the Father except through me" (John 14:6 NIV), encapsulates the magnetic power of His approach.

As we explore the principles laid out in this book, the goal is clear: to help modern salespeople channel the age-old wisdom exemplified by Jesus. By internalizing and manifesting these principles, they can redefine success in sales, ensuring that it's not just about profits but about purpose and profound impact. It's a path that aligns with the core values of the IDEAS Sales System, emphasizing the importance of serving and helping others. In doing so, salespeople can not only achieve success but also leave a lasting mark that resonates with the timeless teachings of Jesus.

Handling Rejection: A Timeless Challenge

Navigating the treacherous waters of rejection is a rite of passage in the realm of sales. No matter how experienced or skilled, every salesperson will encounter those who remain indifferent or even opposed to their message. Whether promoting a revolutionary product or advocating for a transformative idea, the inevitability of refusal stands tall. However, the true prowess of a salesperson is not judged by the number of successes alone but also by the ability to face and persevere through these refusals.

Even Jesus, the best salesperson ever, whose industry was the Kingdom of God and whose product was salvation, faced rejection. In His own hometown, He was dismissed as merely Joseph's son, a sentiment captured in His words: "A prophet is not without honor except in his own town, among his relatives and in his own home." (ESV, Mark 6:4). This rejection did not deter Him; His belief in Himself and His mission was unwavering.

The prophets of old faced similar challenges. Jeremiah, known as the 'weeping prophet,' passionately warned Judah of impending doom, only to be ignored. His frustration is palpable in his lament: "I've got something to say. Is anybody listening? I've a warning to post. Will anyone notice? It's hopeless! They've tuned out God. They don't want to hear from me." (MSG, Jeremiah 6:10-11a).

Isaiah's prophetic call met with indifference, a reality he expressed in his words: "Be ever hearing, but never understanding; be ever seeing, but never perceiving." (ESV, Isaiah 6:9). Zechariah's lament offers another perspective on people resisting divine guidance, "But they refused to pay attention. They turned a cold shoulder and stopped listening." (ESV, Zechariah 7:11).

These biblical accounts resonate with the experiences of contemporary salespeople. They teach that rejection is not necessarily a reflection of the product's value or the salesperson's skill. It often arises from factors beyond one's control. What matters is the ability to face rejection with resilience, learning from each interaction, and moving on with grace.

In the IDEAS Sales System, the process of INTRODUCING, DISCOVERING, EVALUATING, ADAPTING, and SERVING emphasizes the importance of understanding the customer and adapting the presentation. Rejection can be a valuable feedback mechanism in this process, helping to refine and perfect the approach.

The lessons drawn from these timeless biblical examples provide solace, perspective, and motivation. If even the most divine messages faced refusal, earthly offerings are bound to encounter similar challenges. The goal is to remain steadfast, absorb wisdom from each interaction, and stay deeply committed to the genuine mission of serving and helping others. In this way, rejection becomes not a stumbling block but a stepping stone on the path to success.

The Power of Persistence: Learning from Divine Tenacity

In the competitive and demanding world of sales, persistence is a crucial determining factor of success. This journey, often meandering through the maze of communication, negotiation, and adaptation, reinforces a singular truth: immediate success is rare. The enduring spirit of persistence isn't merely a contemporary virtue; it finds profound resonance in the annals of biblical history, emphasizing its timeless relevance.

Consider the intricate spiritual tapestry of the Israelites. Their narrative, spread across centuries, often veered away from God's intended path. Yet, God's response wasn't abandonment but persistent intervention. Time and again, He dispatched prophets, His divine "salespeople," to convey messages of hope, repentance, salvation, and a return to righteousness.

One of the foundational scriptures underpinning this divine drive is found in 2 Peter: "For no prophecy was ever produced by the will of man, but men spoke from God as they were carried along by the Holy Spirit." (2 Peter 1:21 NIV). It serves as a powerful reminder that these weren't just historical figures speaking; they were divinely chosen vessels communicating God's will.

The prophets' journey, however, was far from smooth. Jeremiah, for instance, was tasked with an incredibly difficult message, leading him to lament, "O Lord, you deceived me, and I was deceived; you overpowered me and prevailed. I am ridiculed all day long; everyone mocks me." (Jeremiah 20:7 NIV). Yet, in his pain and distress, he remained resolute, emphasizing God's message of repentance.

Isaiah, another prophet, delivered a poignant prophecy, asserting, "Though your sins are like scarlet, they shall be as white as snow; though they are red as crimson, they shall be like wool." (Isaiah 1:18 NIV). His words not only conveyed God's disapproval but also His promise of redemption to those who repent and return to Him.

Hosea's life became a living metaphor for God's relationship with the Israelites. When speaking of Israel's infidelity to God, Hosea was told: "Go, marry a promiscuous woman and have children with her, for like an adulterous wife this land is guilty of unfaithfulness to the

LORD." (Hosea 1:2 NIV). His personal life and the pain he endured symbolized the depth of God's love and the pain of betrayal.

These stories serve as a beacon of hope and inspiration for salespeople today. If these divinely-appointed prophets, armed with the weight of God's message, encountered resistance, skepticism, and rejection, then contemporary challenges in the sales realm can be viewed with perspective. Drawing strength from these tales can invigorate one's drive.

Conclusively, the world of sales, with its ever-shifting paradigms, retains certain immutable truths. Echoing through the corridors of time, scriptures like Proverbs 24:16 (NIV) remind us, "For though the righteous fall seven times, they rise again." This spirit, an amalgam of persistence, adaptability, and faith, can lead any endeavor, whether sacred or secular, to success.

Navigating Competition

The bustling world of commerce is a vivid reminder of the dynamic marketplace of human engagement. Sellers, much like ancient prophets and messengers, must find their voice among competing narratives. This challenge is as old as civilization itself, and it's a reality that modern salespeople face daily.

Solomon's wisdom in Ecclesiastes captures the essence of this reality: "What has been will be again, what has been done will be done again; there is nothing new under the sun." (Ecclesiastes 1:9 ESV). This timeless truth resonates with sales professionals who must differentiate their products in a saturated market.

In today's market, prospects are overwhelmed with choices. A modern salesperson may face rejection due to the sheer volume of competing voices. The Apostle Paul's words ring truer than ever: "Do you not know that in a race all the runners run, but only one gets the prize? Run in such a way as to get the prize." (1 Corinthians 9:24 ESV). This isn't just about winning; it's about striving to offer real value, something that sets you apart from the competition.

Understanding the competition is vital. A salesperson must discern their offerings' strengths and weaknesses to present their solution effectively. But it's not merely about understanding the market; it's about wielding knowledge wisely. Proverbs provides clarity: "A wise man is full of strength, and a man of knowledge enhances his might." (Proverbs 24:5 ESV). This wisdom can guide a salesperson in tailoring their approach, adapting to rejection, and finding new ways to connect with prospects.

However, sincerity alone doesn't guarantee success. Even with the most genuine offerings, rejection is a possibility. This lesson is evident in Jesus' ministry. He healed the sick and performed miracles, yet faced skepticism and resistance. Modern salespeople can learn from this, recognizing that rejection is not always a reflection of the product's value but may stem from misunderstandings or entrenched beliefs.

The presence of misleading voices further compounds the challenges. Christ's cautionary words highlight this danger: "For many will come in my name, saying, 'I am the Christ,' and they will lead many astray." (Matthew 24:5 ESV). Salespeople must be aware of competitors who misrepresent their offerings, and they must be prepared to articulate why their product or service is the genuine solution.

Amidst such a backdrop, the path forward is illuminated by authentic engagement and the genuine intent to serve. The Book of Proverbs offers guidance: "Let not steadfast love and faithfulness forsake you; bind them around your neck; write them on the tablet of your heart. So you will find favor and good success in the sight of God and man." (Proverbs 3:3-4 ESV). This calls for an approach that goes beyond mere selling, embracing the principle of "selling to help," which is at the core of the IDEAS Sales System.

The marketplace, whether ancient or modern, presents a challenging yet rewarding landscape. With competition at every turn, the timeless wisdom of the scriptures offers invaluable insights. By understanding rejection as a part of the process and responding with resilience, integrity, and genuine care, modern salespeople can not only navigate this terrain but truly make a lasting impact. The lessons drawn from the divine marketplace serve as a compass, guiding sales professionals towards success that transcends mere profits, reaching into the realm of purpose and profound impact.

The Sales System That Jesus Used

In the bustling marketplaces of ancient Israel, Jesus embarked on the mission of conveying a message to an unfamiliar audience. Despite the vast differences in context, the challenges Jesus faced were surprisingly similar to those encountered by salespeople today. He navigated the intricacies of getting recognized, ensuring his message was heard, and asserting that he held the right solutions.

The world Jesus entered was skeptical, filled with competing ideas and numerous teachers. He needed a strategy, not merely to be heard but to be believed and followed. While Jesus wasn't "selling" in the commercial sense, he was certainly promoting ideas, values, and a new way of life. And in doing so, he provided a blueprint for effective communication that remains relevant to sales professionals today.

This brings us to the IDEAS Sales System, a process that aligns with the teachings of Jesus and emphasizes the Triad Of Belief: belief in your industry, belief in your company, product, or service, and belief in yourself. Just as Jesus presented revolutionary ideas that transformed societies, every salesperson has the potential to introduce concepts that can alter the course of a business or an individual's life.

The IDEAS system is adaptable, allowing each salesperson to harness their unique strengths. At its core, IDEAS encourages an open mindset, much like the teachings of Jesus. As written in Matthew 7:7-8, "Ask, and it will be given to you; seek, and you will find; knock, and it will be opened to you." This scripture highlights the importance of persistence, curiosity, and resilience—values deeply embedded in the IDEAS framework.

The principles of the IDEAS Sales System resonate with the teachings of Jesus and the Triad Of Belief:

The principles of the IDEAS Sales System resonate with the teachings of Jesus and the Triad Of Belief:

Openness to New Experiences: Just as Jesus dined with tax collectors and spoke with Samaritans, salespeople should be open to unconventional approaches and unfamiliar terrains. This aligns with the principle of INTRODUCING in the IDEAS system, reflecting the words of Paul in 1 Corinthians 9:22, "I have become all things to all people."

Embracing Failure and Learning from Mistakes: Jesus himself was rejected many times, most notably in Nazareth (Luke 4:16-30). Yet, he moved forward, undeterred. In sales, rejections are inevitable, but they are also valuable learning experiences. This reflects the process of EVALUATING and ADAPTING in the IDEAS system, echoing Proverbs 24:16, "For though the righteous fall seven times, they rise again."

Relentless Endeavor and Persistence: Jesus' ministry was marked by continuous effort, culminating in the ultimate sacrifice. Similarly, genuine dedication can elevate a salesperson's career. This embodies the SERVING aspect of the IDEAS system, where selling is seen as a way to help the customer, aligning with Galatians 5:13, "Through love serve one another."

The IDEAS Sales System isn't just about techniques or tactics; it's a mindset. It pushes salespeople to adopt qualities—curiosity, resilience, adaptability—that were emblematic of Jesus' ministry. By internalizing these principles, salespeople can not only achieve professional success but also ensure their ideas genuinely benefit their clients. In this way, rejection becomes not a stumbling block but a stepping stone on the path to success, aligning with the genuine mission of serving and helping others, as expressed in Philippians 2:4, "Let each of you look not only to his own interests but also to the interests of others." It's a timeless call that still resonates today, offering not merely a temporal solution but a pathway to everlasting success in sales.

> **"And whatever you do, in word or deed, do everything in the name of the Lord Jesus, giving thanks to God the Father through him."**
>
> Colossians 3:17 (ESV)

CHAPTER NINE

INTRODUCING

THE PIVOTAL FIRST STEP

EVERY GREAT ENDEAVOR BEGINS with a single, intentional step. In the realm of sales, this foundational component is the art of INTRODUCING. The "I" in the IDEAS Sales System encapsulates this crucial step, which isn't merely about making acquaintances but initiating meaningful relationships. Like the opening act of a grand performance, INTRODUCING sets the tone, establishes momentum, and paves the way for everything that follows.

The act of INTRODUCING is more than a mere formality; it's a deliberate and thoughtful process of identifying a customer and making an intentional introduction. It's about recognizing potential needs and approaching with genuine interest and care. This is where the sales journey begins, and it's a step that requires both skill and sincerity.

In the life and teachings of Jesus, we find a profound example of this art of INTRODUCING. Jesus began His ministry by calling His disciples, individuals He identified and intentionally approached. He saw something in them, a potential for growth and a willingness to follow. His call to them was simple yet profound: "Follow me, and I will make you fishers of men." (Matthew 4:19, ESV). This was not a casual invitation but a life-changing proposition.

In the IDEAS Sales System, the act of INTRODUCING is similarly transformative. It's about identifying those who could benefit from your product or service and making a deliberate connection. It's about seeing the potential in others and approaching them with a genuine desire to help. This is not about manipulation or coercion; it's about building trust and laying the groundwork for a meaningful relationship.

Many salespeople often find themselves caught in the net of external limitations: a lack of leads, insufficient advertising by their company, challenging locations, or even intricate and convoluted websites. These challenges, albeit real, can be transcended. The IDEAS Sales System seeks to equip salespeople with the capability to generate their leads, independent of external dependencies. By curating a master list and ensuring a consistently full pipeline, a salesperson transforms into a self-sufficient entity, unshackled by external hindrances.

There is a lot to absorb in this section, but I assure you every suggestion, every example, is curated to equip you with the very best. The objective is clear: to transform salespeople from being mere transactional entities to forming genuine relationships, from fleeting interactions to lasting connections.

As you delve deeper into the art of INTRODUCING, remember that you're tracing the steps of a time-tested, universally effective strategy. You're following the path laid out by Jesus, the best salesperson ever, whose industry was the Kingdom of God, and whose product was Salvation. His belief in Himself was unwavering, and His method of INTRODUCING was both intentional and transformative. In embracing this approach, you're not only enhancing your sales skills but aligning yourself with a principle that has proven effective across time and cultures.

Stepping Out of Obscurity: The Art of Personal Connection

In the IDEAS Sales System, INTRODUCING is more than a mere handshake or a fleeting greeting. It's the art of personal connection, the moment you step out of obscurity and present not just your product or service, but yourself.

In today's crowded marketplace, products and services abound, each clamoring for attention. What sets you apart isn't just the quality or innovation of what you offer, but the authenticity and passion with which you present it. This is where the art of storytelling comes into play.

Imagine your product or service as a character in a grand narrative. It has a backstory, a purpose, and a mission. But who is the narrator? That's you. Your personal story, your convictions, your belief in what you offer – these are the threads that weave into a compelling narrative. It's not just about telling people what you have; it's about sharing why it matters, and why it matters to you.

This approach aligns beautifully with the principles of Jesus' approach to INTRODUCING. When Jesus spoke, he didn't just present facts or commandments; he told parables. He connected with people on a deeply personal level, using stories and metaphors that resonated with their lives and experiences. His introductions were never shallow or transactional; they were invitations to a deeper understanding and relationship.

As a salesperson, you have the opportunity to emulate this approach. Your introductions can be more than mere transactions;

they can be transformative experiences. By intertwining your personal narrative with your product's story, you create a connection that transcends mere commerce. You invite your prospects into a relationship, one built on trust, understanding, and shared values.

In essence, INTRODUCING is your opportunity to step out of the shadows and into the spotlight, not for self-aggrandizement, but to shine a light on something you genuinely believe in. It's about owning your narrative and using it to enrich the lives of those you serve.

As we delve deeper into this critical first step, we'll explore strategies and techniques that can help you master the art of personal connection, storytelling, and authentic engagement. The journey begins here, with you stepping out of obscurity and into a world of meaningful connections.

Becoming the Face of Your Product: A Personal Connection

In the previous section, we explored the importance of INTRODUCING as the first step in the IDEAS Sales System. It's about stepping forward, owning your narrative, and intertwining it with the value proposition of what you offer. But how does this concept translate into real-world success? Let's delve into some compelling examples that illustrate how personal connection can transform a product from a mere item on a shelf into a symbol of trust, reliability, and community.

Mike Lindel, known as the "My Pillow" guy, didn't just sell a pillow. He became its embodiment. His personal touch and relatability turned a simple pillow into an emblem of restful sleep for millions. It wasn't just about the pillow's innovation; it was Lindell's personal story and conviction that made it resonate with people.

Dave Thomas, the face of Wendy's, didn't position it as just another burger joint. He made it an experience, with him at its heart. His candid demeanor and earnest advertisements made Wendy's feel like an extension of Dave's own welcoming kitchen. His personal connection to the product made it stand out in a crowded marketplace.

Debbi Fields is another shining example. She wasn't just selling cookies; she was selling the warmth of her kitchen, the love in her baking, and the passion she had for her craft. Mrs. Fields Cookies became synonymous with fresh, delicious treats, and Debbi herself became the face of that promise.

Colonel Harland Sanders, the founder of Kentucky Fried Chicken, is an iconic figure in the fast-food world. His face, with its distinctive beard and glasses, is instantly recognizable. But more than that, Sanders represented his own recipe, his own commitment to quality, and his personal guarantee of finger-licking good chicken.

Victor Kiam made a name for himself when he said, "I liked the shaver so much, I bought the company." This wasn't just a catchy slogan for Remington shavers; it was Kiam's personal endorsement, his own story of belief in the product, and his commitment to its quality.

Orville Redenbacher didn't just sell popcorn; he was popcorn. His genuine enthusiasm for his product, combined with his distinctive appearance, made him a household name. When people saw Orville, they thought of high-quality, delicious popcorn.

These examples underscore the power of INTRODUCING in the IDEAS Sales System. It's not merely about presenting a product; it's about infusing it with your personality, your story, your conviction. It's about stepping out of obscurity and putting a face to the product. In the world of sales, a product, no matter how groundbreaking, often needs more than just features and benefits. It needs a human connection, a story, a spirit behind it. By intertwining your personal narrative with your product's story, you enrich the selling proposition. Your authenticity and conviction can resonate powerfully with potential clients, forging deeper bonds and trust.

In the world of sales, a product, no matter how groundbreaking, often needs more than just features and benefits. It needs a human connection, a story, a spirit behind it. By intertwining your personal narrative with your product's story, you enrich the selling proposition. Your authenticity and conviction can resonate powerfully with potential clients, forging deeper bonds and trust.

Lifting Out of Obscurity: The Jesus Way

In the annals of history, few figures have risen from obscurity to global influence quite like Jesus of Nazareth. Born in humble circumstances and growing up in a place often overlooked, Jesus' early life was marked by simplicity and ordinariness. His appearance was unremarkable, and his lineage, though prestigious as a descendant of King David, did not set him apart in society.

"For he grew up before him like a young plant, and like a root out of dry ground; he had no form or majesty that we should look at him, and no beauty that we should desire him." (Isaiah 53:2, ESV)

Skepticism surrounded Jesus, with doubts about his hometown, Nazareth, and dismissive remarks about his family's ordinary background:

"Isn't this the carpenter's son? Isn't his mother's name Mary, and aren't his brothers James, Joseph, Simon, and Judas? Aren't all his sisters with us? Where then did this man get all these things?" (Matthew 13:55-56, NIV)

"Nazareth! Can anything good come from there?" Nathanael asked. (John 1:46, NIV)

Yet, it was from this unassuming beginning that Jesus embarked on a transformative journey. His rise was not meteoric, nor was it marked by grand gestures or eloquent speeches. Instead, it was a gradual ascent, fueled by authenticity, consistency, and genuine connection with those around him.

Jesus' approach to lifting out of obscurity offers invaluable lessons for anyone looking to make an impact, particularly in the world of sales. He didn't just 'sell' a message; he lived it, breathed it, and personified it. His interactions were not transactional but transformative, turning ordinary encounters into life-changing experiences.

In the context of sales, this approach translates into building deep, meaningful connections with clients. It's about rising above the noise, not through flashy advertising or aggressive tactics, but through sincerity and understanding. It's about becoming not just a seller but a trusted partner, someone who doesn't just offer a product but provides value and meaning.

Jesus' rise from obscurity is a testament to the power of authenticity and connection. It's a reminder that true influence doesn't come from status or appearance but from the ability to resonate with others on a profound level.

Crafting Your Identity Through Purpose and Service

In the competitive landscape of the sales industry, standing out requires more than just clever marketing or a unique selling proposition. It demands a genuine intention to serve and a commitment to a purpose that goes beyond mere transactions. This is where crafting your identity through purpose and service becomes paramount.

Every professional has a story, a reason behind their chosen path. It's this narrative, imbued with authenticity and dedication, that resonates with potential customers. Whether it's a lawyer driven by justice or a personal trainer inspired by transformation, these stories are not mere backdrops; they are the essence of who you are and what you represent.

Consider the ministry of Jesus, who, despite being the Son of God, commenced His mission without earthly wealth or grandeur. His teachings, actions, and miracles stemmed from a deep-rooted love for humanity and an earnest intention to serve. His approach wasn't about impressing the masses but about meeting their needs, both physical and spiritual.

When faced with feeding a crowd of 5,000, Jesus didn't see mere followers; He saw souls yearning for nourishment. With only five loaves and two fish, the task seemed insurmountable. Yet, with genuine intent to serve and unwavering faith, Jesus not only fed everyone but had an abundance left over:

"But Jesus said, 'There is no need to dismiss them. You give them supper.'...They all ate their fill. They gathered twelve baskets of leftovers. About five thousand were fed." (MSG, Matthew 14, 16-21)

This miracle wasn't just an illustration of divine power but a testament to what's achievable with sincere intent. It's a lesson that transcends time and applies directly to the world of sales. When you approach your profession with a heart to serve, resources, even in the direst situations, appear.

Similarly, when confronted with the need to pay taxes, Jesus' unwavering faith and reliance on divine providence led Him to find the required coin inside a fish's mouth:

"...Go to the sea and cast a hook and take the first fish that comes up, and when you open its mouth you will find a shekel. Take that and give it to them for me and for yourself." (ESV, Matthew 17:27)

This example further emphasizes that genuine service, coupled with faith, can overcome even the most unconventional challenges.

In sales, this translates into a focus on genuine service rather than mere profit. Yes, financial stability is crucial, but it should be a byproduct of genuine service, not its driving force. When you align your sales approach with a sincere desire to help and improve the lives of your customers, you not only create a memorable brand but forge deeper connections that last.

Crafting your identity through purpose and service is about embracing a higher calling in your profession. It's about seeing beyond the product and recognizing the profound impact you can have on people's lives. By following the Jesus way, you can transform your sales journey from mere transactions to meaningful relationships, creating a legacy that resonates with authenticity, compassion, and genuine service.

Service as a Mission, Sales as a Ministry

In sales, it's easy to get caught up in numbers, targets, and transactions. But what if we were to approach sales not just as a job but as a mission, a ministry even? Drawing inspiration from Jesus' ministry, we can find a model that transcends the conventional understanding of sales. It was about service, compassion, and transformation. He approached His ministry with a genuine belief in His message and a desire to make a positive difference in people's lives. This wasn't a mere job for Him; it was His calling, His purpose.

Similarly, if you approach sales with the same level of devotion and sincerity, it becomes more than just a means to an end. It becomes a mission to serve, to improve lives, to offer solutions that genuinely help. When you believe in your product and see it as a tool to make a positive difference, you're not just selling; you're ministering to the needs of your customers.

This perspective transforms the entire sales experience. It's no longer about closing deals but about opening hearts. It's about establishing a unique identity that resonates with genuine intent and compassion. Just as Jesus was provided with resources in the most unexpected ways, you too will find abundance in every corner when your focus shifts from mere profit to purposeful service.

"Give, and it will be given to you. Good measure, pressed down, shaken together, running over, will be put into your lap. For with the measure you use it will be measured back to you." (Luke 6:38, ESV)

This scripture encapsulates the essence of approaching sales as a ministry. It's a reminder that when you give with sincerity, when you serve with authenticity, the rewards—both personal and financial—will follow.

Embracing sales as a mission and a ministry is about aligning your professional journey with a higher purpose. It's about seeing beyond the transaction and recognizing the profound impact you can have through genuine service. By following the Jesus model, you can elevate your sales experience from a mere job to a gratifying endeavor, one that not only enriches your life but the lives of those you serve.

Initiating the Connection: The Proactive Pursuit of Service

Prospecting, the relentless endeavor to find potential customers, is often seen as the lifeblood of the sales process. But it's more than just a hunt for numbers; it's a mission to identify those who can genuinely benefit from what you offer. This proactive pursuit is about bridging the gap between needs and solutions, and it echoes a principle found in the very heart of Jesus' ministry.

In today's interconnected world, prospecting has evolved beyond traditional methods like cold calls or door-to-door visits. Modern salespeople have a plethora of tools at their disposal, from global email campaigns to targeted social media marketing. Yet, amidst these technological advancements, the timeless value of personal connection remains undiminished.

But what truly sets prospecting apart is its proactive nature. It's not about waiting for customers to find you in a world brimming with options. It's about taking the initiative, seeking out those winds that will propel your ship forward. This active pursuit is not just a business strategy; it's a commitment to service.

Jesus' ministry exemplified this proactive approach. He didn't wait for people to come to Him; He went to them. His mission was clear and purpose-driven:

"For the Son of Man came to seek and to save the lost." (Luke 19:10, ESV)

This principle of active pursuit is also symbolized in the Old Testament:

"For thus says the Lord God: Behold, I, I myself will search for my sheep and will seek them out." (Ezekiel 34:11, ESV)

These scriptures resonate with the essence of prospecting. It's not about merely finding customers; it's about seeking those who can truly benefit from what you offer and serving them with genuine intent.

The methods of prospecting will vary, influenced by your product, your target audience, and your personal style. Whether you excel in direct communication or digital interactions, the key is to find what resonates with you and aligns with your audience.

As you embark on this journey of prospecting, remember that it's more than a sales tactic; it's a reflection of your mission to serve. It's about initiating connections that lead to relationships, trust, and growth. In the grand tapestry of sales, prospecting is not just about increasing numbers; it's about enriching lives.

In embracing this proactive pursuit, you align your sales journey with a higher purpose, one that resonates with the very principles Jesus exemplified. It's a path that transcends mere transactions and leads to meaningful connections, transforming sales from a mere job to a fulfilling mission.

> **"Do not neglect to do good and to share what you have, for such sacrifices are pleasing to God."**
> Hebrews 13:16 (ESV)

Your Master List

A Treasure Trove of Opportunities

Understanding your audience is akin to a fisherman knowing which bait to use for different fish. This wisdom leads to the creation of your **Master List,** a categorized list of potential clients, each requiring a unique approach. Drawing inspiration from Jesus' ministry, we can liken these categories to different groups he encountered, emphasizing the importance of personal connection and genuine service. The potential size and scope of your Master List indicates that meticulous record-keeping is not merely an administrative task; it's the heartbeat of your success. Your Master List, a living document that evolves with your journey, becomes one of your most invaluable assets. It's more than a list; it's a gold mine of opportunities, a treasure trove that captures your victories (sold customers), the prospects still on the horizon (unsold customers), those who have been left behind by previous representatives (orphans), and even the customers of your competitors.

Whether you're a seasoned professional or just starting, the importance of maintaining a comprehensive Master List cannot be overstated. Ideally, you will use a computerized system that makes information gathering and storage nearly effortless, However, it's not about the medium, whether high-tech Customer Relationship Management tools, traditional index cards, post-it notes, or business cards with meticulous notes on the back. What matters is the consistency, thoroughness, and dedication to this endeavor. Even if your method has its imperfections, remember, it's infinitely better than no method at all.

Every interaction, no matter how fleeting, is a potential future opportunity. From brief exchanges at networking events or trade shows to more significant engagements where you've offered product information, every contact matters. Capture the essence of these interactions, noting down their details and any specific touchpoints or preferences. Retain as much information as you were given, for this list, abundant with names, numbers, emails, and annotations, is likely the most valuable thing you will ever own.

Your Master List is not just a record; it's the embodiment of your effort, dedication, and potential growth in sales. It's a testament to your commitment to your industry, product, or service, and a reflection of your belief in yourself. Utilize it wisely, nurture it, and watch as it transforms from a mere list into a vibrant network of connections, opportunities, and successes. It's your roadmap, guiding you forward, connecting you with prospects, and helping you serve your customers with integrity and excellence.

Your Powerbase

Your immediate circle of friends, family, acquaintances, and colleagues. These are the people you know intimately, much like Jesus knew his disciples. They were his inner circle, and he spoke to them with depth and understanding. In your sales journey, this powerbase is where you can connect on a personal level, offering products or services that align with their needs and values.

Sold Customers

Those who have already experienced your product or service and are likely to return or refer others. Jesus had followers who had witnessed his miracles and teachings, and their faith was firm. When addressing such believers, he unveiled profound truths, much like how you might engage with satisfied customers, offering them deeper insights or additional value.

Unsold Customers

Potential clients who have shown interest but haven't committed. Jesus encountered individuals who were curious but hesitant, like the rich young ruler. Approaching such customers requires a blend of understanding, patience, and gentle persuasion, recognizing their interests and addressing their reservations with clarity and assurance.

Orphans

Customers who lack a direct point of contact due to changes in sales personnel. Jesus reached out to those who felt marginalized or estranged, like tax collectors or sinners. In your sales approach, these individuals need compassion and reassurance, making them feel valued and reconnected with the product or service.

Customers of Your Competitors

Those who have chosen a competitor's product but align with what you offer. Jesus engaged with many who followed other teachers or beliefs, not through confrontation but through dialogue.

Similarly, approaching these customers requires showcasing the unique benefits and values of your offerings, engaging them in meaningful conversation rather than aggressive persuasion.

Adapting Your Approach

It's clear that while the core message might remain consistent, the presentation method can, and should, vary based on the audience. Jesus, a master communicator, tailored his messages based on who he was speaking to. To the scholarly Pharisees, he often quoted scripture, while with common folk, he used parables rooted in everyday life.

Similarly, when you approach someone from your power base, your pitch might be more personal, rooted in shared experiences. With a sold customer, it's about deepening the relationship, perhaps introducing advanced products or after-sales services. Orphans would require reassurance, a demonstration that even though their initial contact is gone, they're still valued. And when approaching a competitor's customer, it's about showcasing what sets your offering apart, without demeaning the competition.

Crafting your "Master List" is more than a strategic exercise; it's a reflection of your understanding and empathy towards different segments of your audience. It's about recognizing their unique needs, interests, and reservations, and aligning your approach with genuine intent to serve.

In emulating the principles Jesus showcased in his interactions, you transform your sales process from mere transactions to meaningful connections. It's not just about selling a product; it's about offering value, building trust, and enriching lives. By knowing your audience and approaching them with sincerity and service, you not only enhance your sales journey but also create lasting relationships that resonate with the very essence of the IDEAS Sales System.

In the forthcoming sections, we'll delve deeper into each category, equipping you with strategies and insights to effectively engage with each group. Remember, in sales, as in life, understanding and empathy go a long way. It's not about pushing a product but about meeting a need, and to do that, one must first understand the person across the table.

> **"Let your speech always be gracious, seasoned with salt, so that you may know how you ought to answer each person."**
>
> Colossians 4:6 (ESV)

Powerbase

Building Trust and Creating Ardent Supporters

Your powerbase is your treasure trove of trust and familiarity. It's a collection of relationships that have been nurtured over time, filled with people who know you, trust you, and may even recognize your qualifications to talk about the product or service you're selling. These relationships are not just about immediate transactions; they are about networking, referrals, and word-of-mouth advertising from people who will almost assuredly answer your call, respond to your texts, and give "thumbs up" to your social media posts.

Identifying Your Powerbase

Your powerbase consists of those closest to you, the people you feel most comfortable with, and those you can always count on. They are the individuals you have the most in common with and enjoy spending time with. Reflect on the people who have had the most significant impact on your life and who you care about the most. These connections form the core of your powerbase, and while they may not directly need your product or service, they may know others who do.

Building Your Powerbase Prospecting List

Start by making a list of everyone you know, including friends, family, colleagues, and former classmates. Contact everyone on your list to share your excitement about what you're doing. Your belief in your industry, product, and yourself should fuel this excitement, allowing you to connect with them genuinely. Even if you don't see a direct connection between the people in your powerbase list and your best prospects, this activity is vital for networking and subsequent word-of-mouth advertising.

Keeping Your List Dynamic

Your powerbase is not a static entity; it evolves. Keep your list up-to-date by adding new people as you meet them and as acquaintances transition from one prospecting list to another. Regular follow-ups, even when not actively looking for opportunities, keep the connections alive and thriving.

The Jesus Way

The first people Jesus added to his powerbase prospecting list were his mother and father. When they found him in the temple, Jesus confirmed to them that He was the Son of God, qualified to talk about what God sent him to offer. His belief in himself and his mission was unwavering, as depicted in the scriptures:

"Everyone who heard him was amazed at his understanding and his answers. When his parents saw him, they were astonished. His mother said to him, 'Son, why have you treated us like this? Your father and I have been anxiously searching for you.' 'Why were you searching for me?' he asked. 'Didn't you know I had to be in my Father's house?'" (NIV, Luke 24: 47 - 49)

The Long-Term Value

Building a strong network takes time and effort, but it's worth it in the long run. Your powerbase is not just a sales tool; it's a reflection of your journey, your values, and your commitment to genuine service. By recognizing and leveraging these personal relationships, you create a network that resonates with trust, empathy, and mutual growth. It's about weaving a tapestry of genuine care and mutual growth, echoing the devotion and sincerity that characterized Jesus' ministry.

In the grand scheme of the IDEAS Sales System, your powerbase serves as a foundational pillar, setting the stage for relationships, trust, and growth. It's not just about increasing numbers but about enriching lives – both theirs and yours. By approaching your power base with the same authenticity and conviction as Jesus did, you lay the groundwork for a sales journey that transcends mere transactions and becomes a mission to serve.

Degrees of Separation – Connecting with Influence

In the fascinating world of cinema, there's a playful game known as "Six Degrees of Kevin Bacon." This game illustrates the idea that any two actors can be connected through a chain of common film appearances. It's a concept that transcends the boundaries of Hollywood and offers a profound insight into the interconnectedness of our world.

The game's underlying principle can be applied to sales, particularly when considering your powerbase. Think about the degrees of separation that stand between you and a significant influencer, such as the President of the United States. It might seem like an impossible distance, but it becomes a tangible and achievable path when broken down into a series of connections.

Your Path to Influence:

A scan of the Powerbase portion of your Master List should reveal at least one person who can connect you to an Alderman, City Councilman, or perhaps directly to your Mayer. From there, how many connections would you need to reach POTUS?

Your Mayor: A phone call to your Mayor's office can lead to an appointment. Once convinced of your message, your Mayor can introduce you to your State Representative.

Your State Representative: Easily reachable, especially with the Mayor's recommendation, your State Representative can introduce you to your Governor or Congressperson.

Your State Governor or Congressperson: With direct access to the President's inner office, your Governor or Congressperson can pave the way for your message to reach the President.

Your Meeting With The President: After just four telephone calls, your message could be heard by the leader of the free world.

This concept isn't limited to political figures. Whether your goal is to reach a leader of industry or the owner of a local chain of pizza parlors, your existing powerbase can shorten your path and pave the way for an introduction.

Leveraging Your Powerbase

The effectiveness of your Master List, and specifically, the Powerbase portion solely depends on your willingness to utilize it.

Compile Your List: Identify friends, family, colleagues, neighbors, or anyone close enough for an easy and comfortable conversation.

Share Your Enthusiasm: Contact them through emails, social media posts, letters, one-on-one visits, events, texts, or phone calls. Remember, these people are familiar with you and will be interested in what excites you.

Utilize Connections: Consider who in your powerbase has a direct line to someone who could benefit from your product or service. Your powerbase can help you climb to the top, no matter how high that top might be.

In the grand scheme of sales, the concept of degrees of separation emphasizes the untapped potential within your network. It's a reminder that the world is interconnected, and opportunities are often just a few connections away. By recognizing and leveraging these connections, you can transform your sales journey into a mission to serve, echoing the principles of the IDEAS Sales System and the teachings of Jesus. It's about building bridges, forging connections, and recognizing that even the most distant goals are within reach when approached with belief, intention, and genuine service.

Jesus' Powerbase: Building Trust and Aligning Missions Through Miracles and Affirmations

The concept of a powerbase is not merely a modern sales strategy; it finds its roots in the very ministry of Jesus Christ. His approach to building relationships was strategic, purpose-driven, and deeply rooted in trust and shared mission. Two pivotal moments in Jesus' ministry illustrate how he solidified his powerbase, aligning those closest to him with his divine purpose.

The first of these moments occurred at the Wedding in Cana. Though initially hesitant to perform a miracle in this setting, Jesus was encouraged by his mother to intervene when the wine ran out. The wedding, likely attended by friends or relatives of Jesus' family, provided a unique setting for his first public miracle. This miracle was not meant for widespread fame but served as a profound affirmation of his divine mission among those closest to him. By transforming water into wine, Jesus subtly revealed his divine nature to his inner circle, strengthening their belief in him and his mission.

Another significant connection within Jesus' powerbase was his relationship with John the Baptist, his cousin. John's miraculous birth, as described in Luke 1:8-25, already set the stage for a divine connection between the two. When Jesus approached John for baptism, John's proclamation, "Behold, the Lamb of God, who takes away the sin of the world! This is he of whom I said, 'After me comes a man who ranks before me, because he was before me.'" (John 1:29-30, ESV), was more than a familial endorsement. It was a public affirmation of Jesus' identity and mission, a powerful endorsement from within his powerbase.

These examples from Jesus' life offer profound insights for anyone seeking to leverage their powerbase in the realm of sales or any other endeavor. It's about recognizing the potential within those closest to you, those who already believe in you, trust you, and share your enthusiasm. By letting them know about your belief in your industry, product, or service, and your ability to help others, you can harness the power of your powerbase to spread your message, just as Jesus did.

In your journey, consider how you can emulate Jesus' approach. Utilize your connections, your family, friends, and closest allies, not just as a support system but as active participants in your vision. Build trust, align missions, and create a network of individuals who not only believe in what you're offering but also share in your purpose.

Your powerbase can be the cornerstone upon which your greater vision stands, propelling you toward success, fulfillment, and genuine impact. By aligning your mission with those in your powerbase, you're not merely selling; you're serving, connecting, and creating a legacy of transformation and positive change.

Your Powerbase May Challenge You: Navigating Skepticism and Building Belief

Those closest to us often find it hardest to see us transition into new roles, especially if those roles challenge the preconceived images they've held of us. Despite its foundation of trust and mutual respect, your powerbase might inadvertently resist supporting your new ventures or fail to see the growth and passion you've developed over time.

This hesitation within your powerbase may stem from various reasons. Perhaps they remember you as the person you once were and struggle to see the transformation you've undergone. They may have had negative experiences with you in the past or have witnessed you give up on things easily. Sometimes, it's a protective instinct, hoping to shield you from potential disappointment. These reservations are not necessarily a reflection of your worth but could be an attempt to protect you or a misunderstanding of your potential.

Overcoming skepticism from loved ones begins with open communication. It's essential to articulate your feelings regarding their reservations and genuinely understand the roots of their hesitations. By showing through your actions and determination that you're deeply committed to your new venture, you can slowly dismantle these doubts. However, it's crucial to remember that enduring such skepticism and maintaining resilience is a part of the journey. Just as you're growing and evolving, your powerbase too will need time to adapt and see the newfound passion and belief that drives you. But above all, it's your unwavering self-belief that will be the cornerstone of your endeavors.

This phenomenon isn't new; even the most revered figures faced skepticism from those closest to them. Jesus, during his ministry, often encountered doubt and disbelief, particularly from those who had known him since his youth. The familiar faces from his hometown questioned, "Isn't this the carpenter's son? Isn't his mother's name Mary, and aren't his brothers James, Joseph, Simon, and Judas? Aren't all his sisters with us?" (MSG, Matthew 13:55-56). Even more poignantly, his own brothers struggled with their belief in his mission: "For even his own brothers did not believe in him." (NIV, John 7:5). Yet, with time and witnessing his unwavering commitment, many in his immediate circle, including his brothers, became staunch advocates of his mission, evident when later scriptures highlight the unity and prayerful commitment of his family: "All these with one accord were devoting themselves to prayer, together with the women and Mary the mother of Jesus, and his brothers." (MSG, Acts 1:14).

Your journey, too, might experience these moments of familial skepticism. But as with Jesus, perseverance, conviction, and compassion can transform doubters into some of your staunchest supporters. It's about recognizing the potential within those closest to you, those who already believe in you, trust you, and share your enthusiasm. By letting them know about your belief in your industry, product, or service, and your ability to help others, you can harness the power of your powerbase to spread your message, just as Jesus did. The path may be fraught with challenges, but with determination, empathy, and unwavering belief in yourself, you can navigate the complexities and build a powerbase that not only supports you but actively participates in your vision.

> "A friend loves at all times, and a brother is born for adversity."
>
> Proverbs 17:17 (ESV)

Sold Customers

The Pinnacle of Your Master List

The term "sold customers" extends beyond a mere tally of past successes; it symbolizes established trust, mutual respect, and the value you've consistently delivered. These individuals, who have already demonstrated their belief in you, form the bedrock of your sales career and should occupy a prominent space on your master list. This list is not a static document but a dynamic and evolving tool, central to your sales strategy. This concept finds its roots even in the teachings of Jesus, who referred to himself as "The Way" and sought to reach the Jewish people, his previously sold customers, to guide them to salvation.

Sales isn't a one-off transaction; it's a relationship built over time. Your master list ensures you never lose touch with those who've placed faith in you. Satisfied customers can be your best advocates, introducing you to potential clients and amplifying your sales prospects. Regular interaction with your sold customers offers insights into your product's strengths and areas for improvement. When cataloging sold customers, it's essential to understand their buying patterns, preferences, and frequency, providing a clearer picture of their needs and potential upsell opportunities. Documenting every interaction, whether a simple email exchange or an in-depth product discussion, ensures every subsequent communication is informed and personalized. Any feedback they've provided or concerns they've raised should be meticulously noted, aiding in refining your approach and addressing potential issues proactively. Remembering a client's birthday or anniversary might seem trivial, but it's these small gestures that deepen relationships. If they've referred someone to you, note it down, as acknowledging and appreciating such gestures fosters goodwill.

In essence, your master list, with a keen emphasis on sold customers, serves as a strategic compass. It's not just a record but a repository of experiences, insights, and relationships that guide future engagements. Ensuring it's comprehensive and regularly updated is pivotal to sustaining and expanding your sales horizons. It's a reflection of your belief in your industry, product, or service, and your belief in yourself. Like Jesus, who reached out to his previously sold customers to guide them, your master list is your way to connect, serve, and create lasting value.

Jesus and His "Sold Customers": Understanding the Israelites' Journey

To grasp the full scope of Jesus' mission, it's essential to delve into the Israelites' profound connection to the Kingdom of God. They were more than mere followers; they were the children of promise, their identity firmly anchored in the teachings and covenants of the Old Testament. This foundational 'purchase' was their unwavering belief in the One true God, encapsulated in the Shema: "Hear, O Israel: The Lord our God, the Lord is one." (Deuteronomy 6:4). As descendants of Abraham, they held onto God's promise: "And I will make of you a great nation, and I will bless you and make your name great, so that you will be a blessing" (Genesis 12:2).

Jesus' arrival was not a disruption but a fulfillment of this legacy. He presented the Israelites with the New Covenant, not as a replacement but an enhancement to their existing beliefs. He was their bridge to the Kingdom of God, introducing them to the path of salvation and emphasizing belief in Him as the Messiah. This 'sales pitch' was eloquently expressed in His declaration: "I am the way and the truth and the life. No one comes to the Father except through me." (John 14:6). The term "The Way" was not merely a descriptor; it was the essence of His doctrine, a phrase that the apostles would continue to use to highlight Jesus as the route to salvation.

The Jewish populace, well-versed in divine interactions through patriarchs and prophets, was Jesus' primary audience. These legacy customers, familiar with divine promises and awaiting the Messiah, were the focus of Jesus' message: "I was sent only to the lost sheep of the house of Israel." (Matthew 15:24, ESV). Even after His resurrection, He emphasized the propagation of salvation beginning from Jerusalem (Luke 24:46-48, MSG), a strategic approach to reach those already in allegiance.

In essence, Jesus' mission was a masterclass in understanding and nurturing an audience. He recognized the Israelites as his 'sold customers,' those who had already bought into the divine covenant. By building upon this prior trust, he demonstrated the timeless principle that previous engagements can often pave the way for deeper, renewed commitments. His approach serves as a timeless reminder for anyone in sales or life coaching, emphasizing the importance of nurturing existing relationships and recognizing the potential within those who already believe in you. It's a lesson in connection, trust, and the art of building upon a strong foundation.

The Art of Reconnection: Twenty Reasons to Contact Previously Sold Customers

Reaching out to previously sold customers is an art that transcends the mere act of selling. It's about nurturing relationships, providing continuous value, and recognizing that the sale was just the beginning of a journey. Here are twenty reasons to reconnect with previously sold customers, each grounded in the desire to help and serve:

Ensuring Satisfaction: Checking in to ensure they are satisfied with the product or service helps in building trust and shows that you care about their experience.

Offering Support: Providing ongoing support or assistance with the product or service fosters a sense of loyalty and appreciation.

Understanding Their Evolving Needs: People's needs change, and understanding those changes allows you to offer relevant solutions.

Sharing Useful Tips: Offering tips on how to get the most out of the product or service adds value to their purchase.

Introducing Complementary Products: If you have other products or services that complement their purchase, it might be helpful to them.

Requesting Feedback: Their insights can help you improve and innovate, making your offerings even more valuable to future customers.

Keeping Them Informed: Updating them on new developments, features, or enhancements keeps them engaged and might lead to further opportunities.

Celebrating Success: Acknowledging how the product or service has positively impacted them can strengthen the relationship.

Inviting to Community: Inviting them to join community forums, groups, or events can create a sense of belonging.

Providing Exclusive Offers: Offering them exclusive deals or early access to new products shows appreciation for their loyalty.

Educating on Industry Trends: Sharing industry news or trends keeps them informed and positions you as a thought leader.

Encouraging Referrals: Happy customers are often willing to refer others, and gentle encouragement can facilitate this.

Reinforcing Your Mission: Reminding them of your mission and how they are a part of it creates a deeper connection.

Offering Personalized Solutions: Tailoring new solutions to their specific needs or challenges shows attentiveness and understanding.

Building Long-term Relationships: Regular, meaningful contact turns a one-time sale into a long-term relationship.

Acknowledging Special Occasions: Recognizing birthdays, anniversaries, or other special occasions adds a personal touch.

Gathering Testimonials: If they are satisfied, they might be willing to provide a testimonial, which can be valuable for your business.

Inviting to Participate in Research: Their participation in surveys or research can help you understand your market better.

Expressing Gratitude: A simple thank you for their business and trust can go a long way in maintaining a positive relationship.

Aligning with Their Growth: As they grow and evolve, so can your relationship with them, leading to new opportunities to serve.

These reasons are not about selling in the traditional sense; they are about selling to help, to enhance, to grow. They align with the Triad of Belief, emphasizing belief in your industry, belief in your product or service, and belief in yourself. By approaching the act of contacting previously sold customers with this mindset, you transform it into an opportunity to deepen relationships, provide continuous value, and truly make a difference. It's a win-win scenario where both you and the customer benefit, creating a positive cycle that can lead to lasting success.

Overcoming The Fear Of Contacting Sold Customers

The bond between salespeople and clients often transcends the initial transaction. As the marketplace evolves, nurturing these relationships becomes more than a sound business practice; it's a vital aspect of ongoing success. However, a variety of fears and hesitations may deter salespeople from reengaging with their sold customers.

In this section, we will delve into sixteen specific fears, examining their origins and consequences. Drawing inspiration from the scriptures, we will uncover how faith and the Triad of Belief—confidence in one's industry, trust in one's product or service, and faith in oneself—can guide salespeople in overcoming these obstacles. These fears are not merely hurdles in the business landscape; they are catalysts for growth, introspection, and a profound connection to our faith and mission.

Our ultimate objective is to use our faith as a tool to carefully examine every fear that we encounter and transform them from obstacles into connections. By doing so, we aspire to bring salespeople and clients together and gain a more profound comprehension of the spiritual significance of our profession. This journey is not solely about overcoming fears, but, in fact, about embracing them as opportunities to cultivate stronger relationships, improve professional ethics, and align our sales pursuits with the timeless wisdom of our faith.

Fear of Negative Feedback

One of the fears that can paralyze salespeople from contacting sold customers is the Fear of Negative Feedback. This fear often stems from the possibility that the product or service did not meet the customer's expectations, and the salesperson might be confronted with dissatisfaction or criticism. It's a fear that can erode the Triad of Belief, shaking confidence in one's industry, product or service, and even oneself.

This concept is not foreign to the scriptures. In John 6:26-66, Jesus faced a situation where His teachings were met with discontent and abandonment by many of His followers. After feeding the five thousand, He began to teach about being the Bread of Life. This teaching was difficult for many to accept, and they grumbled about it. Jesus did not shy away from their dissatisfaction but addressed it head-on, asking, "Does this offend you?" (John 6:61). He continued to teach with conviction, even though many of His disciples turned back and no longer followed Him.

Jesus' response to this negative feedback is a profound lesson for salespeople. He did not compromise His message or lose belief in His mission. His belief in His 'industry' (the Kingdom of God), His 'product' (Salvation), and Himself (as the Son of God) remained unwavering. He understood that not everyone would accept what He offered, but He continued to present it with integrity and compassion.

For salespeople facing the Fear of Negative Feedback, the lesson is clear: Embrace the feedback, whether positive or negative, as an opportunity to learn and grow. Maintain belief in your industry, your product or service, and yourself. Understand that dissatisfaction from a customer is not a failure but a chance to improve, adapt, and serve better. By aligning with the Triad of Belief and following Jesus' example, this fear can be transformed into a pathway for growth, resilience, and deeper connections with customers.

Transition to a New Industry

Transitioning to a new industry can be a daunting experience for salespeople, especially when it comes to reconnecting with old customers. The fear here is multifaceted: a concern that previous customers may not be relevant to the new products or services, coupled with a lack of confidence in one's ability to transfer existing relationships into a new context. This fear can challenge the Triad of Belief, as it requires a reevaluation of belief in a new industry, a new product or service, and a renewed belief in oneself.

While there may not be a direct scriptural reference to Jesus transitioning industries, we can draw inspiration from His approach to engaging with diverse audiences. Jesus spoke to fishermen, tax collectors, religious leaders, and ordinary people, adapting His message to resonate with each unique group. He was not confined to a specific 'industry' but transcended boundaries to reach hearts and minds.

In Matthew 4:18-22, Jesus called His first disciples, who were fishermen, with the words, "Come, follow me, and I will send you out to fish for people." Here, He connected their existing profession with their new calling, making the transition relatable and compelling.

Salespeople transitioning to a new industry can learn from Jesus' adaptability and connection. Rather than severing ties with old customers, consider how your new products or services might still serve them. Focus on the relationships you've built and how those connections can be a bridge to your new venture.

Drawing a parallel from popular culture, consider the "Six Degrees of Kevin Bacon" game, which posits that any two people on Earth are, on average, about six acquaintance links apart. Similarly, even if you're transitioning industries, it's highly probable that connections, direct or indirect, exist between your past customers and your new venture. This interconnectedness means that the relationships you've nurtured over the years can still be of immense value.

Maintain your belief in your new industry, your new offerings, and most importantly, in yourself. By embracing the Triad of Belief and recognizing that the core principles of service, trust, and value remain constant across industries, you can overcome the fear of transition and thrive in your new path.

Perceived Lack of Relevance

The fear of a perceived lack of relevance can be a significant barrier for salespeople when considering reaching out to sold customers with a new product or service. This fear stems from the belief that what they are now offering may not align with the needs or interests of their previous customers. It's a concern that can shake the very core of the Triad of Belief, as it questions the relevance of the industry, the product or service, and even the salesperson's ability to make a meaningful connection.

A scriptural reference that can shed light on this fear is Jesus' interaction with the Samaritan woman at the well in John 4:7-26. Here, Jesus engages with someone who, at first glance, might seem irrelevant to His mission. Samaritans and Jews typically had no dealings with each other, and the woman herself was surprised that Jesus, a Jew, was speaking to her. However, Jesus saw beyond the surface and recognized a deeper need. He offered her "living water," a spiritual truth that transcended cultural and personal barriers.

Jesus knew that His message of salvation was relevant to all, regardless of their background or perceived needs. He listened, understood, and adapted His presentation to make it valuable to the person in front of Him.

Salespeople facing the fear of a perceived lack of relevance can learn from Jesus' example. It's essential to approach each customer with an open mind, recognizing that needs and interests can evolve. Engage in active listening, ask questions, and seek to understand how your new product or service might align with their current situation. Believe in your industry, your offering, and yourself, and be willing to adapt your presentation to demonstrate the relevance of what you're selling.

You can overcome this fear by focusing on the relationship and the potential value you can provide, rather than preconceived notions of relevance. Embrace the Triad of Belief, and allow it to guide you in serving your customers, even when the connection might not seem immediately apparent. Like Jesus at the well, you may find that what seems irrelevant on the surface can become a profound opportunity for connection and transformation.

Embarrassment from Previous Missteps

Embarrassment from previous missteps is a fear that can paralyze salespeople when considering contacting sold customers. If there were any issues, misunderstandings, or mistakes in previous interactions, the salesperson might feel a sense of shame or apprehension about re-initiating contact.

A scriptural reference that can provide insight into this fear is Peter's denial of Jesus as described in the Gospels (e.g., Luke 22:54-62). Peter, one of Jesus' closest disciples, denied knowing Jesus three times, a significant misstep that could have led to embarrassment and a breakdown in their relationship. However, after His resurrection, Jesus did not shun Peter. Instead, He sought him out and asked him three times if he loved Him (John 21:15-17), providing Peter with the opportunity to reaffirm his commitment and mend the relationship.

Jesus' approach to Peter's denial demonstrates a profound understanding of human frailty and a willingness to forgive and move forward. He believed in His mission (industry), His teachings (product or service), and in Peter himself. His belief was not shaken by Peter's mistake; instead, He used it as an opportunity for growth and reconciliation.

Salespeople facing embarrassment from previous missteps can learn from this example. Acknowledging the mistake and taking responsibility for it is the first step. Reach out to the customer, explain what went wrong, and express your commitment to making it right. Show them that your belief in your industry, your product or service, and in yourself is unwavering. Offer solutions and demonstrate through your actions that you value their relationship and are willing to work to rebuild trust.

By approaching the situation with humility, honesty, and a genuine desire to make amends, you can turn a previous misstep into an opportunity for growth and deeper connection. Embrace the Triad of Belief, and let it guide you in overcoming embarrassment and fear, just as Jesus did with Peter. In doing so, you not only mend a professional relationship but also strengthen your character and resilience in your sales journey.

Concerns about Calling Too Often

Concerns about calling too often is a fear that plagues many salespeople. The worry of appearing pushy or bothersome can create a barrier that prevents them from reaching out to sold customers. However, this fear can be addressed by understanding the purpose and the "reason" behind the call.

In the context of Jesus' ministry, we can find a parallel in how He approached His followers and those He sought to reach. Jesus didn't merely preach to the masses; He healed the sick, fed the hungry, and taught with parables. Each interaction had a specific purpose and was tailored to the needs and circumstances of those He was addressing. He wasn't pushing a message; He was offering what was needed.

Similarly, salespeople can approach their sold customers with specific reasons that go beyond selling. Whether it's introducing them to a new product line that complements their previous purchases, sharing a tip on how to better use what they already have, or making a service call to ensure satisfaction, these reasons provide value. They reflect a belief in the industry, showing that the salesperson is engaged and wants to enhance the customer's experience. They demonstrate belief in the product or service, as the salesperson is actively ensuring that the customer continues to benefit from their purchase. And they show belief in oneself, as the salesperson takes on the role of a consultant or supporter rather than just a seller.

This approach aligns with the Triad of Belief, emphasizing the importance of belief in the industry, the product or service, and oneself. By focusing on these aspects, the salesperson can transform the call from a potential annoyance into an opportunity for continued service and relationship-building.

The fear of calling too often can be overcome by shifting the focus from selling to serving. By identifying specific reasons for the call that provide value to the customer, the salesperson can approach the interaction with confidence and purpose. This not only alleviates the fear but also strengthens the relationship with the customer, reflecting a commitment to their ongoing satisfaction and success. It's a strategy that resonates with the teachings and approach of Jesus, turning transactions into meaningful, value-driven connections.

Doubt in Product Quality

Doubt in Product Quality is a fear that can significantly hinder a salesperson's ability to reach out to sold customers, especially when introducing a new product. This fear stems from a lack of confidence in the product's quality or utility, leading to hesitation in offering it to previous customers.

In the context of scripture, we can find a parallel in the Old Testament, where God's assurance and promise are evident. Since Jesus and the Father are one, the words of God resonate with the teachings of Jesus. In Isaiah 55:11, God says, "So shall my word be that goes out from my mouth; it shall not return to me empty, but it shall accomplish that which I purpose, and shall succeed in the thing for which I sent it." This verse emphasizes the unwavering confidence in the purpose and the success of God's word.

Translating this to sales, the Triad of Belief can be a guiding principle. Belief in the industry means understanding the value and potential of what's being offered. Belief in the product or service requires thorough knowledge and conviction in its quality and utility. And belief in oneself involves the confidence to present and stand behind the product.

If a salesperson finds themselves doubting the quality of a new product, they must seek to understand the root of this doubt. Is it a lack of information? Then, investing time in learning about the product, its features, benefits, and potential applications can build confidence. Is it feedback from others? Engaging with those who have used the product, including colleagues or other customers, can provide insights and dispel uncertainties.

Connecting with the core values and mission of the company, aligning with the industry's goals, and recognizing the potential impact of the product on the customers' lives can transform doubt into conviction. It's about seeing beyond the product itself and understanding its place in the larger context of service, improvement, and fulfillment of needs.

In essence, overcoming the fear of Doubt in Product Quality requires a holistic approach that aligns with the Triad of Belief. It's about embracing the confidence that God expressed in His word and applying it to the sales process. By focusing on understanding, alignment, and purpose, a salesperson can turn doubt into a driving force that not only enhances their relationship with sold customers but also contributes to personal and professional growth.

Navigating the Fear of Lack of Proper Record–Keeping

A fear that can inhibit salespeople from contacting sold customers is the Lack of Proper Record-Keeping. Without a systematic record or Customer Relationship Management (CRM) system, salespeople might find themselves uncertain about the last communication, its context, or the details of the previous sale. This lack of information can create a barrier to effective communication and hinder the ability to build on previous successes.

While the scriptures may not directly address the concept of record-keeping in a sales context, we can find wisdom in the Old Testament that resonates with this challenge. In Proverbs 24:3-4, it is said, "By wisdom a house is built, and by understanding it is established; by knowledge the rooms are filled with all precious and pleasant riches." This passage emphasizes the importance of wisdom, understanding, and knowledge in building something valuable and lasting.

In practical terms, overcoming this fear begins with recognizing the value of proper record-keeping and committing to implementing a system that supports it. Whether it's a sophisticated CRM system or a simple spreadsheet, the key is consistency and attention to detail. By capturing essential information such as the date of last contact, the nature of the communication, the customer's needs and preferences, and the details of previous sales, a salesperson can create a valuable resource that enhances their ability to serve their customers effectively.

Regularly reviewing and updating this information ensures that it remains relevant and useful. It also provides opportunities to identify patterns and trends that can inform future interactions. By approaching record-keeping as an essential aspect of the sales process, rather than an administrative chore, a salesperson can transform it into a tool that empowers them to build deeper relationships and achieve greater success.

In essence, the fear of Lack of Proper Record-Keeping can be overcome by embracing the wisdom found in scripture and applying the principles of the Triad of Belief. By recognizing the value of knowledge and understanding, and by committing to practices that support them, a salesperson can turn a potential barrier into a pathway to growth and fulfillment.

Challenging the Assumption of Satisfaction: A Proactive Approach

A common reluctance that salespeople may experience when considering contacting sold customers is the Assumption of Satisfaction. This mindset, characterized by thoughts such as "If they need something, they'll contact me," can lead to complacency and missed opportunities to deepen relationships and add value.

In the New Testament, we find an example that challenges this assumption in the way Jesus approached his followers. He didn't wait for them to come to Him with their needs; He actively sought them out and offered guidance, healing, and wisdom. In Luke 19:10, Jesus states, "For the Son of Man came to seek and to save the lost." He didn't wait for the lost to find Him; He actively sought them out.

This proactive approach aligns with the Triad of Belief. Belief in the industry means recognizing that ongoing engagement with customers is essential to success. Belief in the product or service involves understanding that there may be additional ways to meet the customer's needs or enhance their satisfaction. Belief in oneself includes the confidence to reach out proactively, rather than waiting for the customer to initiate contact.

In practical terms, overcoming the Assumption of Satisfaction requires a shift in mindset and behavior. Rather than viewing the sale as a one-time transaction, it's essential to see it as the beginning of an ongoing relationship. Regular follow-up, even when there's no immediate opportunity for an additional sale, can provide valuable insights into the customer's needs and preferences. It can also demonstrate a genuine interest in their satisfaction and well-being.

This follow-up might include a simple thank-you note, a call to ensure that the product or service is meeting their expectations, or an offer to provide additional information or support. A salesperson can create opportunities to add value, build trust, and strengthen the relationship by taking the initiative to reach out.

The Assumption of Satisfaction is a barrier that can be overcome by embracing the example set by Jesus and the principles of the Triad of Belief. By recognizing the value of proactive engagement and committing to practices that support it, a salesperson can transform this reluctance into a strength that enhances their ability to serve their customers and achieve success.

Navigating Change in Personal Circumstances: A Lesson in Resilience

A fear that can deter salespeople from contacting sold customers is the Change in Personal Circumstances. Personal issues, mental health concerns, or low self-esteem can create a hesitancy that affects their ability to reach out to clients. This fear is not just about professional competence but touches on deeper, personal challenges that can affect all areas of life.

In the New Testament, we find an example of how Jesus dealt with personal challenges in the Garden of Gethsemane. Facing the most significant trial of His life, He felt deep anguish. Yet, He turned to prayer and sought the support of His Father. In Matthew 26:39, He prayed, "My Father, if it is possible, may this cup be taken from me. Yet not as I will, but as you will." Jesus acknowledged His feelings but also reaffirmed His commitment to His mission.

This example can be connected to the Triad of Belief. Belief in the industry means recognizing that personal challenges don't have to define professional success. Belief in the product or service involves understanding that the value offered to customers remains constant, regardless of personal circumstances. Belief in oneself includes the confidence to seek support and take care of oneself, knowing that personal well-being is foundational to professional success.

In practical terms, overcoming the fear associated with Change in Personal Circumstances may require both personal and professional strategies. On a personal level, seeking support from friends, family, or professionals can provide the encouragement and perspective needed to navigate personal challenges. On a professional level, focusing on the value provided to customers and the importance of the work can create a sense of purpose that transcends personal difficulties.

Additionally, embracing the understanding that personal challenges are a normal part of life and don't have to define professional identity or success can be empowering. By acknowledging these challenges and taking proactive steps to address them, a salesperson can build resilience and continue to serve their customers effectively.

In conclusion, the fear associated with Change in Personal Circumstances is complex but not impossible. By drawing on the example of Jesus and the principles of the Triad of Belief, a salesperson can find the strength and perspective needed to navigate this challenge. By recognizing the interconnectedness of personal well-being and professional success and taking steps to support both, they can continue to thrive in their work and relationships with customers.

Facing the Fear of Rejection: A Lesson in Persistence

One of the most common fears that salespeople face when contacting sold customers is the Fear of Rejection. This fear can be particularly acute if the previous sale was challenging or if the salesperson has faced rejection. The thought of hearing a 'no' can be a significant deterrent, creating anxiety and hesitation.

In the New Testament, we find an example of how Jesus faced rejection and how He responded to it. In His hometown of Nazareth, Jesus was rejected by the very people He had grown up with. They questioned His authority and wisdom, leading Him to remark, "A prophet is not without honor except in his own town, among his relatives and in his own home." (Mark 6:4). Despite this rejection, Jesus continued His mission, undeterred by the refusal of those He sought to reach.

This example aligns with the Triad of Belief. Belief in the industry is akin to Jesus' unwavering commitment to His mission, regardless of rejection. Belief in the product or service is reflected in Jesus' confidence in His message, even when faced with disbelief. Belief in oneself is seen in Jesus' resilience and determination to continue despite the refusal of those around Him.

In practical terms, overcoming the Fear of Refusal or Rejection requires a shift in perspective. Rather than viewing rejection as a failure, it can be seen as a learning opportunity. Understanding why a customer said 'no' can provide insights into how to approach future sales. Building resilience through continuous learning and growth can turn rejection into a stepping stone rather than a stumbling block.

Moreover, focusing on the value and benefits of the product or service, rather than the potential for refusal, can create a positive mindset. Concentrating on what can be offered to the customer and how it can meet their needs makes the fear of rejection less central.

The Fear of Refusal or Rejection is a natural but conquerable challenge. By drawing on the example of Jesus and the principles of the Triad of Belief, salespeople can transform this fear into an opportunity for growth and development. By embracing rejection as a part of the process and focusing on the value and purpose of their work, they can continue to build meaningful relationships with their customers and find success in their industry.

Confronting Perceived Inadequacy in Knowledge: A Path to Confidence and Mastery

In the ever-evolving landscape of products and services, salespeople may encounter the fear of Perceived Inadequacy in Knowledge. When products are upgraded or changed, and if the salesperson isn't adequately trained, they might hesitate to engage with old customers. This fear stems from the concern that they won't be able to handle questions or objections effectively.

While this specific scenario might not have a direct parallel in Jesus' ministry, we can find guidance in His approach to teaching and empowering His disciples. Jesus often spoke in parables, using familiar concepts to explain complex spiritual truths. As stated in Mark 4:34, "He did not say anything to them without using a parable. But when He was alone with His own disciples, He explained everything." This method of teaching reflects the Triad of Belief, particularly the belief in oneself and one's product or service. By explaining these parables to His disciples and ensuring they understood, Jesus demonstrated the importance of clarity, connection, and commitment in any form of communication or teaching.

Understanding the broader context of your industry and the role your product plays within it can provide a solid foundation. This understanding allows you to see the bigger picture and not get lost in the minutiae of changes or upgrades. Emphasizing continuous learning and staying abreast of product changes is vital. Just as Jesus ensured His disciples understood His teachings, salespeople must seek understanding and clarity about their products. This may involve regular training sessions, self-study, or engaging with product experts within the company.

Confidence in one's ability to learn and adapt is crucial. Jesus' disciples were ordinary men without formal theological training, yet He entrusted them with His message. Similarly, salespeople must trust in their ability to learn, adapt, and convey the value of their products, even when changes occur. In practical terms, overcoming this fear requires a commitment to continuous learning and a proactive approach to understanding product changes. Salespeople can seek out training, collaborate with product experts, and engage in hands-on experience with the product. By embracing a mindset of growth and curiosity, they can turn perceived inadequacy into mastery and confidence.

Furthermore, open communication with customers about the learning process can build trust. Admitting that you're still learning about a new feature but assuring the customer that you'll find the information they need can be a genuine and effective approach.

Perceived Inadequacy in Knowledge is not a dead-end but a call to growth and empowerment. By embracing the principles of the Triad of Belief and following the example of Jesus' patient and empowering teaching, salespeople can transform this fear into an opportunity for personal and professional development. The path to overcoming this fear lies in continuous learning, confidence in one's ability to adapt, and a genuine commitment to serving the customer's needs.

Navigating the Reluctance to Disrupt the Status Quo: A Lesson in Growth and Trust

In the realm of sales, a fear that can subtly creep into the mindset of a salesperson is the Reluctance to Disrupt the Status Quo. This fear manifests when a previous deal has been particularly lucrative or favorable, and the salesperson hesitates to introduce new offers or changes, fearing that it might disrupt the existing relationship with the customer.

This reluctance can be likened to the parable of the talents in the New Testament (Matthew 25:14-30). In this parable, Jesus tells the story of a master who entrusts his servants with varying amounts of talents (a form of currency). Two of the servants invest and double their talents, while the third, out of fear, buries his talent in the ground, maintaining the status quo. The master praises the first two servants but condemns the third for his lack of initiative.

This parable resonates deeply with the Triad of Belief. The third servant's failure was not in his inability to generate more but in his lack of belief in himself and his fear of taking a risk. He chose to maintain the status quo rather than seek growth.

In sales, maintaining the status quo might seem like a safe option, especially when the relationship is favorable. However, this approach can lead to stagnation and missed opportunities for both the salesperson and the customer. The belief in one's industry, product or service, and oneself must guide the salesperson to recognize that growth and improvement are integral to a thriving relationship.

To overcome this reluctance, salespeople must first acknowledge that change and growth are natural and often beneficial. Just as the servants who invested their talents were rewarded, salespeople must see the potential in offering new solutions or improvements to their customers. This requires a strong belief in the value that these new offers can bring to the customer.

Communication is key in this process. By openly discussing the new offers and explaining how they align with the customer's needs or goals, the salesperson can build trust and understanding. This approach ensures that the relationship is not disrupted but rather enhanced.

In conclusion, the Reluctance to Disrupt the Status Quo is a fear that can be overcome by embracing growth, trust, and open communication. By following the example set by Jesus in the parable of the talents and adhering to the principles of the Triad of Belief, salespeople can transform this reluctance into an opportunity for deeper engagement and success with their customers. The path forward is not in clinging to the status quo but in seeking growth and trusting in the value that one's industry, product, and personal abilities can offer.

Navigating Cultural or Social Barriers: Learning from the Apostle Paul

The fear of Cultural or Social Barriers in sales can be a complex issue, especially when dealing with customers from diverse backgrounds. Such apprehensions often arise from the perception that reconnecting with a customer post-sale might be challenging due to perceived differences or a lack of shared experiences.

A fitting scriptural reference to address this fear can be found in the approach of the Apostle Paul, who was known for his ability to adapt his message to different cultural contexts. In 1 Corinthians 9:19-23, Paul states, "Though I am free and belong to no one, I have made myself a slave to everyone, to win as many as possible. To the Jews, I became like a Jew, to win the Jews. To those under the law, I became like one under the law... I have become all things to all people so that by all possible means I might save some."

Paul's approach uniquely embodies the Triad of Belief. He believed in his mission (industry), the Gospel (product), and in himself, and he was willing to adapt his approach without compromising his message. He recognized the importance of understanding the cultural and social context of his audience and was willing to meet them where they were.

In the realm of sales, this passage offers valuable insights into how to navigate Cultural or Social Barriers. It emphasizes the importance of flexibility and adaptability, recognizing that different customers may have different cultural norms and expectations. The belief in one's industry, product, or service, and oneself must be coupled with a willingness to understand and respect the customer's unique cultural context.

Practical steps to overcome this fear might include taking the time to learn about the customer's cultural background, being mindful of communication styles, and seeking to build genuine relationships that honor and respect cultural differences. It's about finding common ground and connecting on a human level, just as Paul sought to connect with different communities by understanding and respecting their unique perspectives.

In conclusion, the example of the Apostle Paul provides a powerful model for salespeople facing Cultural or Social Barriers. By embracing the principles of understanding, adaptability, and respect, and guided by the Triad of Belief, salespeople can build meaningful connections across cultural divides. The challenge is not to change the message but to adapt the approach, recognizing the value and richness that cultural diversity brings to the relationship. By following Paul's example, salespeople can turn potential barriers into opportunities for connection, growth, and success.

Fear of Appearing Desperate: A Lesson from the Parable of the Lost Sheep

In the world of sales, the fear of appearing desperate can be a significant obstacle. This fear often manifests when a salesperson hesitates to reach out to old customers, worrying that such contact might convey a sense of desperation or a lack of success in their business. It's a concern that can hinder the growth of relationships and limit opportunities for further engagement.

A profound scriptural reference that can shed light on this fear is the Parable of the Lost Sheep, as told by Jesus in Luke 15:3-7. In this parable, Jesus describes a shepherd who leaves ninety-nine sheep in the open field to search for the one that is lost. Upon finding it, he joyfully carries it home and calls his friends and neighbors to celebrate.

This parable can be seen as a metaphor for the salesperson's relationship with their customers. The shepherd's pursuit of the lost sheep is not a sign of desperation but a demonstration of care, commitment, and value. He does not worry about how his actions might be perceived; instead, he focuses on the importance of the individual sheep.

Connecting this to the Triad of Belief, the shepherd's actions reflect a strong belief in his role (industry), the value of each sheep (product or service), and his ability to care for them (belief in himself). His actions are not driven by desperation but by a genuine desire to serve and protect what is valuable to him.

In practical terms, salespeople can overcome the fear of appearing desperate by focusing on the genuine value and care they can offer to their customers. Reaching out to old customers should not be seen as a desperate act but as an opportunity to serve, provide value, and build a lasting relationship. It's about understanding the unique needs and interests of each customer and offering solutions that align with those needs.

By embracing the principles illustrated in the Parable of the Lost Sheep, salespeople can shift their perspective from fear to service. They can recognize that reaching out to old customers is not a sign of weakness but a demonstration of commitment, care, and belief in what they offer. It's a mindset that aligns with the core principles of the Triad of Belief, emphasizing the importance of belief in one's industry, product or service, and oneself.

The fear of appearing desperate can be overcome by adopting a mindset of service and value, guided by the teachings of Jesus in the Parable of the Lost Sheep. By focusing on the genuine care and value that can be offered to each customer, salespeople can transform this fear into an opportunity for growth, connection, and success. It's a lesson that resonates not only in sales but in all aspects of life, reminding us of the importance of individual care, commitment, and the power of belief.

Navigating Technological Challenges: Wisdom from the Tower of Babel

In today's rapidly evolving digital landscape, the fear of technological challenges is not uncommon among salespeople. The need to keep in touch with past customers through various digital platforms can be daunting, especially for those who may not be as comfortable or proficient with technology. This fear can create a barrier, hindering the ability to maintain and nurture relationships with customers.

While the Bible does not provide direct examples of dealing with modern technology, we can draw wisdom from the story of the Tower of Babel in Genesis 11:1-9. In this account, people attempted to build a tower to reach the heavens, but God confused their language, making communication impossible. The story illustrates the importance of clear communication and the challenges that arise when understanding is lost.

Connecting this to the Triad of Belief, we can see that belief in one's industry, product or service, and oneself can guide the way in overcoming technological challenges. Just as the people in the story of Babel faced a barrier in communication, salespeople may face technological barriers. However, the core principles of sales remain the same, whether communicated through traditional means or digital platforms.

Belief in your industry means understanding that technology is a tool, not a barrier. Embrace the technological advancements in your industry as opportunities to reach and serve customers in new and efficient ways. This perspective shifts the focus from the fear of technology to the potential it holds for enhancing relationships and expanding reach.

Belief in your product or service requires focusing on the value and benefits of what you're offering, not the medium through which it's communicated. Whether face-to-face or through a screen, your conviction in what you're selling should shine through. This belief anchors you, allowing you to navigate technological challenges with the confidence that the essence of your message remains unchanged.

Belief in yourself is about recognizing that technological proficiency can be developed with time and effort. Seek training, ask for help, and practice until you become comfortable. Your belief in yourself will fuel your ability to adapt and grow, turning what once seemed like an impossible challenge into a manageable task.

In practical terms, overcoming the fear of technological challenges involves embracing digital tools as a means to an end, not obstacles. It's about recognizing that the core principles of sales, communication, and relationship-building remain the same, regardless of the medium.

The story of the Tower of Babel offers a timeless lesson on the importance of clear communication and the challenges that can arise when understanding is lost. By applying the Triad of Belief and focusing on the core principles of sales, salespeople can navigate the technological landscape with confidence and grace. The tools may change, but the heart of sales remains the same, guided by belief in one's industry, product or service, and oneself. It's a lesson that transcends time, offering wisdom and guidance for the modern salesperson.

Concluding Thoughts: Overcoming Hesitations and Embracing Opportunities

The journey through the various fears and hesitations that salespeople face when contacting previously sold customers has been both enlightening and reflective. From personal doubts to technological barriers, these fears are multifaceted and deeply rooted in the human experience. Yet, as we have explored, they are not insurmountable.

The scriptures have provided us with timeless wisdom, guiding us through these challenges. Whether it's the story of the Tower of Babel teaching us about communication or other scriptural examples that resonate with the modern salesperson's experience, we find that the Bible's teachings are as relevant today as they were thousands of years ago.

Central to our exploration has been the Triad of Belief: belief in your industry, belief in your product or service, and belief in yourself. This triad serves as a compass, directing us towards a path of understanding, empathy, and resilience. It's not merely about overcoming fears but about transforming them into opportunities for growth, reflection, and a deeper connection to our faith and purpose.

Reaching out to previously sold customers is not just a business practice; it's a human connection. It's about recognizing the value in each relationship and nurturing it with care and intention. It's about seeing beyond the transaction and understanding the potential for ongoing collaboration and mutual benefit.

In practical terms, the fears we've identified can be addressed through continuous learning, self-awareness, and a commitment to serving others. By aligning our actions with our beliefs, we can create a sales process that is not only effective but also ethical and compassionate.

As we conclude this chapter, let us remember that our fears and hesitations are not unique to sales or our contemporary setting. They are part of the human condition, challenges that we all face in various aspects of our lives. What sets us apart is how we respond to these challenges, how we allow them to shape us, and how we use them as stepping stones towards greater understanding and fulfillment.

May we approach our work with a sense of purpose and a commitment to excellence, guided by our faith and the timeless wisdom of the scriptures. May we see each fear not as a barrier but as an invitation to grow, to learn, and to serve. And may we always remember that in the intricate dance of sales, belief is our most powerful ally, and serving others is our highest calling.

Embracing Service Beyond the Sale: A Lasting Connection

The relationship with a customer doesn't end with a successful transaction; it merely enters a new phase. Contacting sold customers is not just a follow-up procedure but a continuation of a partnership that began with the first introduction. It's a reflection of the commitment to serve, to understand, and to foster a relationship that transcends the mere exchange of goods or services.

The IDEAS Sales System emphasizes the importance of serving, and this principle resonates deeply when engaging with sold customers. It's about ensuring that the value promised is the value delivered, and it's about being there when questions, needs, or concerns arise. Just as Jesus continued to guide and nurture His followers, salespeople must continue to guide and support their customers.

In the world of sales, where competition is fierce and choices are abundant, the ability to maintain and grow relationships with sold customers can be a defining factor in long-term success. It's a practice that requires empathy, diligence, and a genuine desire to see others succeed. It's about embodying the principle that selling is serving, a concept that is at the core of the IDEAS Sales System.

As you reflect on the strategies and insights shared in this chapter, consider them not as mere tactics but as expressions of a philosophy that values human connection and mutual growth. Remember the words of Jesus in Matthew 20:28 (ESV): "Even as the Son of Man came not to be served but to serve, and to give his life as a ransom for many." In your interactions with sold customers, strive to serve, to add value, and to be a positive force in their lives.

The journey of sales is filled with opportunities, challenges, and lessons. In embracing the art of contacting sold customers, you're not only enhancing your professional practice but aligning yourself with timeless principles that have shaped successful relationships for centuries. May this chapter serve as a guide and inspiration as you continue to navigate the vibrant and ever-evolving landscape of sales, always remembering that at its heart, selling is an act of service, an opportunity to make a lasting impact.

> **"Let each of you look not only to his own interests, but also to the interests of others."**
>
> Philippians 2:4 (ESV)

Unsold Customers

The Untapped Potential

IN THE EVER-EVOLVING SALES landscape, the pursuit of new customers often takes center stage. Yet, there lies a hidden treasure trove of opportunity that is frequently overlooked: the unsold customers. These are individuals who, for one reason or another, did not complete a purchase during their last interaction with you. While dismissing them as lost causes might be easy, this chapter aims to shed light on the incredible benefits of adding unsold customers to your master list and maintaining an ongoing relationship with them.

First and foremost, it's essential to recognize that not closing a sale does not equate to a failure or a rejection of what you offered. Customers might not make purchases for various reasons. Perhaps the timing was not right, or they were facing budget constraints. Maybe they needed more time to consider the offer, or they were waiting for a specific feature or upgrade. These reasons do not necessarily reflect a lack of interest or value in your product or service.

The beauty of unsold customers is that they already know something about you and your offerings. You have already made an impression, lifted yourself out of obscurity, and laid the groundwork for a potential future relationship. This familiarity is a valuable asset, as it can significantly reduce the time and effort required to reintroduce yourself and your products.

Staying in touch with potential customers who haven't made a purchase yet can be very advantageous for any business. By reaching out to them, you have the opportunity to inform them about any updates, exclusive deals, or modifications that might be more suitable for their requirements. This not only helps to keep them engaged but also creates a bond of trust and connection, demonstrating that you appreciate their interest and are dedicated to building a lasting relationship with them, even if they didn't buy anything right away. It's important to remember that every interaction with a potential customer is an opportunity to strengthen your relationship with them and increase the chances of them becoming a loyal customer in the future.

Furthermore, unsold customers can provide invaluable insights and feedback. Understanding why they didn't buy can lead to improvements and refinements in your offerings and sales approach. Their perspectives can guide you in tailoring your products or services to better meet the needs and expectations of your target audience.

In this chapter, we will explore the strategies, techniques, and mindset required to tap into the untapped potential of unsold customers. We will delve into the art of nurturing these relationships, guided by our Triad of Belief, and discover how to transform what might seem like missed opportunities into lasting connections and future successes.

The journey with unsold customers is not a path of consolation but one of exploration and growth. It's about recognizing the potential in every interaction and understanding that every customer, whether sold or unsold, is a part of the intricate web of relationships that defines the success and sustainability of your business. By embracing this perspective, you open the doors to endless possibilities and set the stage for a more holistic and human-centered approach to sales.

The Positive Pursuit: Twenty Reasons to Contact Unsold Customers

Contacting unsold customers is not merely a sales strategy; it's a positive pursuit rooted in the desire to help. It's about recognizing the potential in every interaction and understanding that every customer, whether sold or unsold, can benefit from what you have to offer. Here are twenty compelling reasons to reach out to unsold customers, each reflecting a genuine intention to serve and assist:

Understanding Their Needs: By contacting unsold customers, you can gain insights into their specific needs and preferences, allowing you to effectively tailor your offerings.

Building Relationships: Even if a sale was not made initially, maintaining contact helps build a relationship that might lead to future opportunities.

Providing Value: Sharing tips, updates, or information that can help them in their daily lives or businesses shows that you care about providing value beyond the sale.

Offering Solutions: If they had concerns or objections previously, you might have new solutions or improvements that address those issues.

Keeping Them Informed: Informing them about new products, services, or features that align with their interests can be seen as a service rather than a sales pitch.

Gathering Feedback: Their feedback on why they didn't buy can be invaluable for improving your products, services, or sales approach.

Creating Trust: Regular, non-intrusive contact can foster trust and show that you are interested in more than just a one-time sale.

Enhancing Their Experience: Offering support or guidance on related topics can enhance their experience with your industry, even if they haven't bought from you.

Recognizing Opportunities: Sometimes, their circumstances change, and what was not relevant before becomes relevant now.

Encouraging Referrals: Even if they didn't buy, they might know someone who needs your product or service and can refer you.

Showcasing Your Expertise: Sharing insights or industry trends helps position yourself as an expert in your field.

Expressing Appreciation: A simple thank you for their time and consideration can leave a positive impression.

Aligning with Their Timing: Maybe they weren't ready to buy before, but circumstances have changed, and now they are.

Offering Exclusive Deals: They might be interested if you have special offers or exclusive deals.

Inviting to Events: Inviting them to webinars, workshops, or events can provide value and keep the relationship warm.

Educating Them: Providing educational content that helps them make informed decisions in your industry can be highly beneficial.

Celebrating Milestones: Acknowledging a birthday, anniversary, or other milestones can create a personal connection.

Resolving Past Issues: If there were misunderstandings or issues in the past, reaching out can clear the air and open doors.

Connecting on a Human Level: Sometimes, a genuine human connection can turn an unsold customer into a loyal advocate.

Fulfilling Your Mission: If you genuinely believe in your product or service and its ability to help others, contacting unsold customers is a natural extension of your mission to serve.

In each of these reasons, the underlying theme is the desire to help, to provide value, and to create meaningful connections. It's about approaching sales not as a transaction but as a relationship, guided by the Triad of Belief. When you view contacting unsold customers through this lens, it transforms from a task into an opportunity, from a challenge into a rewarding endeavor. It becomes a pathway to not only grow your business but also to make a positive impact on the lives of others.

Unsold but Not Forgotten: Tackling the Reluctance to Re-Engage

One of the most nuanced and challenging aspects is the re-engagement with unsold customers. This seemingly straightforward task often becomes a complex emotional and strategic maze for sales professionals. The hesitation is palpable, stemming from a blend of uncertainty, fear of rejection, and the delicate balance of persistence and intrusion. It's an everyday struggle, one that resonates across industries and experience levels, and it's rooted in both the art and psychology of sales. As we delve into this subject, we will unravel the layers of this hesitation, exploring the underlying causes, implications, and strategies to navigate this critical aspect of the sales process.

Facing Unresolved Objections: A Lesson from the Apostles

The fear of unresolved objections is a common barrier that salespeople face when considering contacting unsold customers. This fear stems from the anticipation of encountering the same objections that prevented the sale in the first place. The salesperson might feel unprepared or inadequate to address these objections, leading to hesitation and missed opportunities.

In the context of scripture, we can find a parallel in the experiences of the Apostles, particularly in the book of Acts. The Apostles faced objections and resistance from various groups as they spread the teachings of Christ. They were often met with skepticism, disbelief, and even hostility. Yet, they did not shy away from these challenges. Instead, they engaged with those who objected, addressing their concerns with wisdom, patience, and faith.

In Acts 17:2-3, Paul's approach to objections is described: "As was his custom, Paul went into the synagogue, and on three Sabbath days he reasoned with them from the Scriptures, explaining and proving that the Messiah had to suffer and rise from the dead." Paul did not avoid those who disagreed with him; he engaged them, reasoned with them, and sought to address their objections through understanding and dialogue.

This approach aligns with the Triad of Belief in sales: belief in your industry, belief in your product or service, and belief in yourself. Like Paul, a salesperson must have unwavering belief in what they are offering and in their ability to communicate its value. They must also be willing to engage with objections, not as barriers but as opportunities to better understand and serve the customer.

Jesus often engaged with those who questioned or challenged him, responding with wisdom, compassion, and clarity. He did not avoid difficult conversations but used them as opportunities to teach and enlighten.

Practically, a salesperson can overcome the fear of unresolved objections by preparing themselves with knowledge, empathy, and a genuine desire to help. Understanding the objections, finding ways to address them, and approaching the conversation with a service mindset can turn a potential roadblock into a path towards trust and connection.

In conclusion, while typical, the fear of unresolved objections is not insurmountable. By embracing the principles exemplified by Jesus and the Apostles, and by grounding oneself in the Triad of Belief, a salesperson can transform this fear into an opportunity for growth, understanding, and success. It's not about winning an argument but about building a relationship, serving the customer, and ultimately, fulfilling a need.

Overcoming the Belief in Fixed Opinions: Lessons from the Conversion of Saul

The fear that unsold customers have unchangeable opinions can be paralleled with Saul's conversion in the New Testament (Acts 9:1-19). Saul, a zealous persecutor of Christians, seemed to have a fixed and unchangeable opinion against the followers of Jesus. His views were so strong that he actively sought to arrest and imprison those who believed in Christ.

However, on the road to Damascus, Saul had a life-changing encounter with Jesus. This experience transformed his beliefs, and he became one of the most passionate apostles of Christ, known as Paul. His fixed opinions were not only challenged but completely reversed.

This story illustrates that even the most steadfast opinions can change. It reminds salespeople that unsold customers' opinions are not necessarily permanent. Just as Saul's beliefs were transformed, so too can a prospect's views evolve over time or with new information.

Connecting this to the Triad of Belief, salespeople must have an unwavering belief in their industry, their product or service, and in themselves. They must approach unsold customers with the understanding that opinions can change and that genuine engagement can lead to new perspectives.

Practically, salespeople can take inspiration from this story by approaching unsold customers with empathy, patience, and a willingness to listen. By understanding the customers' needs and concerns, they can present their product or service in a way that resonates with them. They must also be open to the possibility that a 'no' today might become a 'yes' tomorrow.

In conclusion, the conversion of Saul teaches us that no opinion is truly fixed. It encourages salespeople to approach unsold customers with an open mind and a compassionate heart, grounded in the Triad of Belief. By doing so, they can transform reluctance into opportunity and fear into faith. The story of Saul's transformation is a powerful reminder that change is possible, and that with belief and persistence, salespeople can connect with unsold customers in meaningful and productive ways.

Overcoming Inadequate Follow-Up Strategy: Learning from the Parable of the Sower

The fear of an inadequate follow-up strategy in contacting unsold customers can be likened to the lessons learned from the Parable of the Sower (Matthew 13:1-23). In this parable, Jesus describes a sower who scatters seeds on different types of soil. Some seeds fall on the path, some on rocky ground, some among thorns, and some on good soil. The seeds' growth and success depend on the type of soil they land on.

This parable can be seen as a metaphor for the different responses salespeople might encounter when engaging with unsold customers. The seeds represent the attempts to reach out, and the soil symbolizes the various reactions and circumstances of the customers.

Jesus' explanation of the parable emphasizes the importance of understanding the conditions and adapting the approach accordingly. The sower's success with the good soil demonstrates the value of a well-thought-out strategy and the understanding of the environment.

Connecting this to the Triad of Belief, salespeople must believe in their industry, their product or service, and themselves. They must recognize that not every attempt will result in success, but with careful planning and understanding of the customers' needs and concerns, they can find the "good soil" where their efforts will thrive.

Practically, this means developing a tailored follow-up strategy for unsold customers. Salespeople should consider the reasons for the initial refusal and address them in their follow-up. They should also be patient and persistent, recognizing that building trust and understanding takes time.

The Parable of the Sower teaches salespeople the importance of a well-planned follow-up strategy. It encourages them to approach unsold customers with insight, adaptability, and persistence, grounded in the Triad of Belief. By doing so, they can turn the challenge of an inadequate follow-up strategy into an opportunity for growth and success. The lessons from this parable are a valuable guide for salespeople in their efforts to engage unsold customers, reminding them that with belief, understanding, and a thoughtful approach, they can cultivate fruitful relationships.

Patience in the Process: Embracing Long Sales Cycles with the Wisdom of Noah

The fear of anticipating long sales cycles with unsold customers can be a significant obstacle for salespeople. This fear stems from the expectation that engaging with unsold customers may require more time, effort, and patience, leading to a prolonged and potentially tedious negotiation process.

A scriptural reference that can be drawn upon to address this fear is the story of Noah and the Ark (Genesis 6-9). Despite the long and arduous process, Noah's obedience to God's command to build the ark is a powerful example of patience, faith, and perseverance.

In the context of sales, the story of Noah can be related to the Triad of Belief. Just as Noah believed in God's promise, salespeople must believe in their industry, their product or service, and themselves. Building relationships with unsold customers may be long, but it is not without purpose or potential reward.

Noah's unwavering faith and patience in constructing the ark over many years teach salespeople the value of persistence and trust in the process. The long sales cycle should not be seen as a deterrent but rather as an opportunity to build a more profound and meaningful connection with the customer.

Practically, salespeople can overcome the fear of long sales cycles by setting realistic expectations and focusing on the quality of the relationship rather than the speed of the sale. They should recognize that some customers may require more time to understand, trust, and invest in the product or service. By approaching these interactions with empathy, patience, and a genuine desire to help, salespeople can turn the challenge of a long sales cycle into a rewarding experience.

The story of Noah and the Ark offers a timeless lesson in patience, faith, and perseverance that can inspire salespeople facing long sales cycles with unsold customers. By embracing the process and focusing on the Triad of Belief, salespeople can navigate these challenges with confidence and grace. The journey may be long, but the potential for meaningful connections and successful outcomes makes it a path worth pursuing.

Overcoming Perceived Value Mismatch: The Healing of Naaman

The story of Naaman, the commander of the Syrian army, who suffered from leprosy, provides a unique perspective on perceived value mismatch. Naaman was told by the prophet Elisha to wash in the Jordan River seven times to be healed. Initially, Naaman was angry and disappointed with the simple instruction, as he expected a grand gesture from the prophet. However, when he followed the instruction, he was healed. (2 Kings 5:1-14)

This story can be connected to the Triad of Belief in various ways. Naaman's initial rejection of the simple solution reflects how customers may dismiss a product or service due to preconceived notions or expectations. The salesperson's belief in the industry helps them understand that even simple solutions can provide immense value. Elisha's confidence in the simple act of washing in the Jordan River symbolizes the salesperson's belief in the product or service, knowing that it can meet the customer's needs, even if it doesn't align with their initial expectations.

Elisha's unwavering stance in his instruction represents the salesperson's confidence in their approach, maintaining integrity and belief in what they offer, even when faced with skepticism or rejection. The story of Naaman teaches that value may not always be perceived in the way we expect. It encourages salespeople to remain steadfast in their belief in what they offer and to guide customers past their initial misconceptions or expectations.

Salespeople can apply this lesson by focusing on clear communication, empathy, and education. By helping unsold customers understand the actual value and applicability of the product or service, salespeople can overcome initial objections and perceived value mismatches.

The Healing of Naaman offers a rich lesson in recognizing the potential for value in unexpected places. It encourages salespeople to approach unsold customers with a strong belief in the industry, product or service, and themselves, guiding them past initial misconceptions to see the true value in what is offered. Like Naaman's healing through a simple act, salespeople can find success by helping customers see beyond their initial expectations and recognize the value in what is being offered.

Fear of Appearing Desperate: Lessons from the Feeding of the Four Thousand

The apprehension salespeople might feel about contacting unsold customers, stemming from concerns about appearing desperate, can be paralleled with the situation Jesus encountered when He showed compassion for the multitude that had been with Him for three days without sustenance. In the account of the feeding of the four thousand, Jesus took what seemed like a limited supply of food (seven loaves and a few small fish) and miraculously nourished a vast crowd. (Matthew 15:32-39)

This narrative underscores the Triad of Belief deeply. Jesus' unwavering belief in His mission (industry) enabled Him to see opportunity where others might see a lack or desperation. His trust in His ability to cater (product or service) spurred Him to act. His self-belief empowered Him to perform a miracle that addressed the people's needs.

In sales, the apprehension of appearing desperate when reaching out to unsold leads can be mitigated by focusing on a genuine intent to assist and deliver value. Just as Jesus discerned potential in what appeared to be scant resources, salespeople should have faith in the worth they bring and understand that reconnecting with unsold leads isn't a sign of desperation but a chance to serve.

To navigate this apprehension, it's beneficial to view the engagement with unsold leads as a continuous relationship-building endeavor rather than a fallback strategy. By sustaining consistent, value-centric communication and emphasizing how the product or service can cater to the distinct requirements of the unsold customer, salespeople can uphold the brand's reputation and ethos.

Moreover, being transparent and sincere in interactions can transform the act of re-engaging unsold leads into a positive brand gesture. It conveys that the company cherishes every potential customer and is devoted to identifying solutions tailored to their needs, irrespective of the duration it might take.

The tale of the feeding of the four thousand imparts that situations perceived as lacking or desperate can be avenues for service and provision. By internalizing the Triad of Belief and centering on an authentic desire to assist, salespeople can approach unsold leads with assurance, fortifying the brand image and converting perceived vulnerabilities into assets.

Rekindling Lost Momentum: Lessons from the Rebuilding of Jerusalem's Walls

The fear or hesitation that salespeople might have for contacting unsold customers due to lost momentum can be likened to the situation faced by Nehemiah when he sought to rebuild the walls of Jerusalem. The task was daunting, and the momentum to rebuild had been lost over time. However, Nehemiah's belief in his mission, his strategy, and his faith in God allowed him to rekindle the energy and engagement needed to complete the task. (Nehemiah 2:17-20)

Nehemiah's story aligns with the Triad of Belief. His belief in the importance of rebuilding the walls (industry) drove him to take on the challenge. His belief in the plan and the support of the people (product or service) gave him the confidence to proceed. His belief in himself and his faith in God (belief in oneself) empowered him to overcome opposition and rekindle the lost momentum.

In the context of sales, the fear of lost momentum with unsold customers can be overcome by focusing on the core values and benefits that the product or service offers. Just as Nehemiah was able to rally the people around a shared vision, salespeople must reconnect with the unsold customer by emphasizing the unique value they can provide.

Practical steps to overcome this fear include revisiting the initial conversation and identifying what engaged the customer in the first place. By understanding their needs and interests, salespeople can tailor their approach to rekindle that initial energy. Regular follow-ups, personalized communication, and demonstrating a genuine interest in the customer's success can help rebuild the momentum.

Moreover, salespeople should not shy away from acknowledging the time that has passed. Being transparent about the desire to reconnect and provide value can create a positive and honest foundation for re-engaging the unsold customer.

In conclusion, the story of Nehemiah rebuilding Jerusalem's walls teaches us that lost momentum can be regained through belief, strategy, and genuine engagement. By embracing the Triad of Belief and focusing on the unique value that can be provided, salespeople can overcome the fear of lost momentum and successfully re-initiate conversations with unsold customers. The key lies in understanding the customer's needs, being transparent, and demonstrating a consistent commitment to serving them.

Nothing New To Say: Lessons from Isaiah's Consistent Prophesying

Salespeople often hesitate to contact unsold customers due to a lack of updated offers or new aspects of the product or service to introduce. This fear stems from the belief that without something new to present, the conversation may seem redundant or uninteresting.

In the scriptures, we find a parallel in the prophet Isaiah's consistent prophesying. Isaiah's message was often the same, emphasizing the eternal nature of God's word: "The grass withers and the flowers fall, but the word of our God endures forever" (Isaiah 40:8). Isaiah did not need new promotions or changing aspects of his message to continue his prophetic mission. His belief in the timeless value of God's word was enough.

This example aligns with the Triad of Belief. Isaiah's unwavering belief in his mission (industry), his confidence in the eternal truth of God's word (product or service), and his faith in his prophetic calling (belief in oneself) allowed him to continue his work without needing to change or update his message.

Salespeople can learn from Isaiah's example by focusing on the timeless value and core benefits of their product or service. Even without new promotions or updates, the essential value that the product or service provides to the customer remains. By emphasizing these core benefits and how they align with the customer's needs and goals, salespeople can re-engage unsold customers effectively.

One practical strategy to overcome this fear is to understand the timeless value of the product or service. Salespeople can identify the core benefits that remain relevant to the customer, regardless of new promotions or updates. This understanding can form the foundation of a conversation that emphasizes the enduring value of what is being offered.

Another approach is to personalize the conversation, tailoring it to the specific needs and interests of the unsold customer. By focusing on how the product or service can provide value to them, salespeople can create a connection that transcends the need for new offers.

Building relationships is also key. Salespeople should focus on building a relationship with the customer, not just selling a product. By showing genuine interest in their success and well-being, they can create a connection that goes beyond the transactional nature of sales.

The fear of having nothing new to say can be overcome by focusing on the timeless value and core benefits of the product or service. Isaiah's consistent prophesying teaches us that the essential message's value does not diminish over time. By embracing the Triad of Belief and focusing on serving the customer, salespeople can re-engage unsold customers with confidence and purpose, even without new promotions or updates.

Venturing into the Unknown: Lessons from Abraham's Faith

The fear of venturing into unknown territory is not uncommon among salespeople, especially when contacting unsold customers. If the reasons for the initial non-purchase were not clearly communicated, the salesperson might feel they are stepping into an uncertain situation. This fear can be paralyzing, hindering the salesperson from trying to reconnect with the potential customer.

In the scriptures, we find an inspiring example in the story of Abraham, who was called by God to leave his homeland and go to a place he did not know. Hebrews 11:8 tells us, "By faith Abraham, when called to go to a place he would later receive as his inheritance, obeyed and went, even though he did not know where he was going." Abraham's faith in God's promise allowed him to venture into the unknown with confidence.

This story resonates with the Triad of Belief. Abraham's belief in God's promise (industry), his trust in God's guidance (product or service), and his faith in his calling (belief in oneself) empowered him to overcome his fear of the unknown.

Salespeople can learn from Abraham's example by embracing faith in their industry, product or service, and themselves. Even when the feedback from unsold customers is unclear, the core principles of the Triad of Belief can guide them.

One practical way to overcome this fear is to seek clarity. If the reasons for non-purchase were not communicated, the salesperson can approach the customer with a genuine desire to understand their needs and concerns. By asking open-ended questions and actively listening, they can gain insights into what held the customer back and how they might address those concerns.

Another strategy is to focus on building a relationship rather than making a sale. By showing genuine interest in the customer's needs and offering value without immediate expectation of a purchase, the salesperson can create a connection that may lead to future opportunities.

The fear of unclear feedback from unsold customers can be overcome by embracing the principles of the Triad of Belief and learning from Abraham's faith. By seeking clarity, building relationships, and emphasizing value, salespeople can venture into the unknown with confidence, turning potential obstacles into opportunities for growth and success. The timeless lesson from Abraham's journey reminds us that faith and belief can guide us even when the path ahead seems uncertain.

Overcoming the Fear of Presumed Loyalty to Competitors: Lessons from the Call of Matthew

In the world of sales, the fear of presumed loyalty to competitors can be a significant barrier. Salespeople might hesitate to contact unsold customers, believing that they have chosen a competing product or service and are now loyal to that choice. This presumption can lead to missed opportunities and a lack of engagement with potential customers.

A scriptural reference that can shed light on this fear is the call of Matthew, the tax collector, found in Matthew 9:9-13. Jesus saw Matthew sitting at the tax collector's booth and said to him, "Follow me." Matthew got up and followed Him. Tax collectors were often seen as loyal to the Roman authorities, and their allegiance was presumed to be fixed. Yet, Jesus saw beyond this presumed loyalty and called Matthew to a higher purpose.

This story can be connected to the Triad of Belief. Jesus believed in the Kingdom of God and the transformative power of His message. He did not shy away from those who seemed loyal to other authorities. His belief in the unique value of His teachings and the salvation He offered allowed Him to approach Matthew without hesitation. He saw the potential in Matthew, not just the current reality. Jesus' unwavering belief in His mission, His teachings, and Himself provides a powerful example for salespeople.

Salespeople can learn from this example by recognizing that presumed loyalty to competitors is not an insurmountable barrier. By engaging in conversation and asking questions, salespeople can uncover the real reasons behind a customer's choice. Understanding their needs and concerns can open the door to presenting your product or service in a new light. If the salesperson believes in the unique value of their product or service, they can confidently present it to the customer, highlighting what sets it apart from competitors and creating interest that challenges presumed loyalty.

Furthermore, loyalty is often built on relationships. By focusing on building a genuine connection with the customer, salespeople can create trust and openness. This relationship can lead to opportunities to present the product or service again. Just as Jesus did not hesitate to call Matthew, salespeople should not be deterred by initial rejection or presumed loyalty to competitors. Persistence, coupled with respect and understanding, can lead to success.

In conclusion, the fear of presumed loyalty to competitors can be overcome by embracing the principles of the Triad of Belief and learning from the call of Matthew. By understanding the customer's needs, highlighting unique value, building relationships, and embracing persistence, salespeople can approach unsold customers with confidence and purpose. The story of Matthew reminds us that presumed loyalty is not permanently fixed, and with the right approach, new opportunities can be found. This perspective aligns with the belief in one's industry, product or service, and oneself, reinforcing the positive activity of selling with the intent to help.

Overcoming Ego and Pride: Embracing Humility in Reconnecting with Unsold Customer

Ego and pride can be significant barriers in the sales process, particularly when it comes to contacting unsold customers. The fear of appearing unsuccessful or the reluctance to admit that a sale was not closed can prevent salespeople from reapproaching potential clients.

This hesitation is rooted in the fear of a hit to their self-esteem, believing that they gave their best pitch and still didn't close the deal.

A powerful scriptural reference that can be applied to this situation is found in the story of John the Baptist's humility in John 3:30, where he states, "He must become greater; I must become less." John the Baptist recognized that his role was to prepare the way for Jesus, not to seek glory for himself. His humility allowed him to focus on the mission rather than his ego.

This example can be connected to the Triad of Belief by emphasizing the importance of humility and recognizing the greater purpose in the sales process. Belief in your industry, product or service, and yourself should not be overshadowed by personal pride or ego. Instead, the focus should be on how the product or service can genuinely benefit the customer.

Jesus himself demonstrated humility throughout his ministry. He washed the feet of his disciples (John 13:1-17), a task typically reserved for the lowest servants. He did not let pride or status prevent him from serving others. This example can inspire salespeople to approach their work with humility, recognizing that their role is to serve the customer's needs, not to boost their ego.

Practically, salespeople can overcome the fear of ego and pride by adopting a mindset of continuous learning and growth. Recognizing that not every pitch will result in a sale, and that's okay, can alleviate the pressure to always succeed. Instead, focusing on what can be learned from the experience and how to improve for the next opportunity can turn a perceived failure into a valuable lesson.

Additionally, salespeople can remind themselves of the core purpose of their role: to help the customer. By shifting the focus from self to service, the fear of a hit to self-esteem becomes less significant. The goal is not personal glory but the satisfaction and benefit of the customer.

The fear or hesitation rooted in ego and pride can be overcome by embracing the examples of humility found in the scriptures, particularly in the lives of John the Baptist and Jesus. By focusing on continuous growth, learning from experiences, and prioritizing service over self, salespeople can approach unsold customers with confidence and purpose. Connecting this approach to the Triad of Belief reinforces the positive and selfless nature of selling with the intent to help, aligning with the core values of belief in one's industry, product or service, and oneself.

Balancing New and Unsold Leads: A Lesson in Comprehensive Engagement

Pursuing new leads is an essential aspect of sales, but it can sometimes lead to neglecting unsold customers. When a salesperson juggles multiple new potential customers, they might deprioritize or even overlook the unsold ones. This fear or hesitation is not merely about time management but also about understanding the value each lead brings to the table, whether new or unsold.

In the New Testament, we can find a parallel in the way Jesus handled the multitudes that followed Him. In the Gospel of Mark, Chapter 6, Jesus feeds the five thousand. Despite the overwhelming number of people, He didn't turn anyone away or prioritize one group over another. Instead, He took what was available, blessed it, and ensured that everyone was fed. This miracle wasn't just about food; it was a lesson in managing abundance without neglecting anyone.

The Triad of Belief can be applied here as well. Belief in your industry means recognizing the potential in every lead, whether new or unsold. Belief in your product or service requires understanding that what you offer can be valuable to both new and previous prospects.

And belief in yourself involves having the confidence to manage multiple leads without losing sight of the individual value each one holds.

Practical suggestions to overcome this fear include implementing a robust lead management system that doesn't allow unsold customers to fall through the cracks. Regularly reviewing and categorizing leads can ensure that no opportunities are missed. Training and support in time management and lead prioritization can also be invaluable.

Being overburdened by new leads at the expense of unsold ones can be overcome by taking a holistic approach to lead management. By learning from the example of Jesus and applying the principles of the Triad of Belief, salespeople can ensure that they are serving all potential customers, recognizing the unique value and opportunity that each one presents.

Misjudging the Sales Window: The Persistent Pursuit

The fear of misjudging the sales window, believing that the optimal time for making a sale has passed, is a common concern among salespeople. This fear can lead to missed opportunities and a lack of engagement with potential customers.

A scriptural example that can shed light on this fear is found in the Parable of the Persistent Widow (Luke 18:1-8). In this parable, Jesus tells the story of a widow who persistently seeks justice from an unjust judge. Despite her initial failures, she continues to plead her case, never giving up or believing that her window of opportunity has closed. Her persistence pays off, and the judge finally grants her request.

This parable teaches us about the importance of persistence and faith, even when it seems like the opportunity has passed. It aligns with the Triad of Belief in sales: belief in your industry, belief in your product or service, and belief in yourself. Just as the widow did not give up on seeking justice, a salesperson should not give up on unsold customers, assuming that the opportunity has passed. The window for making a sale may still be open, and it requires persistence, faith, and a genuine desire to serve the customer.

If a salesperson feels that they have missed the optimal window for a sale, they should take inspiration from the Persistent Widow. They must continue to engage with the customer, understanding their needs, and demonstrating how their product or service can meet those needs. This approach requires a strong belief in the value of what is being offered and a commitment to serving the customer's best interests.

The fear of misjudging the sales window can be overcome by embracing the lessons from the Parable of the Persistent Widow. By applying these lessons and maintaining a strong belief in the industry, product or service, and oneself, salespeople can turn what seems like a missed opportunity into a chance for connection and success. Much like in the parable, the window of opportunity in sales may remain open far longer than we initially perceive.

Worry Over Consistency: The Unwavering Message

Salespeople often face the fear or hesitation of contradicting or altering what was said in the initial interaction with unsold customers. This concern over consistency can be daunting and may lead to reluctance in reapproaching potential clients.

A scriptural reference that can be drawn upon to address this fear is the consistency of Jesus' teachings throughout His ministry. One example is His Sermon on the Mount (Matthew 5-7), where He lays out the core principles of His teachings. These principles were not altered or contradicted throughout His ministry. Whether speaking to the crowds, His disciples, or the Pharisees, Jesus maintained a consistent message.

This consistency in Jesus' teachings can be related to the Triad of Belief in sales: belief in your industry, belief in your product or service, and belief in yourself. Just as Jesus had unwavering belief in His message and mission, a salesperson must have unwavering belief in what they are offering. This belief forms the foundation for a consistent and authentic approach to potential customers.

If a salesperson is worried about consistency in their approach to unsold customers, they should reflect on the core values and benefits of what they are offering. By understanding these deeply, they can communicate them consistently, without contradiction. This requires a genuine belief in the value of the product or service and a commitment to serving the customer's best interests.

Practical suggestions to overcome this fear include preparing and understanding the key points that need to be communicated, practicing the pitch to ensure that it aligns with the core values of the product or service, and focusing on the customer's needs rather than on making a sale. By aligning the approach with the customer's needs and the inherent value of what is being offered, the salesperson can maintain consistency in their interactions.

The fear of inconsistency can be overcome by drawing inspiration from the unwavering consistency of Jesus' teachings. By focusing on the core values and benefits of what is being offered and aligning these with the customer's needs, a salesperson can maintain a consistent and authentic approach. This approach, rooted in the Triad of Belief, can turn the fear of inconsistency into a strength, building trust and credibility with potential customers.

Memory Gaps: The Challenge of Recollection and the Wisdom of Documentation

The fear of memory gaps is a shared concern among salespeople, both when contacting sold and unsold customers. This hesitation stems from uncertainty about the specifics of previous interactions, leading to fears of making mistakes or overlooking essential details. The recurrence of this concern in different contexts emphasizes the importance of utilizing all available resources, not just relying on memory.

A scriptural reference that can be drawn upon to address this fear is found in the Book of Proverbs. Proverbs 3:5-6 advises, "Trust in the Lord with all your heart and lean not on your own understanding; in all your ways submit to him, and he will make your paths straight." This wisdom can be applied to the sales context, reminding salespeople not to rely solely on their memory but to seek guidance and use available tools to ensure accuracy.

Connecting this scripture with the Triad of Belief in sales, we can see how belief in your industry, belief in your product or service, and belief in yourself can be fortified by not leaning solely on one's understanding or memory. By seeking guidance and utilizing resources, salespeople can approach unsold customers with confidence and precision.

In practical terms, this means employing tools such as Customer Relationship Management (CRM) systems, taking detailed notes, and setting reminders. These practices align with the belief in serving the customer by ensuring that their specific needs and previous interactions are accurately remembered and addressed.

The wisdom found in Proverbs also reinforces the belief in the industry and the product or service being offered. By not leaning solely on one's understanding and embracing available resources, salespeople can approach unsold customers with renewed confidence. This approach, rooted in the Triad of Belief and aligned with serving the customer's needs, turns a common fear into an opportunity for growth and success.

The fear of memory gaps in contacting unsold customers can be overcome by drawing inspiration from the wisdom found in Proverbs. Trusting in guidance and utilizing practical tools allows salespeople to have accurate recollections of their interactions with customers. This approach, grounded in the Triad of Belief and focused on serving the customer's needs, transforms a common fear into a pathway for enhanced engagement and achievement. By recognizing that this fear is common and can be addressed through practical means, salespeople can move forward with confidence, knowing that they are well-equipped to serve their customers effectively.

Embracing the Challenge: Transforming Hesitations into Opportunities with Unsold Customers

The journey through the myriad of hesitations and fears that salespeople may experience when contacting unsold customers has been both enlightening and empowering. Unlike the path we explored with sold customers, the terrain here is filled with unique challenges and opportunities that require a distinct approach.

In sales, unsold customers represent a landscape rich with potential. They are not closed doors but rather unopened gateways, waiting for the right key. The hesitations we've examined in this chapter are not insurmountable barriers but rather signposts, guiding us towards understanding, empathy, and strategic action.

Drawing from the wisdom of scripture and aligning with the Triad of Belief, we've seen how belief in the industry, belief in the product or service, and belief in oneself can be the compass that navigates through these hesitations. The lessons from Jesus, the apostles, and the prophets have provided timeless insights that resonate with the modern salesperson's journey.

The unsold customer is not a failure but a future success story waiting to be written. Each hesitation we've explored is a lesson in disguise, teaching us more about ourselves, our customers, and our industry. By recognizing these fears and hesitations as opportunities for growth, we can transform them into strengths.

In practical terms, this means adopting a mindset of continuous learning and adaptation. It means recognizing that every 'no' is a step closer to a 'yes,' and every hesitation is a chance to refine our approach. It means embracing technology, honing our listening skills, and adapting our presentations to serve the unique needs of each customer.

As we conclude this section, let us carry forward the understanding that contacting unsold customers is not a task to be feared but a mission to be embraced. It's a journey filled with potential, guided by the principles of service, belief, and continuous growth. The road ahead is open, and the opportunities are endless. Let us move forward with confidence, knowing that we are equipped to turn hesitations into triumphs and unsold customers into lasting relationships.

> **"For God gave us a spirit not of fear but of power and love and self-control."**
>
> 2 Timothy 1:7 (ESV)

Orphans

Reconnecting with the Lost and Forgotten

In sales, an "orphan" is not a child without parents but a customer who, despite having previously engaged with your company, is left unattended. They have purchased from your organization, but no one is currently reaching out to them to introduce new products, update them on current ones, or ensure that they are utilizing your product or service to its fullest potential. These customers, though once connected, have become isolated and forgotten, much like orphans in the traditional sense.

Understanding the importance of taking ownership of these orphans is vital for any salesperson. An "orphan owner" is someone who assumes the responsibility of managing a client account that has been left without a designated owner. This can occur for various reasons, such as an employee leaving the company or a reorganization of accounts. The role of the orphan owner is not merely administrative; it's about building and maintaining relationships, ensuring that the client's needs are met, and addressing any concerns or issues that may arise.

The necessity of having an orphan owner cannot be overstated. Without one, the account may be neglected, and the customer could be lost to a competitor. The orphan owner's role is to show the client that we value their business and are committed to providing excellent customer service. It's about demonstrating our willingness to go the extra mile to ensure that their needs are met, even in challenging situations. This commitment helps build trust and loyalty, essential elements for long-term success.

In the context of the Old Testament, the prophets were, in a sense, the salespeople of the Kingdom of God. They were there to educate, instruct, manage, and lead the Israelites in how to receive and best achieve God's salvation. Prophets like Isaiah, Jeremiah, Elijah, Ezekiel, and Amos were chosen by God to deliver messages of warning, encouragement, and hope. Though often unpopular in their time, their words have been preserved and continue to inspire millions today.

The Bible's intertestamental period, marked by political upheaval and cultural changes, saw the Jewish people become orphans in a spiritual sense. They experienced foreign rule and significant challenges to their religious practices. New religious movements emerged during this time, and the Jewish people sought to preserve their traditions and adapt to new circumstances.

Jesus sought to reconnect these spiritual orphans, the lost sheep of Israel, and bring them back to God. He referred to himself as a shepherd, and his parables, such as the one about the lost sheep, illustrate his desire to reach out to the orphans of Israel and bring them back. Jesus' words in Matthew 10:12-14 and Luke 15:6-7 emphasize the joy of finding the lost and the importance of not losing even one believer.

Reaching these orphans was central to Jesus' prospecting methodology and was his first step in bringing God's salvation to the world. He only expanded his ministry to others after attempting to contact the orphans of Israel.

The concept of orphans in sales is not merely a business strategy but a profound principle that resonates with our deepest human values. It's about recognizing the worth of every individual and ensuring that no one is left behind or forgotten. Whether in the context of sales or the spiritual teachings of the Bible, the lesson is clear: We must be diligent in seeking out those who have been lost or neglected and make every effort to bring them back into the fold. In doing so, we enhance our business and enrich our understanding of compassion, responsibility, and the interconnectedness of all people.

Integrating Orphans into your prospecting Master List is not a mere addition; it's a vital enhancement that can lead to renewed opportunities, deeper insights, and a more effective approach to sales. It's a strategy that recognizes the potential in every connection and the value of not letting anyone slip through the cracks. It's about seeing the big picture and understanding that every customer, no matter how distant or disengaged they may seem, is a part of that picture. By embracing this approach, you not only strengthen your Master List but also enrich your sales practice with compassion, insight, and strategic wisdom.

Engaging with Orphans

Orphans represent a unique and often untapped opportunity in the dynamic sales world. These are clients who have previously engaged with your company but are currently without a designated point of contact. Reconnecting with Orphans revives dormant relationships and opens doors to new possibilities.

By becoming the primary contact and information source for orphans, you can gain a pre-sold customer base for your company, product, or service.

Guidance on Preparing for a Call to an Orphan

Calling orphans presents unique challenges. The customer's reaction to your call could be positive, negative, or anywhere in between. The following guidelines for preparing for your call will help you strategize.

Set Clear Objectives: Know what you want to achieve from the conversation. Whether it's rekindling a relationship, understanding their current needs, or offering a new product, having clear goals will guide the conversation.

Research: Gather information about the orphan's past purchases, feedback, and any previous issues or successes. This knowledge will help you address their specific situation.

Empathize: Understand that the orphan may have felt neglected or overlooked. Approach the conversation with empathy and a genuine desire to serve.

Be Flexible: While the forthcoming conversation starters provide a guide, be prepared to adapt to the conversation as it unfolds. Flexibility will allow you to respond to the orphan's unique concerns and interests.

Understand the Context: Before reaching out, familiarize yourself with the orphan's history with your company. Knowing their past interactions and experiences will help you tailor your approach.

Align with Values: These conversation starters are rooted in scriptural principles. Reflect on these values and consider how they align with your company's mission and the specific needs of the orphan.

Prepare and Practice: Select a conversation starter that resonates with the situation and practice it. Being prepared will make the conversation flow more naturally.

Be Genuine: While these starters provide a framework, it's essential to be genuine and attentive. Listen actively and respond thoughtfully.

Follow Up: These conversation starters are just the beginning. Be prepared to follow up with detailed information, solutions, and continued engagement.

Conversation Starters

By utilizing these conversation starters and following the guidance provided, salespeople can approach Orphans with confidence, empathy, and a genuine desire to serve. These interactions are not merely transactional but an opportunity to build trust, demonstrate value, and foster long-term relationships. The scriptural connections add a layer of depth, aligning the conversation with timeless principles that can resonate on a profound level.

The following list of conversation starters is crafted to assist salespeople in initiating meaningful dialogues with Orphans. Each starter is tied to a portion or lesson from scripture, infusing the conversation with values and principles that transcend mere business interactions.

Rekindling Connection: "I'm reaching out to reconnect and see how we can serve you better." (Luke 15:4-7 - Parable of the Lost Sheep)

Understanding Needs: "Can we discuss your current needs and how we might align with them?" (Philippians 2:4 - Looking to the interests of others)

Offering Assistance: "How can I assist you today with our products/services?" (Galatians 6:2 - Bearing one another's burdens)

Acknowledging Past Relationship: "I value our past relationship and want to explore how we can continue working together." (Proverbs 17:17 - A friend loves at all times)

New Opportunities: "Have you considered our latest offerings? They might be just what you need." (Isaiah 43:19 - God making something new)

Expressing Value: "We truly value your partnership. How can we strengthen our relationship?" (1 Peter 2:17 - Honor everyone)

Addressing Concerns: "I'm here to address any concerns you may have. Your satisfaction is our priority." (Matthew 7:12 - Golden Rule)

Inviting Feedback: "Your thoughts and feedback are vital to us. Can we discuss your experience?" (Proverbs 19:20 - Listen to advice)

Sharing Updates: "I'd like to share some exciting updates that could benefit you." (Ecclesiastes 3:1 - A time for everything)

Building Trust: "Trust is essential to us. How can we earn yours?" (Psalm 20:7 - Trust in the name of the Lord)

Exploring Goals: "Let's explore your goals and see how we can support them." (Proverbs 16:3 - Commit your work to the Lord)

Offering Support: "I'm here to support you. What can I do to help?" (1 Thessalonians 5:11 - Encourage one another)

Emphasizing Commitment: "We're committed to your success. How can we better serve you?" (Ruth 1:16 - Ruth's commitment to Naomi)

Seeking Collaboration: "I see opportunities for collaboration. Can we explore them together?" (1 Corinthians 12:14 - One body, many parts)

Acknowledging Mistakes: "If we've fallen short, please let us know so we can make it right." (James 5:16 - Confess your sins to one another)

Focusing on Growth: "I believe in our potential for growth. Can we discuss this?" (2 Peter 3:18 - Grow in grace and knowledge)

Inviting Open Dialogue: "I'm here to listen. What's on your mind?" (James 1:19 - Quick to hear, slow to speak)

Offering Solutions: "I have some ideas that might interest you. Can we discuss them?" (Proverbs 3:5-6 - Trust in the Lord for direction)

Expressing Appreciation: "Thank you for your past engagement. How can we continue to serve you?" (Colossians 3:15 - Be thankful)

Creating a Vision: "I envision a renewed partnership. Can we explore this vision together?" (Habakkuk 2:2 - Write the vision)

Emphasizing Integrity: "We strive for integrity in all we do. How can we demonstrate this to you?" (Proverbs 10:9 - Integrity guides)

Building Long-Term Relationships: "I'm interested in building a long-term relationship with you. Can we discuss our future collaboration?" (Ecclesiastes 4:9-10 - Two are better than one)

Providing Assurance: "I want to assure you of our commitment to excellence. How can we prove this to you?" (Deuteronomy 31:6 - Be strong and courageous)

Seeking Understanding: "I want to understand your perspective better. Can you share your thoughts?" (Proverbs 4:7 - Wisdom is supreme)

Offering encouragement: "I believe in your vision and want to support it. How can we help?" (1 Thessalonians 5:11 - Build each other up)

Emphasizing Respect: "We respect your decisions and want to align with your needs. Can we discuss this further?" (Romans 12:10 - Show honor to one another)

Promoting Partnership: "I see us as partners working towards common goals. How can we strengthen our partnership?" (Ecclesiastes 4:12 - A cord of three strands is not easily broken)

Valuing Time: "I value your time and want to make our conversation productive. What would you like to focus on?" (Ephesians 5:16 - Making the best use of time)

Promoting Peace: "I want our relationship to be harmonious and beneficial. How can we achieve this?" (Romans 12:18 - Live peaceably with all)

Fostering Commitment: "I'm committed to your success and satisfaction. How can we make our relationship even better?" (Proverbs 16:3 - Commit your work to the Lord)

Conclusion: Embracing the Opportunity with Orphans

The journey of reconnecting with Orphans is more than a sales strategy; it's a commitment to service, understanding, and relationship-building. Salespeople can transform overlooked opportunities into thriving partnerships by approaching these unique clients with empathy, preparation, and the timeless wisdom found in scripture.

The conversation starters and guidance provided in this chapter are tools to help you navigate this nuanced terrain. They are not merely scripts to be recited but starting points to be adapted and personalized. Each interaction with an orphan is a chance to demonstrate your belief in your industry, your product or service, and most importantly, in yourself. This aligns perfectly with the Triad of Belief, reinforcing the core principles that guide successful sales endeavors.

Remember, the prophets of old were sent to guide, educate, and reconnect the people to the Kingdom of God. In a similar vein, salespeople are called to reach out to Orphans, not just to sell a product but to offer solutions, build trust, and create lasting relationships. The lessons drawn from scripture serve as a moral compass, guiding these interactions with integrity and purpose.

As you move forward, may you see Orphans not as lost opportunities but as invitations to grow, serve, and excel. Embrace them with the same passion and dedication that Jesus showed in seeking the lost sheep, knowing that every connection made is a step towards fulfilling your mission as a salesperson.

In the end, reaching out to Orphans is not just about closing a deal; it's about opening a door to collaboration, understanding, and mutual success. It's about selling as serving, guided by principles that have stood the test of time.

> **"For I was hungry and you gave me something to eat, I was thirsty and you gave me something to drink, I was a stranger and you invited me in."**
>
> Matthew 25:35 (NIV)

Customers of Your Competitors

Engaging the Competition's Terrain

You are not alone in the bustling marketplace of ideas, products, and services. Your offerings share the stage with competitors, no matter how unique and innovative. These competitors have their customers, individuals who have chosen a path different from what you offer. But does that mean they are out of reach? Absolutely not.

Navigating the Commodity Landscape

In any market, whether you're offering a product or service, there's a high likelihood that others are offering something similar. These competitors have their clientele, but is that clientele genuinely content? Are they receiving everything they desire or require? Herein lies your golden opportunity.

Your unwavering belief in your industry, your product or service, and most importantly, in yourself, sets you apart. You understand that what you offer can meet specific needs, enhance lives, and deliver unmatched service. This conviction is your compass, guiding you even in markets saturated with similar products.

Take Mike Lindell of My Pillow, for instance. Was his pillow genuinely groundbreaking compared to the plethora of other pillows on the market? Probably not in the conventional sense. However, Lindell's distinguishing factors were his fervent passion, his personal journey, and his self-assuredness. His belief in his product, his industry, and himself resonated with consumers, allowing My Pillow to dominate in a market where differentiation was challenging.

Colonel Sanders serves as another poignant example. While he didn't invent restaurant-served fried chicken, his distinct recipe and tenacious marketing, despite numerous setbacks, etched KFC into the global consciousness. The allure wasn't solely the chicken but the narrative, the brand persona, and an unwavering belief in his offering. The brand became so iconic that today, fried chicken is almost synonymous with Colonel Sanders.

Reflect on Netflix's trajectory in the home movie sector. In an era where Blockbuster and Hollywood Video were the titans, Netflix disrupted the scene with their mail-order DVD service, eliminating notorious late fees and broadening selection. As the digital age advanced, they seamlessly transitioned to streaming, altering our media consumption habits. Their success wasn't merely about movie rentals; it was their foresight, innovation, and keen understanding of evolving consumer needs. They didn't just join a bustling marketplace; they redefined it.

Apple's iPhone launch offers a similar narrative. While mobile phones weren't novel when Apple ventured in, the iPhone transformed the smartphone landscape with its intuitive interface, aesthetic appeal, and cohesive ecosystem. Apple's strategy wasn't just about a device; it was about curating an experience, a lifestyle. They differentiated not by crafting a radically different device, but by offering unique features and a distinct user experience.

What's remarkable about the examples given is that they didn't just enter crowded markets, they thrived and became leaders in their respective industries. This was due to their ability to envision a new way of doing things, their understanding of what consumers truly wanted, and their ability to tell a story that captivated their audience. It's clear that success is not just about having a good product or service, but also about having the vision and skills to break through the noise and rise to the top.

Reflecting on these tales of success in commoditized markets, ponder what unique attributes you bring to the table. Even if the product remains constant, your approach, your story, and your conviction can be the game-changers. Remember, in the world of sales, you are the differentiator.

The Knowns and Unknowns

Former Secretary of Defense Donald Rumsfeld once famously said, "There are known knowns; there are things we know we know. We also know there are known unknowns; that is to say we know there are some things we do not know. But there are also unknown unknowns—the ones we don't know we don't know." This profound statement acknowledges the limits of our knowledge and reminds us never to become complacent.

When it comes to standing out among your competitors, it's important to recognize that their customers may be convinced that their product or service is the best available. However, it's also possible that those customers are simply not aware of your own products or services. This is where you have the chance to differentiate yourself and make your offerings known. By highlighting the unique benefits and features of your products or services, you can capture the attention of potential customers and show them why you are the better choice. Don't be complacent and assume that your offerings speak for themselves - take proactive steps to showcase what you have to offer and win over new customers.

Learning from Jesus

Since humanity's fall, Jesus has been reaching out to those who sought solutions from His competitors, demonstrating that He offers a superior alternative. He proclaimed, "I am the way, and the truth, and the life. No one comes to the Father except through me" (John 14:6). He also described Himself as the good shepherd (John 10:11), the light of the world (John 8:12), and the resurrection and the life (John 11:25). Through these declarations, Jesus positioned Himself as the optimal answer to humanity's profound needs. While many believed they had found adequate solutions elsewhere, Jesus revealed that His offering, though seemingly similar on the surface, was truly unparalleled in its depth and efficacy.

Embracing the Opportunity

Customers of your competitors already believe in the industry and the product. Your task is to demonstrate your belief in yourself and convey that to your prospect. When you think of it this way, reaching out to these customers becomes 66% easier than trying to sell to a completely new prospect.

By following Jesus' lead and offering yourself as a resource, you can place yourself in front of a group of people who need to know you and how well you will serve them. Show that you care, be their guide, and open the door to new possibilities.

Reaching out to your competitors' customers is not a battle but an opportunity for connection and growth. It's about recognizing the shared landscape and finding the unique paths that lead to your door. It's about belief, passion, and the willingness to engage with those who may not yet know what you can offer.

As a salesperson, you are more than just someone pushing a product - you are a guide and helper who believes in the potential for a better future. Embrace this role, and you will discover that these customers are not lost causes, but rather valuable partners in your success. Building a relationship with these potential customers can lead to long-term partnerships and referrals. By providing exceptional customer service and offering a personalized experience, you can create a loyal customer base that sees you as more than just a salesperson, but a trusted advisor. With patience, persistence, and a commitment to excellence, you can turn your competitors' customers into your own success story.

Offering a Better Solution: Guided by Belief and Inspired by Scripture

The desire to offer a better solution is a driving force in the competitive sales world. Salespeople often find themselves in situations where they genuinely believe that their product or service is superior to what a customer is currently using. This belief is not merely a sales tactic but a conviction that they have something of greater value to provide. It's a belief rooted in the understanding of the industry, confidence in the product or service, and faith in oneself.

Consider a scenario where a salesperson is aware of a competitor's customer struggling with a product that lacks certain features or benefits. The salesperson knows that their offering not only includes those missing elements but also provides additional advantages that could significantly enhance the customer's experience. The salesperson's intention is not to undermine the competitor but to genuinely help the customer by providing a solution that better meets their needs.

This approach aligns with the teachings of Jesus, who consistently offered better solutions to those he encountered. A poignant example can be found in the story of the Samaritan woman at the well, as described in John 4:10-14. Jesus, knowing the woman's need for physical water, offered her something far more valuable: living water. He said, "Whoever drinks of the water that I will give him will never be thirsty again. The water that I will give him will become in him a spring of water welling up to eternal life."

Jesus was not merely offering a physical solution but a spiritual one that transcended the woman's immediate needs. He saw beyond the surface and provided a solution that would satisfy her deepest thirst. This story illustrates the essence of offering a better solution, not just to meet a temporary need but to provide lasting value.

The Triad of Belief resonates with this approach. Belief in the industry means understanding the broader context and recognizing where true value lies. Belief in the product or service means knowing its potential to make a real difference in people's lives. And belief in oneself means having the courage and integrity to reach out and offer that better solution, even when it means stepping into a competitor's territory.

Salespeople can take inspiration from this scriptural example by approaching customers of competitors with empathy, insight, and a genuine desire to help. It's not about winning a sale but about enriching a life. Salespeople can build trust and create lasting relationships by focusing on the customer's real needs and offering a solution that truly serves them.

Offering a better solution is not just a sales strategy but a philosophy guided by belief and inspired by the teachings of Jesus. It's about seeing the bigger picture, understanding the deeper needs, and having the conviction to offer something that makes a difference. It's a path that leads not just to a successful sale but to a meaningful connection and a satisfied customer.

Educational Opportunity: Enlightening Customers with Knowledge and Insight

In the competitive landscape of sales, customers often find themselves committed to products or services without fully understanding the broader industry, latest technological advancements, or emerging trends. This lack of awareness can lead to missed opportunities or suboptimal choices. A salesperson, driven by the Triad of Belief, can seize this as an educational opportunity, reaching out to competitors' customers to enlighten them with knowledge and insight.

Imagine a scenario where a salesperson is aware of a groundbreaking technological advancement in their industry that could significantly benefit a customer currently engaged with a competitor's product. The salesperson's belief in the industry, the product, and themselves compels them to reach out to the customer, not to push a sale, but to educate them about this new development. The intention is to help the customer make an informed decision that aligns with their needs and goals.

This approach of educating and enlightening finds a profound parallel in the teachings of Jesus. In Luke 24:13-35, we find the story of the Road to Emmaus, where Jesus encounters two disciples who were unaware of the events of His resurrection. Rather than merely revealing Himself, Jesus takes the time to explain the Scriptures to them, starting with Moses and all the Prophets, interpreting everything concerning Himself. It's an enlightening journey that opens their eyes to the truth, culminating in their recognition of Jesus when He breaks bread with them.

Jesus' approach was not about imposing His identity or demanding belief. It was an educational journey, a gentle guiding through the Scriptures, leading to a profound realization. He believed in His mission, His message, and His ability to convey it, and He used this belief to enlighten others.

Salespeople can emulate this approach by seeing their interactions with competitors' customers as educational opportunities. It's about sharing knowledge, offering insights, and guiding customers towards understanding. It's about belief in the industry's importance, confidence in the product's value, and faith in one's ability to convey this knowledge.

In practical terms, this means preparing oneself with the latest information, understanding the customer's needs, and approaching the conversation with empathy and respect. It's not about undermining the competitor but about enriching the customer's understanding. It's about being a guide, a teacher, and a trusted advisor.

The educational opportunity is a noble and impactful approach to engaging with competitors' customers. Inspired by the teachings of Jesus, it's an approach that transcends mere selling and enters the realm of enlightenment and empowerment. It's about seeing the customer not as a target but as a fellow traveler on a journey towards better choices and greater satisfaction. It's an approach that resonates with the core beliefs in the industry, product or service, and oneself, leading to relationships built on trust, respect, and mutual growth.

Price Comparisons: Guiding Customers to Cost-Effective Choices

In the world of sales, price often plays a pivotal role in a customer's decision-making process. While some customers may be committed to a competitor's product, they may not be aware of more affordable or cost-effective options available in the market. A salesperson, guided by the Triad of Belief, can approach this scenario as an opportunity to help the customer compare prices and possibly find a solution that better aligns with their budget without compromising quality.

Consider a situation where a salesperson is aware that their product offers similar features and benefits as a competitor's but at a more reasonable price. The salesperson's belief in the industry, the product, and themselves motivates them to reach out to the customer to present this alternative. The intention is not to undermine the competitor but to provide the customer with information that allows them to make an informed and financially wise decision.

This approach of guiding customers to cost-effective choices finds resonance in the teachings of Jesus. In the Parable of the Wise Builder (Matthew 7:24-27), Jesus speaks of a wise man who builds his house on the rock and a foolish man who builds on the sand. The wise man's house withstands the storms, while the foolish man's house falls. The underlying message is about making wise choices, considering not just the immediate appearance but the long-term value and stability.

Jesus' teaching is not about price comparison in a literal sense, but it emphasizes the importance of evaluating options and making decisions that offer lasting value. It's about wisdom, discernment, and understanding the true cost of choices.

Salespeople can adopt this approach by presenting price comparisons not as a mere numbers game but as a thoughtful evaluation of value, quality, and long-term benefits. It's about helping the customer see beyond the price tag and understand what they are truly gaining or losing. It's about belief in the industry's significance, confidence in the product's worth, and faith in one's ability to guide the customer to a wise decision.

In practical terms, this means being transparent about pricing, offering clear comparisons, and explaining the differences in features, benefits, and potential long-term savings. It's about being a trusted advisor, helping the customer navigate the complexities of pricing, and guiding them to a choice that aligns with their needs and budget.

The opportunity to provide price comparisons is more than a sales tactic; it's a service to the customer, inspired by the wisdom of Jesus' teachings. It's an approach that goes beyond mere selling and enters the realm of guidance, discernment, and empowerment. It's about seeing the customer not just as a potential sale but as a fellow traveler on a journey towards wise choices and financial well-being. It's an approach that resonates with the core beliefs in the industry, product or service, and oneself, leading to relationships built on trust, transparency, and mutual respect.

Better Features: Guiding Customers to Enhanced Solutions

In the competitive sales landscape, discovering a product or service with improved features, functionalities, or added benefits can be a game-changer for a customer. It's not uncommon for customers to settle for a competitor's offering without being fully aware of the superior options available. A salesperson, driven by the Triad of Belief, can approach this scenario as an opportunity to enlighten the customer about these enhanced solutions.

Imagine a situation where a salesperson knows that their product has a unique feature that significantly improves efficiency or adds a new dimension to the user experience. This feature is not just a minor upgrade but a substantial enhancement that could make a real difference to the customer. The salesperson's belief in the industry, the product, and themselves motivates them to reach out to the customer, not to disparage the competitor but to present this alternative that could better meet the customer's needs.

This approach finds resonance in the teachings of Jesus, specifically in the Parable of the Mustard Seed (Matthew 13:31-32). Jesus compares the Kingdom of Heaven to a mustard seed, which, though the smallest of all seeds, grows into a large tree where birds come and nest. The message here is about the potential for something small and seemingly insignificant to grow into something grand and beneficial.

Jesus' teaching is not about product features in a literal sense, but it emphasizes the importance of recognizing potential and the value of minor differences that can lead to significant benefits. It's about seeing beyond the immediate appearance and understanding the transformative power of unique attributes.

Salespeople can adopt this approach by presenting the improved features not as mere add-ons but as transformative enhancements that can bring substantial value to the customer. It's about helping the customer see the potential in these features and how they align with their needs, goals, or aspirations.

In practical terms, this means being clear about what sets the product apart, demonstrating how these features work, and explaining their tangible benefits. It's about being a guide, helping the customer navigate the complexities of product features, and showing them how these enhancements can make a real difference in their lives or businesses.

The opportunity to present better features is an act of service to the customer, inspired by the wisdom of Jesus' teachings. It's an approach that goes beyond mere selling and enters the realm of guidance, enlightenment, and empowerment. It's about seeing the customer not just as a potential sale but as a fellow traveler on a journey towards better solutions and enriched experiences. It's an approach that resonates with the core beliefs in the industry, product or service, and oneself, leading to relationships built on trust, understanding, and mutual growth. It's about planting the seed of possibility and nurturing it to fruition, just as the mustard seed grows into a nurturing tree.

Special Offers: Extending the Invitation to Greater Value

In the world of sales, special offers, promotions, and discounts are powerful tools to attract customers. They not only provide financial incentives but also create a sense of exclusivity and opportunity. When a salesperson reaches out to a competitor's customer with a special offer, it's more than just a sales pitch; it's an invitation to explore something valuable that they might not have discovered otherwise.

Consider a scenario where a salesperson has a limited-time offer that provides significant savings or additional benefits on a product or service. This offer is not widely advertised and is available only to a select group of customers. The salesperson, believing in the industry, the product, and their ability to serve the customer, takes the initiative to contact a competitor's customer. The intention is not to undermine the competitor but to present an opportunity that aligns with the customer's interests and needs.

This approach can find inspiration in the Parable of the Great Banquet (Luke 14:15-24). In this parable, Jesus tells the story of a man who prepared a great feast and invited many guests. When the invited guests made excuses and refused to come, the host sent his servant to invite the poor, the crippled, the blind, and the lame. The host's intention was to fill his house and share the feast with those who would appreciate it.

The parallel here is the generous invitation extended to those who might not have been the original or expected recipients. The host's desire to share the feast with others reflects the salesperson's intention to extend the special offer to a broader audience, including competitors' customers. It's about recognizing the value in what is being offered and wanting others to benefit from it.

The Triad of Belief plays a crucial role in this approach. The salesperson's belief in the industry signifies the understanding that the special offer is not just a marketing gimmick but a genuine opportunity. The belief in the product or service reinforces the conviction that the offer brings real value. The belief in oneself empowers the salesperson to reach out confidently, knowing they are acting in the customer's best interest.

In practical terms, this means being transparent about the offer, explaining why it's special, and how it aligns with the customer's needs or preferences. It's about building trust, showing empathy, and demonstrating that the offer is not just a sales tactic but a thoughtful gesture aimed at providing greater value.

Extending special offers to competitors' customers is a practice that goes beyond mere selling. It's an act of generosity, inspired by the teachings of Jesus, and rooted in a deep belief in the value of what is being offered. It's about seeing the potential in every customer, regardless of their current affiliations, and inviting them to partake in something that could enhance their lives or businesses. It's a practice that resonates with the core principles of sales as a service, guided by belief, integrity, and the desire to make a positive difference.

Upgraded Customer Service: A Commitment to Excellence

In the competitive business landscape, customer service often becomes a distinguishing factor. It's not just about the product or the price; it's about the experience, support, and relationship a company builds with its customers. When a salesperson knows that their company provides superior customer service, reaching out to a competitor's customer becomes an act of care. It's an offer to elevate the customer's experience and provide them with a level of service they may not have encountered before.

Imagine a scenario where a salesperson is aware that a competitor's customer has faced repeated issues and delays in resolving them. The salesperson decides to reach out, confident in their company's commitment to customer satisfaction. They explain how their company prioritizes customer support, detailing the various channels of communication, the responsiveness, and the personalized care they provide. It's not just a sales pitch; it's an invitation to a better experience.

This approach finds inspiration in the story of Jesus healing the man at the Pool of Bethesda (John 5:1-9). In this account, Jesus encounters a man who had been an invalid for thirty-eight years. The man explains that he has no one to help him into the healing waters when they are stirred, and as a result, he has remained unhealed. Jesus, moved by compassion and understanding the man's need for support, tells him to pick up his mat and walk. The man is healed instantly.

The connection here is the attentive care and immediate response that Jesus provided. He didn't just offer words of comfort; he provided a solution. He understood the man's frustration and took action to resolve his issue. This mirrors the salesperson's intention to offer upgraded customer service, to understand the customer's pain points, and to provide a tangible solution.

The Triad of Belief is integral to this approach. The belief in the industry signifies that customer service is not an afterthought but a core component of the business. The belief in the product or service reinforces the commitment to support the customer in every possible way. The belief in oneself empowers the salesperson to reach out with genuine concern and the confidence that they can make a difference.

In practical terms, this means being empathetic to the customer's previous experiences, highlighting the specific ways in which your company's customer service excels, and assuring them that their satisfaction is a priority. It's about building trust through transparency and a genuine desire to enhance their experience.

Offering upgraded customer service to a competitor's customer is more than a business strategy; it's a human connection. It's inspired by the compassionate care that Jesus demonstrated and is rooted in a profound belief in the value of customer satisfaction. It's about recognizing the individual needs of each customer and committing to meet them with excellence. It's a practice that resonates with the essence of sales as a service, guided by empathy, integrity, and the relentless pursuit of customer happiness.

Tailored Solutions: Meeting Individual Needs with Precision

In the realm of sales, one size does not fit all. Customers have unique needs, preferences, and challenges that require specific solutions. A salesperson who recognizes this and offers tailored solutions is not just selling a product or service; they are providing a personalized experience that can make a profound difference in the customer's life.

Consider a scenario where a salesperson learns about a competitor's customer who is struggling with a generic product that doesn't quite fit their needs. The salesperson knows that their company specializes in creating customized solutions that can precisely address the customer's unique requirements. They decide to reach out, not just to make a sale, but to offer a solution that could genuinely enhance the customer's life or business.

This approach finds resonance in the story of Jesus healing the blind man in Bethsaida (Mark 8:22-26). When Jesus encounters the blind man, He doesn't merely speak a word of healing as He had done in other instances. Instead, He takes the man by the hand, leads him out of the village, puts saliva on his eyes, and lays His hands on him. When Jesus asks if the man sees anything, the man replies that he sees people but they look like trees walking. Jesus then lays His hands on the man's eyes again, and his sight is fully restored.

This healing is unique in the way Jesus approached it. He didn't heal the man instantly; He took the time to understand the man's condition and applied a specific method to heal him. It was a tailored solution, designed to meet the individual's unique need.

The Triad of Belief is evident in this approach. The belief in the industry signifies the understanding that customized solutions are essential in meeting diverse needs. The belief in the product or service is reflected in the confidence that the salesperson's offering can be adapted to fit the customer's specific requirements. The belief in oneself empowers the salesperson to approach the customer with the assurance that they can provide a solution that will make a real difference.

In practical terms, this means taking the time to understand the customer's unique challenges, preferences, and goals. It involves asking probing questions, listening attentively, and designing a solution that is aligned with the customer's specific needs. It's about demonstrating empathy, expertise, and a commitment to delivering value that goes beyond the generic.

Offering tailored solutions to a competitor's customer is an act of service that reflects a deep understanding of the customer's individuality. It's inspired by Jesus' compassionate and personalized approach to healing and is rooted in a profound belief in the power of customization. It's a practice that transcends mere selling and becomes a partnership in achieving the customer's goals. It's a testament to the salesperson's dedication to excellence, empathy, and the relentless pursuit of solutions that truly resonate with the customer's unique journey.

Risk Diversification: A Wise Approach to Stability

Risk diversification is a principle that encourages individuals not to place all their trust in one source or method. It's a strategy that can be applied in various aspects of life, including business, where it helps in reducing dependency on a single vendor or product.

A salesperson who understands the importance of risk diversification may approach a competitor's customer to offer an alternative solution. This isn't about replacing what the customer already has but adding to it, providing a safety net, and enhancing the customer's options.

This concept relates to the wisdom in the Book of Proverbs. Proverbs 11:14 states, "Where there is no guidance, a people falls, but in an abundance of counselors there is safety." This verse emphasizes the importance of having multiple sources of advice and guidance, rather than relying solely on one.

In the context of sales, this scripture can be seen as a metaphor for the wisdom of having multiple suppliers or options. Just as having many counselors provides safety and a well-rounded perspective, having options from various suppliers ensures that the customer isn't overly reliant on one, reducing the risk and providing a more stable foundation.

The Triad of Belief is reflected in this approach. The belief in the industry is recognizing that risk diversification is a sound business practice. The belief in the product or service is knowing that what is being offered can genuinely add value to the customer's existing setup.

The belief in oneself is the confidence that the salesperson has the insight and integrity to guide the customer in a direction that truly benefits them.

In practical terms, this means the salesperson must be knowledgeable about the customer's current situation, understanding their needs, and how the offered product or service can fit into their existing structure. It's about building trust, showing empathy, and demonstrating a genuine desire to enhance the customer's experience.

As illustrated in Proverbs 11:14, the principle of risk diversification is a wise and compassionate approach to sales. It's not about pushing a product but about understanding, caring, and offering solutions that truly resonate with the customer's unique needs and goals. It's a practice that aligns with the core principles of belief in the industry, the product or service, and oneself, embodying a holistic approach to customer engagement and satisfaction. It's a testament to the salesperson's commitment to excellence, integrity, and the relentless pursuit of solutions that genuinely serve the customer's best interests.

Negotiation Leverage: Abraham's Negotiation with God for Sodom

The story of Abraham's negotiation with God over the fate of Sodom, found in Genesis 18:22-33, provides a powerful example of negotiation that can be applied to the sales context.

In this passage, God reveals to Abraham that He plans to destroy the cities of Sodom and Gomorrah due to their wickedness. Abraham, concerned for the righteous people who might be living there, including his nephew Lot, begins to negotiate with God. He asks if God would spare the city if fifty righteous people were found there. God agrees, and Abraham continues to negotiate, lowering the number to forty-five, then forty, and so on, until God agrees to spare the city if even ten righteous people are found.

This story illustrates the concept of negotiation leverage in a profound way. Abraham's negotiation with God demonstrates a deep understanding of compassion, justice, and the value of human life. He leverages his relationship with God and his understanding of God's nature to advocate for the people of Sodom.

In the context of sales, the concept of negotiation leverage can be applied with integrity and empathy. A salesperson can use their understanding of the customer's needs, the competitive landscape, and the unique value of their product or service to negotiate in a way that benefits both parties.

The Triad of Belief is integral to this approach. The belief in the industry involves understanding the broader landscape and how the product or service fits into the customer's world. The belief in the product or service reflects confidence in the value and benefits that the offering can provide to the customer. The belief in oneself embodies the skill and integrity to negotiate in a way that aligns with the customer's interests and creates a positive relationship.

Abraham's negotiation with God serves as a reminder that negotiation is not just about self-interest but about understanding others and creating solutions that serve the greater good. It requires empathy, integrity, and a willingness to engage in dialogue.

In practical terms, this means approaching negotiations with a clear understanding of the customer's needs and the unique value that can be provided. It means crafting solutions that resonate with the customer's situation and leveraging the information and relationships to create positive outcomes.

Abraham's negotiation with God over the fate of Sodom offers a profound perspective on negotiation leverage. It challenges us to think deeply about the dynamics of negotiation and the balance between self-interest and ethical behavior. It's a reminder that negotiation is not just about getting what we want but about understanding others and creating solutions that serve the greater good. By applying these principles with integrity and wisdom, the salesperson can create meaningful connections with customers and achieve success in a way that reflects the core values of belief in the industry, the product or service, and oneself.

Fresh Perspective: Jesus Healing the Blind Man

The concept of bringing a fresh perspective to a problem is not only a powerful tool in sales but also a recurring theme in the teachings and actions of Jesus. One such example can be found in the story of Jesus healing a blind man in John 9:1-12.

In this account, Jesus encounters a man who has been blind from birth. His disciples ask Him whose sin caused the man's blindness, reflecting a common belief of the time. Jesus, however, offers a fresh perspective, stating that the man's blindness is not a result of sin but an opportunity for God's works to be displayed.

Jesus then proceeds to heal the man, not through conventional means, but by making mud with His saliva and applying it to the man's eyes. He instructs the man to wash in the Pool of Siloam, and the man comes back seeing. This unconventional approach not only healed the man but also challenged the prevailing beliefs and expectations of those around Him.

In the context of sales, this story illustrates the importance of looking beyond conventional wisdom and being willing to approach problems from a unique angle. Just as Jesus saw the blind man's condition as an opportunity rather than a punishment, a salesperson might see a customer's challenge as a chance to provide a novel solution.

Consider a company struggling with employee engagement. A salesperson offering organizational development services might recognize that the root issue is not lack of motivation but a misalignment between company values and employee incentives. By approaching the problem from this fresh perspective, the salesperson can offer a tailored solution that addresses the underlying issue, rather than just treating the symptoms.

The Triad of Belief is also evident in this story. Jesus' belief in His mission allowed Him to see the opportunity in the blind man's condition. His belief in His ability to heal and His method (the product or service) gave Him the confidence to proceed in an unconventional way. His belief in Himself enabled Him to challenge prevailing beliefs and offer a fresh perspective.

The story of Jesus healing the blind man in John 9 offers a powerful lesson in the importance of a fresh perspective in sales. By looking beyond conventional wisdom and being willing to approach problems from a unique angle, salespeople can uncover opportunities and provide solutions that truly meet the customer's needs. This approach, aligned with the Triad of Belief, allows salespeople to connect with customers on a deeper level and offer solutions that are not only effective but also resonate with the customer's true needs and desires.

Performance Benchmarking: The Parable of the Talents

Performance benchmarking is a vital aspect in the business world, allowing companies to gauge their standing compared to competitors. This concept parallels the teachings of Jesus, particularly in the Parable of the Talents found in Matthew 25:14-30.

In this parable, a master entrusts his servants with varying amounts of talents (a form of currency) based on their abilities. Two of the servants invest and increase their talents, while the third hides his talent in the ground. Upon the master's return, the servants are assessed based on their performance.

The master praises the first two servants for their wise investment and diligent work, while the third servant is reprimanded for his lack of initiative. The comparison between the servants' performances serves as a form of benchmarking, where the master evaluates their success relative to the opportunities and resources given to them.

In a sales context, this parable can be applied to the idea of engaging with multiple vendors to benchmark the performance of a current product or service. Just as the master in the parable assessed the performance of his servants, a company might evaluate different vendors to understand how their current provider measures up.

For example, a business might be using a particular software solution but wants to ensure that it is receiving the best value and functionality. By engaging with competitors and assessing their offerings, the company can benchmark its current solution's performance against others in the market. This process can lead to a more informed decision, whether to continue with the current provider or switch to a new one that offers better value or features.

The Triad of Belief is also reflected in this process. Belief in the industry drives the desire to seek the best solutions. Belief in the product or service motivates the search for the most effective option. Belief in oneself empowers the decision-making process, trusting that the right choice will be made.

The Parable of the Talents not only offers a scriptural basis for the concept of performance benchmarking but also provides a timeless lesson in stewardship, responsibility, and the importance of making the most of our opportunities. By applying these principles, salespeople can approach their interactions with potential customers with integrity, offering solutions that truly meet their needs and reflecting the values that underpin the Triad of Belief. This alignment between scriptural wisdom and modern sales practices can inspire both salespeople and customers, fostering a relationship built on trust, understanding, and shared values.

Improved Contract Terms: The Covenant with Abraham

In the realm of sales, the pursuit of improved contract terms is a common goal. Customers often seek flexibility, favorable payment terms, or other beneficial clauses that align with their needs. This concept resonates in the Old Testament, particularly in the covenant God made with Abraham, as described in Genesis 17.

The covenant with Abraham is a profound example of a contractual agreement, where God promises to make Abraham the father of many nations, multiply his descendants, and give them the land of Canaan. In return, Abraham and his descendants must keep God's commandments and walk in His ways. The terms of this covenant were clear, binding, and offered immense benefits to Abraham and his lineage.

This scriptural reference can be applied to the sales context, where a salesperson might approach a competitor's customer with the intention of offering improved contract terms. Just as God offered Abraham a covenant with specific benefits and responsibilities, a salesperson can present a contract that is tailored to the customer's unique needs and preferences.

For instance, a company might be locked into a long-term contract with a supplier that lacks flexibility. A competing salesperson, recognizing this pain point, might approach the customer with a proposal that includes more favorable payment terms, options for scaling services, or clauses that allow for adjustments based on changing business needs. This approach not only addresses the customer's specific challenges but also aligns with the principles of the Triad of Belief.

Belief in the industry drives the salesperson to understand the competitive landscape and the contractual norms that govern it. Belief in the product or service fuels the confidence to offer terms that truly benefit the customer. Belief in oneself empowers the salesperson to negotiate and present a contract that reflects the customer's best interests.

The covenant with Abraham is a timeless example of a mutually beneficial agreement, grounded in trust, commitment, and clear communication. By drawing inspiration from this scriptural reference, salespeople can approach their interactions with integrity and a genuine desire to serve the customer's needs.

Future Collaborations: The Parable of the Mustard Seed

The idea of future collaborations and growth potential can be beautifully illustrated through the Parable of the Mustard Seed in Matthew 13:31-32. This parable speaks to the potential of small beginnings and how they can lead to significant growth over time.

Jesus compares the kingdom of heaven to a mustard seed, which, though it is the smallest of all seeds, grows into a tree where birds come and perch in its branches. The mustard seed's growth is not immediate; it takes time, care, and nurturing. But the potential within that tiny seed is immense.

In the context of sales, this parable can be applied to the approach of engaging a competitor's customer with an eye toward future collaborations. A salesperson might reach out to a potential customer with a small offer, a new perspective, or a unique solution that might not seem significant at first glance. However, like the mustard seed, this initial engagement has the potential to grow into something much larger.

For example, a salesperson might offer a free consultation or a trial of a product. This small gesture can lead to a deeper understanding of the customer's needs and challenges, laying the groundwork for a future collaboration. It's not about making an immediate sale but about building a relationship that has the potential to grow over time.

This approach aligns with the Triad of Belief, reflecting a belief in the industry, the product or service, and oneself. The belief in the industry allows the salesperson to see the long-term potential in even the smallest engagements. The belief in the product or service gives the confidence to offer it without immediate expectations, knowing that it has value. The belief in oneself guides the salesperson to approach the interaction with patience and vision, recognizing that small beginnings can lead to significant growth.

The Parable of the Mustard Seed teaches us that even the smallest actions can profoundly impact over time. In the world of sales, this means that a tactful call to a competitor's customer, even if it doesn't result in an immediate conversion, can lay the foundation for future collaborations. By approaching sales with patience, vision, and a belief in the growth potential, salespeople can build meaningful relationships that benefit both parties in the long run. This perspective, rooted in ancient wisdom, offers a timeless lesson for modern sales practices.

Staying Informed: The Watchman's Duty

The role of a watchman as described in Ezekiel 33:1-6 illustrates the idea of staying informed and vigilant. In this passage, the Lord speaks to Ezekiel about the duty of a watchman. The watchman's role is to stand on the walls of the city and keep watch. He must blow the trumpet to warn the people if he sees the sword coming against the land. If he fails to sound the alarm, the people's blood will be on his hands.

This metaphor of the watchman serves as a profound lesson for salespeople in understanding the importance of staying informed and communicating valuable insights to potential customers. Just as the watchman must be vigilant and alert to potential threats, a salesperson must be aware of market shifts, potential risks, or upcoming innovations that might affect a customer's decision-making process.

Consider a salesperson who regularly reaches out to a competitor's customer to provide insights into new developments in the industry. This salesperson acts as a watchman, keeping an eye on the landscape and ensuring that the customer is aware of possible opportunities or challenges. This approach reflects a strong belief in the industry, recognizing the dynamic nature of the market and the need to stay ahead. It also demonstrates a belief in the product or service, aligning insights with the customer's unique needs and goals. Finally, it shows a belief in oneself, approaching the customer with confidence and a genuine desire to serve.

The Triad of Belief is at the core of this approach, guiding the salesperson to act with integrity, foresight, and empathy. By keeping the customer informed, the salesperson builds trust and positions themselves as a valuable resource, ready to assist with future projects or needs.

The watchman's duty in Ezekiel teaches us that staying informed and being prepared to communicate vital information is essential for the well-being of those we serve. In the context of sales, this means engaging with potential customers, offering insights that align with their needs, and being a trusted advisor who helps them navigate the complexities of their industry. This timeless lesson, rooted in ancient wisdom, resonates with modern sales practices, emphasizing the importance of vigilance, communication, and genuine engagement. It's not merely about making a sale; it's about building a relationship and being a reliable guide who helps the customer make informed decisions.

Networking: Building Connections for the Greater Good

Networking is not merely a modern concept tied to professional growth; it's a timeless principle that can be traced back to biblical times. The idea of building connections and relationships for mutual benefit is deeply rooted in the teachings and actions of Jesus Christ.

One striking example can be found in the Gospel of Luke, specifically in the story of Zacchaeus (Luke 19:1-10). Zacchaeus, a chief tax collector, was a man of wealth but had a reputation for dishonesty. When Jesus was passing through Jericho, Zacchaeus climbed a tree to see Him, driven by curiosity and a desire for something more meaningful in his life.

Jesus, recognizing the opportunity to connect and transform, called Zacchaeus down and invited Himself to his house. This act was more than a simple visit; it was a deliberate effort to network with someone on the fringes of society, someone who needed guidance and a fresh perspective.

The result of this connection was profound. Zacchaeus's life was transformed, and he committed to giving half of his possessions to the poor and restoring fourfold anything he had taken dishonestly. This story illustrates the power of networking, not for personal gain but for the greater good, leading to transformation and positive change.

In the context of sales, this networking principle can be applied in a way that aligns with the Triad of Belief. A salesperson who reaches out to a competitor's customer may not only be seeking an immediate sale but also looking to build a broader professional network. This network can serve as a platform for sharing insights, exploring collaborations, and fostering a community that transcends individual interests.

For example, a salesperson in the technology industry might approach a competitor's customer with an invitation to a seminar or a professional group focused on emerging trends. This approach is not about pushing a product but about creating a space for dialogue, learning, and growth. It reflects a belief in the industry as a dynamic and collaborative field, a belief in the product or service as something that can add value beyond immediate needs, and a belief in oneself as a connector and facilitator.

The story of Zacchaeus teaches us that networking is not about superficial connections or self-serving agendas. It's about seeing the potential in others, reaching out with genuine interest, and building relationships that can lead to positive change. In sales, this means approaching networking with a spirit of service, curiosity, and a desire to contribute to the broader community. It's a lesson that transcends time, reminding us that true success comes from connecting with others in meaningful ways, guided by integrity, empathy, and a vision for the greater good.

Feedback Opportunity: A Pathway to Growth and Improvement

The opportunity to provide feedback is a powerful tool for growth and improvement. It allows for the refinement of products, services, and even personal development. This concept is not only applicable in the modern business world but can also be traced back to the teachings and practices of Jesus Christ.

In the Gospel of Matthew, Jesus provides a profound example of seeking feedback in the form of the question he poses to his disciples:

"Who do people say the Son of Man is?" (Matthew 16:13-20). This question was not asked out of ignorance or vanity; instead, Jesus used it as a way to gauge the understanding and perception of his mission among the people. He then directed the question to his disciples, asking, "But what about you? Who do you say I am?" This direct inquiry allowed Jesus to assess their understanding, affirm their faith, and provide further clarification.

This scriptural example can be applied to the sales process, particularly in the context of engaging with a competitor's customer. A salesperson who approaches a competitor's customer with an open mind and a genuine interest in understanding their needs and experiences creates an opportunity for feedback. This feedback can be invaluable in understanding the market, identifying areas for improvement, and even innovating new solutions.

Consider a salesperson in the automotive industry who reaches out to a competitor's customer to understand their satisfaction with their current vehicle. By asking open-ended questions and actively listening, the salesperson can gather insights into what the customer values, what they feel might be lacking, and what they hope to see in future models. This information is not just valuable for making a sale; it can be channeled back into product understanding, leading to improvements that benefit the entire industry.

This approach aligns with the Triad of Belief. It reflects a belief in the industry as a space for continuous growth and innovation, a belief in the product or service as something that can always be refined and improved, and a belief in oneself as a conduit for positive change. It's about recognizing that every interaction, even with a competitor's customer, is an opportunity to learn, grow, and contribute to something greater.

The example of Jesus seeking feedback from his disciples teaches us that asking questions and seeking understanding is not a sign of weakness but a pathway to growth. It's about humility, curiosity, and a commitment to excellence. In sales, this means approaching interactions with a spirit of inquiry, recognizing that every conversation is a chance to learn and improve. It's a lesson that transcends time and industry, reminding us that true success comes from a willingness to listen, learn, and strive for better.

Closing Thoughts: Embracing the Opportunities in Competition

The journey through the various reasons for tactfully engaging with a competitor's customer has been enlightening, revealing a landscape rich with opportunities and potential growth. From price comparisons to networking, from tailored solutions to the chance for valuable feedback, the reasons are diverse and compelling. Yet, they all converge on a central theme: the pursuit of excellence, service, and genuine connection.

These principles, deeply rooted in the teachings of Jesus Christ and reflected in the Triad of Belief, guide us to approach competition not as a battlefield but as a fertile ground for collaboration, learning, and innovation. It's a perspective that transcends the transactional nature of sales and elevates it to a higher calling.

In the world of sales, competitors are often viewed through a lens of rivalry and conflict. However, this chapter has shown that there's a more nuanced and constructive way to approach the relationship with competitors and their customers. By seeing them as potential partners in growth, sources of insight, and even catalysts for self-improvement, we can transform what might seem like a threat into an opportunity.

The examples drawn from scripture have provided inspiration and a moral compass, guiding us to act with integrity, empathy, and respect.

Whether it's the wisdom of Solomon or the compassionate outreach of Jesus to those outside his immediate circle, these stories remind us that the principles of good salesmanship are timeless and universal.

As we move forward, let us carry these lessons with us, remembering that every interaction, even with a competitor's customer, is a chance to reflect our belief in our industry, our product or service, and ourselves. Let's embrace the opportunities hidden in competition, recognizing that they are pathways to growth, innovation, and a deeper connection with the values that drive us.

In the end, selling is not just about closing deals; it's about opening doors to new possibilities, relationships, and understanding. It's a journey that requires courage, curiosity, and a commitment to excellence. By following these principles, we are not just selling products or services; we are serving others and contributing to a greater good. That's a mission worth pursuing, a calling that resonates with the very best of who we are and what we can become.

The Power of INTRODUCING: Building a Boundless Pipeline

The INTRODUCE stage of the IDEAS Sales System is not merely the beginning; it's the foundation upon which the entire sales process is built. It's the strategic alignment of your efforts with those who stand to benefit most from your product or service. It's the creation of a Master List, a reservoir of opportunity that ensures you are never without prospects, never dependent on external factors, and never confined by limitations beyond your control.

In this stage, we've explored the various facets of your Master List, encompassing your powerbase, sold customers, unsold customers, customers of your competition, and orphans. Each category represents a unique opportunity, a chance to connect, serve, and build relationships that transcend mere transactions.

Jesus, in His earthly ministry, exemplified the essence of INTRODUCING. Though His time was limited, He never rushed His interactions. He listened, taught, helped, and served, embodying the principle of "Sell To Help." His words, "In a little while you will see me no more" (John 16:16, NIV), remind us of the urgency of our mission, yet His actions teach us to invest the time necessary to make a genuine impact.

The salesperson who embraces the INTRODUCE stage with seriousness and dedication is not merely seeking a sale but forging a pathway to lifelong business. They recognize that convincing a prospect to purchase a product that doesn't actually help them is not just a waste of time but a breach of trust. They understand that speed and efficiency are vital, but never at the expense of integrity and genuine connection.

The Master List is more than a tool; it's a living, evolving testament to your commitment to your industry, your belief in your product, and your faith in yourself. It's a visual representation of your sales pipeline, a tangible assurance that your efforts are not in vain but investments in a future filled with potential.

As Romans 9:28 (NIV) states, "For the Lord will carry out his sentence on earth with speed and finality." Let this be a reminder that our time is precious, our mission urgent, and our approach must be both swift and substantial.

Ultimately, the INTRODUCE stage is a call to action, a challenge to build a pipeline so full that opportunity is not a fleeting chance but a constant companion. It's a commitment to excellence, guided by principles that have stood the test of time, inspired by the greatest salesperson ever, Jesus of Nazareth.

May your Master List be a beacon of opportunity, your approach a reflection of purpose, and your success a testament to the power of INTRODUCING.

> **"Let us not become weary in doing good, for at the proper time we will reap a harvest if we do not give up."**
>
> Galatians 6:9 (NIV)

Chapter Ten

DISCOVERING

More Than Active Listening

DISCOVERING IS A PROFOUND journey into the heart of the customer's needs, desires, and dreams. It's not about selling a product; it's about connecting with a person. It's about finding out how our customers can use our product or service to their best advantage.

DISCOVERING isn't something you can just skip or rush through. It's a vital part of selling, and you can't ignore it if you want to really succeed. Think about all the hard work you put into making your master lists. You've looked at your powerbase, learned from customers who bought from you and those who didn't, studied what your competitors are doing, and reached out to orphan customers. All of that leads to this key moment of DISCOVERING.

Think about how you built your Master List. Maybe you used every contact you ever made, every business card you ever got, and every conversation you ever had. Maybe you kept in touch with customers after they bought something, learning from what they told you. With customers who didn't buy, you might have asked why, so you could understand what held them back. When looking at competitors' customers, you might have watched the market, joined online groups, or taken part in community events. And for orphan customers, you might have sent newsletters or held events to bring them back.

After the INTRODUCING stage, you've worked hard to reach out and get noticed. You've started conversations, made phone calls, sent personal emails, texted reminders, visited people, or used other ways to connect with your audience. You've let people know you're there.

But all that work won't mean anything if you don't follow it up with real DISCOVERING. If you don't take the time to really get what your customer needs and wants, everything else is a waste. It's like a farmer who plants seeds but doesn't bother to find out what the soil needs to make them grow.

DISCOVERING means putting the focus on the customer, not on you. It's about seeing things from their point of view, understanding what they feel, and knowing what they really want. That's how you can ensure what you're offering fits their needs. That's how you go from just trying to sell something to being someone your customer can trust and rely on.

In short, without DISCOVERING, all your effort won't get you the results you want. This part of selling, where you listen and understand and make real connections, is what makes everything else work.

The Essence of DISCOVERING

Imagine you're selling an amazing new widget with top-notch tech, a super easy-to-use touch screen, and AI capabilities that make it stand out from the rest. Sounds great, right? But if your customer doesn't need your widget, all those fancy features don't mean a thing.

Salespeople often go into a sale thinking they already know everything they need to. They ask a few basic questions and think they've got their customer figured out. But that's not going to cut it. In the IDEAS system, the DISCOVERING Stage is kind of like a "needs assessment." But instead of just skimming the surface, we want to go deep. Like Jesus did.

If we skip over the DISCOVERING Stage or rush through it, we're not doing our job right. We're not giving our customer the best service we can.

So, what's involved in 'DISCOVERING?' It's asking questions, listening carefully, and really noticing what the other person is saying. It's about picking up on things like body language, eye contact, and gestures. You need to understand how your customer will use your product or service. That's how you get the information you need to evaluate what you've learned and show your customer that you've really heard them.

The concept of discovering, listening is so simple that we overlook it. Most of us are simply waiting for our turn to talk. We don't actually hear what the other person is saying; we're just using what they say as the catapult for us to talk about ourselves.

One of the most essential parts of the DISCOVERING Stage goes beyond just finding out about what a customer wants or needs. It's about understanding the person in front of you. Everyone wants to feel understood. To feel heard. To feel seen. It's a basic human need, and it's at the heart of this stage of the IDEAS system.

This is the time to really listen. It's not about coming up with solutions or fixes just yet. It's about giving your full attention to the customer and showing them that you really care about what's going on in their world.

By focusing on the customer, by really trying to understand them, you build a connection. That connection can make a big difference in the sales process. When a customer feels like you get them, they're more likely to trust you. They're more likely to be open to your ideas. But that comes later.

Right now, in the DISCOVERING Stage, it's all about opening up to the customer's world. It's about listening with empathy. It's about recognizing their hopes, dreams, fears, and worries. It's about showing them that you're not just trying to make a sale. You're trying to understand them.

This is what sets the IDEAS Sales System apart in a world where sales pitches can feel fake and automated. It makes the sales process more than just a transaction. It makes it a real human connection.

Learning to listen this way might take some time and practice. But it's worth it. It leads to better relationships with your customers. It's not just about selling something. It's about seeing and honoring the person in front of you. That's the real power of the DISCOVERING Stage in the IDEAS Sales System.

The act of listening is a powerful and compassionate gesture, and throughout the Bible, there are numerous instances where God, Jesus, the prophets, and the disciples showcased this trait. The scriptures teach us the timeless wisdom of empathy, understanding, and connection.

In embracing the principles of DISCOVERING, we align ourselves with a tradition of compassion and empathy that resonates through the ages. We become not just salespeople but connectors, listeners, and helpers.

The Art of Patient Discovery

It's human nature, especially for a well-intentioned salesperson, to leap into action the moment we sense a problem or detect a hint of struggle. Our instincts scream at us to fix it, to present a solution, to demonstrate our value. But the DISCOVERING stage isn't about that. It's about the discipline of restraint and the power of active listening.

To the eager reader, tempted to skip ahead to the problem-solving, solution-offering stages of the sales system: hold your horses. There's immense wisdom in the order of these stages, and it's crucial to respect that sequence. Right now, your goal is singular — to deeply understand your customer.

Imagine you're a detective in a classic noir film. Your job isn't to solve the crime in the first five minutes; it's to gather clues, to observe, to listen to testimonies, and to piece together the narrative. Similarly, in the DISCOVERING stage, you're collecting invaluable pieces of information about your customer's struggles, needs, and desires.

When engaging your customer, arm yourself with a pen and notepad or a digital tool of choice. Your primary role during this stage is to hear and record. As your customer opens up, detailing their struggles and aspirations, jot down even what might seem inconsequential at the moment. These notes will be the cornerstone of your strategy and approach later on. Every word they share is a clue into their world, and it's your job to document it faithfully.

Resist the temptation to don your problem-solving hat just yet. While your mind might race to connect dots, formulate responses, or strategize solutions, it's imperative to stay present. Every time you find yourself wandering towards solution mode, gently remind yourself: "Now, I'm here to discover, not to solve."

This might seem counterintuitive. After all, isn't the goal of sales to provide solutions? Yes, but true mastery in sales comes from understanding the depth and breadth of a client's needs before crafting a tailored solution. The time to address and resolve will come, and when it does, you'll be better prepared because you took the time to truly listen.

In the quiet discipline of discovery, you're building trust, rapport, and a deep reservoir of understanding. The foundation you lay here will determine the strength and stability of every subsequent interaction. Dive deep, remain curious, and embrace the art of patient discovery.

Delving deeper into the DISCOVERING stage of the IDEAS Sales System, it's evident that this stage is about far more than simply ascertaining a customer's desires or requirements. At its core, DISCOVERING aims to truly grasp the essence of the individual you're engaging with.

Every individual has an innate longing to be acknowledged, to be genuinely listened to, and to be indeed seen. These desires aren't mere whims; they're foundational human needs. Acknowledging this fact is pivotal to fully embracing the DISCOVERING Stage of the IDEAS Sales System.

This isn't the juncture to craft solutions or offer fixes. Nor is it the time to mirror the customer's words back to them. Instead, it's about deep, intentional listening. It's a period of posing questions, taking meticulous notes, posing further questions, and making more notes. It's about dedicating your undivided attention to the customer, demonstrating that their experiences, emotions, and insights genuinely matter to you.

By wholeheartedly investing in understanding the customer, you're not only accumulating valuable information but also forging a genuine bond. This bond, this authentic connection, often becomes the linchpin in the sales journey. A customer, feeling truly understood, is invariably more inclined to place their trust in you, making them more receptive to future propositions. However, those discussions are for a later stage.

Currently, in the DISCOVERING Stage, the priority is immersing oneself into the customer's realm. It's a time of empathetic listening, of discerning their aspirations, dreams, fears, and concerns. It's an opportunity to signal to them that your objective isn't solely about making a sale, but genuinely understanding and valuing them.

In today's sales environment, characterized by its automated pitches and impersonal interactions, the IDEAS Sales System is a breath of fresh air. It elevates the sales experience from a mere transaction to a genuine, human connection.

Mastering this level of attentive listening might require effort and persistence, but the dividends it pays in strengthened customer relationships are unparalleled. This stage isn't merely about securing a sale, but genuinely valuing and honoring the individual you're interacting with. This profound understanding and connection form the essence and true strength of the DISCOVERING Stage within the IDEAS Sales System.

True Listening: Beyond Waiting for Your Turn to Speak

Diving into the very heart of the DISCOVERING Stage, it's astonishing to realize that the essence of listening, something so fundamental, often eludes our grasp. This oversight is particularly evident when one peruses the scriptures. Sacred texts repeatedly underscore the vitality of authentic listening, yet its importance remains perennially undervalued.

Upon introspection, we might conclude that we're adept listeners during our conversations with others. Yet, a deeper, more authentic reflection often unravels a different story. Instead of genuinely absorbing the words and sentiments of our conversation partners, many of us are merely biding our time, impatiently waiting for our moment in the spotlight. Our minds often prematurely latch onto fragments of what's being shared, using it as a springboard to interject our thoughts and experiences. We delude ourselves into believing we've grasped the essence of the conversation when, in reality, we're often just skimming the surface.

We don't truly understand or empathize with the other person by doing it the way we've always done it. Instead, we continue using their narrative as a launchpad to pivot the conversation back to our own narratives, experiences, and insights. This isn't genuine listening; it's opportunistic self-expression.

However, the IDEAS Sales System urges us to rewrite this script, particularly in its DISCOVERING Stage. It calls for us to embrace and practice genuine, deep listening, where our primary focus is on truly understanding the person we're engaging with rather than seeking opportunities to redirect attention to ourselves. It's a lesson many of us need to relearn, both in sales and in our daily interactions. Only when we genuinely listen can we genuinely understand, connect, and, eventually, offer solutions that resonate.

The Power of Questions: Cornerstone of the DISCOVERING Stage

The DISCOVERING Stage of the IDEAS Sales System revolves around the art of asking questions. Just as a sculptor uses a chisel to shape stone or a painter wields a brush to create masterpieces, a salesperson's most potent tool is their ability to craft and pose questions. This skill, when honed and used with precision, has the potential to transform interactions and lead to successful sales outcomes.

In the world of sales, it's not enough to know your product inside out. While this knowledge is crucial, it's equally vital to understand the person across the table from you. You need to grasp their motivations, their concerns, their aspirations, and their needs. The only way to genuinely unearth this information? Through asking the right questions.

Think about a doctor with a stethoscope. The doctor doesn't use this tool haphazardly. They place it on specific parts of the body, listening intently for any signs of distress. They're searching for clues, for information that might not be visible on the surface. Similarly, a salesperson's questions probe beneath the surface, delving into the heart of what a potential customer truly desires. It's a delicate art, but it's the key to truly understanding a customer's needs.

However, it's not just about the act of asking; it's about *how* you ask. The best salespeople don't just throw out generic questions. They craft them based on the conversation's flow, on the cues given by the potential customer, and on their intrinsic understanding of human nature. These questions are open-ended, inviting the customer to share, to reflect, and to open up. They turn the sales interaction into a conversation, a two-way street where the customer feels heard and understood.

Furthermore, asking questions demonstrates genuine interest. It signals to the customer that you're not just there to push a product but to find a solution that aligns with their needs. This not only builds trust but also positions you as a consultant, an advisor, rather than just another salesperson.

In essence, the questions you ask shape the trajectory of the sales conversation. They determine whether you get a superficial understanding of the customer's needs or a deep, nuanced insight. They can be the difference between a missed opportunity and a successful sale. So, as you navigate the Discovery Stage, remember the power of your questions. Hone them, refine them, and use them as the delicate instruments they are, guiding your interactions towards meaningful connections and successful outcomes.

Jesus: The Master of Questions and The Divine Physician

One of the most profound teachers in history, Jesus, truly recognized the immense power of questions. He wasn't just a declarative speaker; He often employed questions as a primary method of engaging with others, challenging their thoughts, and leading them to introspection. If we consider the overarching narrative of His teachings and interactions, we find a deliberate questioning pattern that probed the depths of human understanding and illuminated the truth.

Tying this back to our analogy, Jesus referred to Himself as a physician. In the Gospel of Mark, He states, "Those who are well have no need of a physician, but those who are sick. I came not to call the righteous, but sinners." (Mark 2:17). This portrayal of Himself not only emphasizes His divine mission but also sheds light on His methodology. Like a doctor employing a stethoscope to diagnose an ailment, Jesus used questions to diagnose the spiritual state of those He encountered.

Several instances in the scriptures highlight this approach. When posed with questions about the greatest commandment, He responded with another question, prompting introspection and reflection. When He encountered the rich young ruler, He didn't immediately prescribe a course of action; He questioned him, leading the young man to confront his own values and priorities. His dialogue with the Samaritan woman at the well is another perfect illustration. Instead of immediately revealing His identity, He engaged her with questions, allowing her to gradually recognize the truth.

This style of questioning serves dual purposes. First, it allows the individual to search their heart, to grapple with their beliefs, and often, to come to a revelation on their own. Second, it fosters a genuine connection between Jesus and the individual, creating a space of trust and openness.

For salespeople, this approach taken by Jesus offers a profound lesson. By positioning questions at the heart of interactions, you're not only striving to understand the customer but also fostering an environment where the customer can come to their own realizations. It's a mutual journey of discovery, one that can lead to more meaningful outcomes and connections.

In essence, if Jesus, the Divine Physician, placed such emphasis on the power of questions to heal and guide the soul, then it behooves salespeople to harness this tool in their own interactions, diagnosing needs and guiding customers towards the best solutions.

Questions as a Catalyst: Learning from Jesus' Art of Inquiry

Mastering the art of inquiry is no small feat. The New Testament showcases Jesus not just as a teacher, orator, or healer but as a masterful questioner. His interactions, more often than not, began or were punctuated with thought-provoking questions. These weren't merely for His own understanding; after all, He, being omniscient, already knew the answers. Instead, His questions were intended to enlighten the person He was speaking to, shed light on their innermost thoughts, challenges, and desires.

Jesus' questions were concise, clear, and purposeful. Each one was meticulously tailored, aimed at making the recipient reflect, sometimes challenging their status quo or nudging them towards self-realization.

He understood that people often hold the answers within them, and a well-placed question can be the key that unlocks that revelation.

As we delve into the richness of Jesus' interrogative approach, salespeople today can glean invaluable insights. The intent behind Jesus' questions was not just to gather information but to guide individuals towards truth and transformation. Similarly, in the world of sales, the right questions can help discern a client's real needs, guiding them not just toward a product but a solution tailored just for them.

Seeking Understanding: Jesus' Inquiry about John the Baptist and Its Application in Sales Discovery.

In the Gospel of Matthew, Jesus poses a thought-provoking question to the crowds concerning John the Baptist: "What did you go out into the wilderness to see?" (Matthew 11:7-9). This question is set against the backdrop of John's disciples questioning Jesus about His identity as the Messiah. Jesus, in turn, directs the attention of the crowd to John's role as a prophet and his purpose in the wilderness. The question is not merely rhetorical; it's a challenge to the listeners to reflect on their expectations, motivations, and understanding of John's mission.

Jesus' question is layered with meaning and intention. By asking what the people went into the wilderness to see, He is prompting them to reflect on their own spiritual journey and their reasons for seeking out John. Was it mere curiosity, or were they genuinely seeking spiritual insight and transformation? Jesus is drawing out their understanding of John's role as a prophet and the fulfillment of prophecy, challenging them to see beyond the superficial and recognize the deeper spiritual significance. He's encouraging them to move past mere observation to a place of personal engagement and response.

This approach of Jesus can be seen as a parallel to the DISCOVERING Stage of the IDEAS Sales System, where the focus is on asking the customer questions that will give them an opportunity to openly share with the salesperson the ways that the salesperson's product or service can help. In a sales context, understanding the customer's motivation and expectations is crucial. Just as Jesus probed the crowd's reasons for seeking John in the wilderness, a salesperson must delve into what the customer is truly looking for. Are they merely curious, or do they have a specific need or problem that requires a solution? By asking insightful questions that prompt reflection, a salesperson can uncover the underlying needs and desires of the customer.

This not only helps in offering a tailored solution but also builds a deeper connection and trust. It moves the conversation from a transactional level to a more meaningful engagement, where the salesperson is not just selling a product but guiding the customer towards a solution that resonates with their unique situation. In essence, it's about shifting the focus from "What are you buying?" to "What are you seeking?" and aligning the sales approach accordingly. The lesson from Jesus' interaction with the crowd about John the Baptist serves as a timeless example of how asking the right questions can lead to a deeper understanding and connection, whether in a spiritual context or in the world of sales.

Unveiling Hypocrisy: Jesus' Question on Healing on the Sabbath and Its Relevance to Sales Discovery"

In the Gospel of Luke, Jesus finds Himself in a situation that reveals the hypocrisy and rigid legalism of the Pharisees. He is dining at the house of a leader of the Pharisees on the Sabbath, a day of rest and worship in Jewish tradition. Observing a man suffering from dropsy,

Jesus heals him, knowing that His actions will provoke a reaction from the Pharisees, who held a strict interpretation of the Sabbath laws. To challenge their thinking and expose their inconsistency, Jesus poses the question: "Which one of you will have a son or an ox fall into a well, and will not immediately pull him out on a Sabbath day?" (Luke 14:5).

Jesus asked a question that exposed the Pharisees' double standards, revealing their hypocrisy and challenging their beliefs and practices. Jesus was often criticized for his actions on the Sabbath, particularly when it came to healing. However, he saw through the hypocrisy of his detractors and used their inconsistency to encourage them to think about the true purpose of the law. He emphasized that the law was meant to promote kindness and mercy above strict adherence to rules, and that helping those in need was more important than following strict legalistic interpretations of the Sabbath. Ultimately, Jesus wanted people to understand that acts of compassion and love were at the heart of the law, and that these values should always guide our actions, regardless of the day of the week.

In the context of the DISCOVERING Stage of the IDEAS Sales System, this question from Jesus offers a profound lesson for modern salespeople. Just as Jesus used a question to uncover the underlying beliefs and inconsistencies of the Pharisees, a salesperson can use thoughtful questioning to uncover the true needs, desires, and potential objections of a customer. By asking questions that prompt the customer to reflect on their own situation, needs, and values, the salesperson can guide them to recognize what they truly need from a product or service. This approach goes beyond mere information gathering; it's about fostering a deeper understanding and connection with the customer, helping them to see how the product or service aligns with their values and needs. It's a method that emphasizes empathy, insight, and genuine engagement, turning the sales process into a collaborative journey of discovery.

The Question of Identity: Jesus' Inquiry into Self-Understanding

In the Gospel of Matthew, we find a profound moment where Jesus questions His disciples about His own identity. The setting is the region of Caesarea Philippi, a place filled with various religious influences. Here, Jesus asks His disciples two interconnected questions: "Who do people say the Son of Man is?" followed by the more personal, "But what about you? Who do you say I am?" (Matthew 16:13-15, ESV).

These questions were not asked out of ignorance or curiosity about public opinion. Rather, Jesus was leading His disciples to a moment of self-discovery and affirmation of faith. He wanted them to articulate their understanding of who He was, not just repeat what others were saying. By asking them directly, He was inviting them to take a stand, to declare their belief, and to understand the implications of that belief for their lives.

What was Jesus trying to draw out of them? He was encouraging them to move beyond hearsay and superficial understanding to a personal, deep-rooted conviction about His identity as the Messiah. He was guiding them to recognize Him not just as a teacher or prophet but as the Christ, the Son of the living God.

This approach has significant applications in the modern sales context, particularly in the DISCOVERING Stage of the IDEAS Sales System. Just as Jesus used questions to guide His disciples to a deeper understanding, a salesperson can use thoughtful questions to guide customers to recognize their true needs and how a product or service can meet those needs. It's not about imposing a preconceived solution or relying on general assumptions. It's about engaging with the customer in a way that helps them articulate their unique situation, needs, and desires. By asking the right questions, a salesperson can help the customer discover for themselves the value and relevance of what's being offered, building a relationship based on genuine understanding and trust. This approach transforms the sales process from a mere transaction into a meaningful journey of discovery, much like Jesus' interaction with His disciples.

The Challenge of Faith: Jesus' Question of Commitment and Understanding

In the Gospel of Matthew, we encounter a moment of frustration and challenge from Jesus towards His disciples. A man had brought his demon-possessed son to the disciples, but they were unable to cast the demon out. When Jesus was informed of this failure, He responded with an exasperated question: "How long shall I stay with you? How long shall I put up with you?" (Matthew 17:17, ESV).

This question was not merely an expression of annoyance. It was a challenge to the disciples, a call to self-examination. Jesus had been with them, teaching and demonstrating the principles of faith, yet they had failed in a task they should have been able to accomplish. His question was an invitation for them to reflect on their lack of faith and understanding, to recognize their need for deeper commitment and reliance on Him.

What was Jesus trying to draw out of them? He was highlighting a gap in their faith and understanding, urging them to recognize their shortcomings and grow in their relationship with Him. He wanted them to see that their failure was not a matter of technique or method but a fundamental issue of faith and dependence on His power.

This scenario has a parallel in the modern sales context, especially in the DISCOVERING Stage of the IDEAS Sales System. A salesperson may find themselves frustrated with a lack of progress or success with a particular customer. Instead of merely expressing frustration, they can use this moment as an opportunity to ask probing questions, both of themselves and the customer. What is missing in the understanding of the customer's needs? Where has the communication or connection fallen short? What deeper insights or commitments are needed to move forward?

By asking these questions, the salesperson can uncover underlying issues that may be hindering the sales process. It's an opportunity to reflect, reassess, and realign with the customer's true needs and desires. Just as Jesus used His question to prompt growth and deeper understanding in His disciples, a thoughtful inquiry in the sales process can lead to a more meaningful connection with the customer and a more successful outcome. It's a shift from frustration to reflection, from impasse to insight, guided by the power of a well-placed question.

Unearthing the True Need: A Lesson from Jesus and the Rich Young Ruler

In the Gospel of Matthew, a rich young ruler approaches Jesus with a question that seems straightforward but leads to a profound dialogue. He asks, "Teacher, what good deed must I do to have eternal life?" Jesus responds with a question of His own: "Why do you ask me about what is good?" (Matthew 19:17, ESV).

The context of this question is vital. The young man's inquiry was not merely about following rules or performing deeds; it was about the nature of goodness itself. By responding with a question, Jesus was inviting the young man to reflect on his understanding of goodness and his motives in seeking eternal life. Was he looking for a formula, a set of actions to perform? Or was he genuinely seeking to understand the nature of goodness and align his life with it?

What was Jesus trying to draw out of him? He was challenging the young man's assumptions and guiding him to a deeper understanding of goodness, not as a mere external standard but as something intrinsic to the nature of God Himself. Jesus wanted the young man to recognize that goodness is not about following a checklist but about a relationship with the One who is the source of all goodness.

In the modern sales context, particularly in the DISCOVERING Stage of the IDEAS Sales System, this interaction between Jesus and the rich young ruler offers a profound lesson. When a customer asks a question, the salesperson's response can be more than just an answer; it can be a tool to unearth the customer's true needs and desires.

For example, if a customer asks about a specific feature of a product, instead of merely describing that feature, the salesperson might respond with a question like, "What is it about that feature that interests you?" or "How do you envision that feature enhancing your experience?" By doing so, the salesperson is drawing something out of the customer, inviting them to share more about their unique situation, needs, and goals.

This approach moves the conversation beyond mere transaction to a genuine exploration of value and alignment. It's not about providing quick answers but about engaging in a journey of discovery, understanding the customer's world, and guiding them to the solutions that truly fit their needs.

Just as Jesus used His question to guide the rich young ruler to a deeper understanding of goodness, a well-placed question in the DISCOVERING Stage can lead to a richer, more meaningful connection with the customer.

It's about using questions not just to gather information but to draw out the customer's true needs and desires, giving you a rich understanding of how to help and leading them to the solutions that will genuinely serve them. It's a technique that transforms the sales process from a mere transaction to a meaningful relationship, reflecting the very heart of the DISCOVERING Stage in the IDEAS Sales System.

Clarifying Desire: The Lesson from Jesus and the Blind Men

In the Gospel of Matthew, Jesus encounters two blind men sitting by the roadside. Hearing that Jesus was passing by, they cried out for mercy. The crowd tried to silence them, but they persisted, and their cries reached Jesus. He stopped and asked them a question that might seem obvious but was deeply significant: "What do you want me to do for you?" (Matthew 20:32, ESV).

The setting of this question is important. These men were blind, and their need for healing was apparent. Yet, Jesus did not assume or impose His understanding of their need. He asked them to articulate their desire, to state explicitly what they wanted from Him. Their response was clear: "Lord, let our eyes be opened." Jesus, moved by their faith, healed them.

What was Jesus trying to draw out of them? He was inviting them to express their need and desire openly. He was recognizing their individuality, their right to ask for what they wanted. He was not treating them as passive recipients of charity but as individuals with voices, desires, and the ability to articulate their needs.

This interaction between Jesus and the blind men offers a valuable lesson for the modern sales context, especially in the DISCOVERING Stage of the IDEAS Sales System. When engaging with a customer, it's easy to assume that we know what they need based on their situation or our understanding of their problem. However, like Jesus, a salesperson must resist the urge to assume and instead ask the customer to articulate their desire.

For example, a customer might express interest in a particular product or service. Instead of immediately offering solutions, the salesperson might ask, "What specifically are you looking to achieve with this product?" or "How do you envision this service fitting into your current situation?" By asking these questions, the salesperson is inviting the customer to clarify their desire, to express what they truly want and need.

This approach recognizes the customer as an active participant in the sales process, not just a recipient of a product or service. It honors their unique perspective, needs, and goals. It transforms the sales interaction from a mere transaction to a collaborative exploration, where the salesperson and customer work together to identify the best solutions.

Just as Jesus' question to the blind men led to a clear expression of their desire and a miraculous healing, a well-placed question in the sales process can lead to a clear understanding of the customer's needs and the identification of the best solutions to meet those needs. It's an approach that respects the customer's individuality, fosters collaboration, and reflects the very essence of the DISCOVERING Stage in the IDEAS Sales System.

Uncovering Hidden Needs: The Lesson of Jesus and the Tribute to Caesar

In the Gospel of Matthew, Jesus is faced with a question designed to trap Him. The Pharisees and Herodians asked Him about paying taxes to Caesar, a question loaded with political implications. Jesus, recognizing their intent, responded with a question of His own: "Why are you trying to trap me? Show me the coin used for paying the tax." ... "Whose portrait is this? And whose inscription?" (Matthew

22:18-20, ESV). By asking these questions, Jesus was able to navigate the situation, uncovering the hidden motives behind their query.

The setting of this question was a public one, where the Pharisees and Herodians were trying to discredit Jesus. They were not genuinely seeking an answer but were attempting to manipulate the situation. Jesus' response was not a direct answer but a question that led them to reveal their own thoughts. He was guiding them to see the implications of their question, and in doing so, He exposed their hidden agenda.

What was Jesus trying to draw out of them? He was attempting to uncover the true nature of their inquiry. By asking them to look at the coin and identify whose image and inscription were on it, He was leading them to the logical conclusion of their own question. He was not merely answering them but engaging them in a process of discovery, guiding them to a deeper understanding of the issue at hand.

This interaction provides a powerful lesson for the modern sales situation, particularly in the DISCOVERING Stage of the IDEAS Sales System. Often, customers may have hidden needs or concerns that they are not openly expressing. A salesperson's role is to ask questions that will uncover these hidden needs, guiding the customer to openly share how the product or service can help them.

For example, if a customer is looking at a particular product but seems hesitant, a salesperson might ask, "What specific concerns do you have about this product?" or "What are you hoping this product will help you achieve?" These questions are designed to draw out the customer's underlying needs and concerns, allowing the salesperson to address them directly.

Just as Jesus used questions to uncover the hidden motives of His questioners, a salesperson can use thoughtful, probing questions to uncover a customer's hidden needs. By asking the right questions, the salesperson can guide the customer to a deeper understanding of their own needs and how the product or service can meet those needs.

In the DISCOVERING Stage of the IDEAS Sales System, the focus is on asking the customer questions that will give them an opportunity to openly share. By following Jesus' example of asking insightful questions, a salesperson can transform the sales interaction from a mere transaction into a collaborative journey of discovery. This approach not only leads to a more satisfying sales experience but also builds trust and rapport, laying the foundation for a successful and lasting relationship.

Clarifying Misconceptions: The Lesson of Jesus and the Sadducees on Resurrection

In the Gospel of Matthew, Jesus is confronted by the Sadducees, a group that did not believe in the resurrection. They posed a hypothetical question to Jesus, involving a woman who had been married to seven brothers, each dying in succession, and asked whose wife she would be in the resurrection. Jesus responded by challenging their understanding of the Scriptures and the nature of God: "Have you not read what God said to you, 'I am the God of Abraham, the God of Isaac, and the God of Jacob'? He is not the God of the dead but of the living." (Matthew 22:31-32, ESV).

The context of this question reveals the Sadducees' attempt to trap Jesus in a theological dilemma. They were not genuinely seeking understanding but were trying to discredit Him. Jesus, recognizing their misunderstanding, used the opportunity to clarify the nature of the resurrection and the character of God. He did not merely answer their question but addressed the underlying misconception that led to the question in the first place.

What was Jesus trying to draw out of them? He was attempting to correct their misunderstanding and guide them to a true understanding of God's nature and the reality of the resurrection. By referencing the Scriptures they held in esteem, He was leading them to recognize their own error and to see the truth that lay beyond their limited perspective.

This interaction provides valuable insights for the modern sales situation, especially during the DISCOVERING Stage of the IDEAS Sales System. Customers may come with misconceptions or misunderstandings about a product or service. These misconceptions can hinder their ability to see how the product or service can truly benefit them. A skilled salesperson, like Jesus, will recognize these misconceptions and ask questions that guide the customer to a clearer understanding.

For example, if a customer believes that a particular software is too complex for their needs, a salesperson might ask, "What specific features are you looking for in a software solution?" or "Can you tell me about a time when you found a software too complex to use?" These questions can help uncover the root of the customer's misconception and provide an opportunity to clarify and demonstrate how the product can indeed meet their needs.

By asking thoughtful questions that address the customer's underlying misconceptions, a salesperson can guide them to a true understanding of how the product or service can help them. This approach not only resolves the customer's concerns but also builds trust and confidence in the salesperson's expertise and the value of the product or service.

In the DISCOVERING Stage of the IDEAS Sales System, the goal is to understand the customer's needs and how the product or service can meet those needs. By following Jesus' example of asking insightful questions that clarify misconceptions, a salesperson can transform a potential obstacle into an opportunity for deeper understanding and connection. This approach lays the foundation for a successful sales interaction, rooted in genuine understanding and tailored solutions.

Reaffirming Commitment: The Lesson of Jesus and Peter's Conversation

After His resurrection, Jesus appeared to His disciples by the Sea of Galilee. Among them was Peter, who had previously denied Jesus three times before His crucifixion. In a poignant and intimate conversation, Jesus asked Peter three times, "Simon son of John, do you love me?" (John 21:15-17, ESV). Each time, Peter affirmed his love for Jesus, and each time, Jesus commissioned him to care for His flock.

The setting of this question was deeply significant. Peter's earlier denial of Jesus was a painful betrayal, and this conversation was an opportunity for healing and restoration. By asking Peter three times if he loved Him, Jesus was allowing Peter to reaffirm his commitment and love, effectively undoing his earlier denial. Jesus was not questioning Peter's love but was drawing out a deeper, more profound affirmation of commitment and readiness to serve.

What was Jesus trying to draw out of Peter? He was seeking a heartfelt declaration of love and commitment from Peter, not for His own assurance, but for Peter's restoration and empowerment. Jesus was preparing Peter for his future role as a leader in the early church, and this conversation was essential in reestablishing trust and confidence.

This profound interaction between Jesus and Peter offers a valuable lesson for the modern sales situation, particularly in the DISCOVERING Stage of the IDEAS Sales System. In sales, understanding a customer's commitment and readiness to proceed is vital. A salesperson may encounter a customer who has previously had a negative experience with a product or service or who may be hesitant to make a decision.

In such cases, asking the right questions can help the customer articulate their concerns, needs, and level of commitment. For example, a salesperson might ask, "Can you tell me about your previous experience with this type of product?" or "What are your main concerns about moving forward with this solution?" These questions are not meant to interrogate but to open a dialogue that allows the customer to express their feelings and needs openly.

By engaging the customer in this way, the salesperson can address any underlying concerns and help the customer reaffirm their commitment to finding the right solution. This approach builds trust and understanding, paving the way for a successful sales relationship.

In the DISCOVERING Stage, the goal is not merely to sell a product but to understand the customer's needs and build a relationship based on trust and mutual respect. By following the example of Jesus in His conversation with Peter, a salesperson can create an environment where the customer feels heard and understood, leading to a more meaningful and successful sales experience.

The Desire for Healing: A Question at the Pool of Bethesda

In the Gospel of John, we find Jesus at the Pool of Bethesda, a place where many disabled people gathered, hoping for healing. Among them was a man who had been paralyzed for thirty-eight years. Jesus, knowing the man's long history of suffering, approached him with a seemingly simple yet profound question: "Do you want to get well?" (John 5:6).

At first glance, the question might seem unnecessary. Why wouldn't the man want to be healed after so many years of suffering? But Jesus' question goes deeper, probing the man's desires and readiness for change. He is drawing out the man's own acknowledgment of his need and his willingness to take the steps necessary for healing. Jesus' question is not just about physical healing but about the man's mental and emotional readiness to embrace a new life.

In a modern sales context, this approach can be incredibly insightful. A salesperson may encounter a potential customer who has been struggling with a problem for a long time, perhaps using an outdated or inefficient product. The question, "Do you want to find a better solution?" might seem obvious, but it serves a similar purpose to Jesus' question. Encouraging customers to evaluate their current situation, recognize their discontentment, and express their aspirations for improvement can be an effective way to foster communication and identify their needs. By clearly communicating their requirements, salespeople can suggest products or services that can genuinely assist them in achieving their goals. This approach can help build trust and establish a long-term relationship between the customer and the salesperson.

Jesus' question to the paralyzed man at the Pool of Bethesda was not about gathering information but about engaging the man in a process of self-reflection and readiness for change. It was a question that recognized the complexity of human desire and the importance of personal agency in the process of healing. Similarly, in the DISCOVERING Stage of the IDEAS Sales System, a well-placed question can guide a customer to recognize their own needs and desires, opening the way for a salesperson to offer a solution that is not just a product but a path to a better future. By understanding the customer's readiness for change and guiding them to articulate their own needs, a salesperson can build a relationship that is not just transactional but transformational.

A Question of Compassion: Understanding the Woman Caught in Adultery

The scene is set in the temple courts, where Jesus is teaching the people. The Pharisees and teachers of the law, seeking to trap Jesus, bring before Him a woman caught in the act of adultery. They remind Jesus of the Law of Moses, which commands that such a woman be stoned, and they ask Him what He says. Jesus' response is to write on the ground, and then He challenges them, saying, "Let him who is without sin among you be the first to throw a stone at her." Convicted by their consciences, the accusers leave one by one, until only Jesus and the woman remain.

Jesus then asks the woman, "Woman, where are they? Has no one condemned you?" (John 8:10). This question is not for Jesus' benefit, as He already knows the answer. Rather, it's a question designed to make the woman reflect on what has just happened. Jesus is drawing her attention to the fact that her accusers have gone, and there is no one left to condemn her. He is leading her to recognize His grace and the opportunity for a new beginning.

In a modern sales situation, this approach can be applied by asking questions that guide the customer to reflect on their own situation and recognize the solutions they need. For example, a salesperson might ask a client about their previous experiences with a product or service, leading them to articulate what they found lacking and what they are looking for now. This not only helps the salesperson understand the client's needs but also helps the client clarify their own thoughts and recognize the value that the salesperson's product or service can offer.

Jesus' question to the woman caught in adultery was not about gathering information but about guiding her to a realization about herself and her situation. It was a question of compassion, understanding, and grace. Similarly, in the DISCOVERING Stage of the IDEAS Sales System, the goal is not just to learn about the customer's needs but to guide them to recognize how the product or service can meet those needs. By asking thoughtful, reflective questions, a salesperson can build a connection with the customer and guide them towards a solution that truly serves them.

Commitment and Choice: The Question to the Twelve Apostles

In the Gospel of John, Chapter 6, Jesus delivers a teaching that is difficult for many of his followers to accept. He speaks of himself as the "bread of life" and emphasizes the spiritual nature of his mission. The teaching is so profound that many of his disciples turn away, unable to grasp what he is saying. In this pivotal moment, Jesus turns to his twelve apostles and asks, "Do you want to leave too?" (John 6:67).

This question is not one of uncertainty on Jesus' part, but rather a profound inquiry into the apostles' commitment and understanding. Jesus is not seeking validation; he is inviting the apostles to reflect on their own beliefs, their understanding of his mission, and their willingness to continue following him. He is drawing out their personal conviction and giving them a choice. It's a moment of self-examination, where the apostles must confront their own faith and decide whether to continue on the path with Jesus.

In the context of modern sales, this question can be seen as a powerful tool in the DISCOVERING Stage of the IDEAS Sales System. Imagine a scenario where a salesperson has presented a product or service that requires a significant change or commitment from the customer. The customer may be hesitant or unsure, and the salesperson might ask, "Are you ready to make this change?" or "Do you want to continue with your current situation?" Like Jesus' question to the apostles, these questions are not about pressuring the customer but inviting them to reflect on their own needs, desires, and readiness to take a new step.

Jesus' question to the apostles was a deliberate and insightful one, a time to decide whether to continue on a challenging but transformative path. In the same way, a well-crafted question in the sales process can guide a customer to recognize their own needs and make a conscious, committed decision. It's not about manipulating or coercing but about helping the customer to see their own situation clearly and choose a path that aligns with their goals and values. By asking the right question at the right time, a salesperson can build a relationship of trust and collaboration, guiding the customer to a choice that is not only beneficial but deeply satisfying.

Faith and Expectation: The Question at Lazarus' Tomb

In the Gospel of John, Chapter 11, we find the deeply moving account of the death and resurrection of Lazarus. Jesus, upon hearing of his friend's illness, delays his arrival, knowing that Lazarus's death and subsequent resurrection will serve a greater purpose. When Jesus finally arrives, Lazarus has been dead for four days, and his sisters Martha and Mary are grieving. Martha expresses her belief in Jesus' power but also her disappointment at his delay. It is in this context that Jesus asks her, "Did I not tell you that if you believe, you will see the glory of God?" (John 11:40).

This question is not a rebuke but a gentle reminder and an invitation to faith. Jesus is drawing out Martha's belief and encouraging her to trust in his promise, even in the face of apparent hopelessness. He is guiding her to look beyond the present circumstances and to expect the miraculous. The question serves to refocus her attention on the divine purpose and to prepare her for the extraordinary event that is about to unfold.

In a modern sales context, this question can be applied in the DISCOVERING Stage of the IDEAS Sales System, particularly when a customer is facing a challenging situation or is skeptical about the potential benefits of a product or service. A salesperson might ask a question like, "Didn't we discuss how this solution could transform your current situation?" or "Do you remember what we identified as the key benefits for your specific needs?" These questions are not about challenging the customer but about reminding them of previous conversations, agreements, or insights that have already been acknowledged.

Just as Jesus guided Martha to recall her faith and expect the glory of God, a salesperson can guide a customer to recall their own recognition of a need or desire and the potential solution that has been identified. It's a way of reconnecting with the customer's own insights and building upon them, leading them to a renewed understanding and commitment. By asking the right question, a salesperson can help the customer to see beyond their doubts or obstacles and to envision the positive outcome that is possible. It's a process of affirmation and encouragement, grounded in a genuine understanding of the customer's needs and the sincere belief in the value of the product or service being offered.

Demonstrating Authority: The Question to the Paralyzed Man's Onlookers

In the Gospel of Mark, Chapter 2, we find the intriguing account of a paralyzed man being brought to Jesus by his friends. Unable to reach Jesus due to the crowd, they lower the man through the roof. Jesus, seeing their faith, tells the paralyzed man that his sins are forgiven. This statement stirs controversy among the teachers of the law, who consider it blasphemous. In response to their unspoken criticism, Jesus poses a question to the crowd and His disciples: "What is easier to say to this paralyzed man: 'Your sins are forgiven,' or to say, 'Get up, take your mat and walk'?" (Mark 2:9).

Jesus' question is not merely rhetorical; it's a challenge that exposes the hearts of the onlookers. He is drawing out their understanding of His authority and their belief in His ability to perform both spiritual and physical healing. By asking this question, Jesus is leading them to confront their own doubts and biases and to witness a tangible demonstration of His divine power. He then heals the paralyzed man, validating His authority to forgive sins.

In modern sales, particularly in the DISCOVERING Stage of the IDEAS Sales System, this question's principle can be applied when a salesperson is faced with skepticism or doubt from a potential customer. A salesperson might encounter a situation where the customer questions the effectiveness or relevance of a product or service. In such a scenario, the salesperson could ask a question that challenges the customer to consider two related aspects of the solution, one abstract and one concrete, much like Jesus' question about forgiveness and healing.

For example, a salesperson might ask, "What do you think is more challenging: understanding how this software can streamline your workflow or actually implementing it to see the results?" This question can prompt the customer to reflect on their own perceptions and expectations, leading them to a deeper understanding of both the conceptual benefits and the practical application of the product or service.

By posing such a question, the salesperson is not only addressing the customer's doubts but also guiding them to recognize the value and feasibility of the solution being offered. It's a way of engaging the customer in a thoughtful exploration of their needs and the ways that the product or service can meet those needs. It's a process of discovery that builds trust and alignment, grounded in a genuine understanding of the customer's situation and a sincere belief in the potential for positive transformation.

The Art of Listening: Jesus as a Patient Listener

In the context of sales and the crucial DISCOVERING stage of the IDEAS Sales System, the emphasis on asking deep, probing questions to uncover the needs and desires of a potential client is paramount. Jesus exemplifies this approach through the compelling questions He asked in various encounters recorded in Scripture. But beyond asking, we glean a vital lesson from Jesus' interactions: His profound ability to listen.

When we study the conversations Jesus had, particularly with those who were hurting and came to Him for healing, we notice something exceptional: Jesus' unwavering patience in listening. He didn't merely pose questions; He genuinely sought to understand the people He was engaging with.

There's no recorded instance in the Bible where Jesus interrupted someone in the midst of their response to His question. Even when faced with emotional pleas or complicated issues, Jesus showed a remarkable ability to wait, to listen attentively, and to fully absorb what was being said before attempting to address the problem. This wasn't just an act of courtesy but a testament to His compassion and empathy.

For those who came to Jesus in their pain and despair, His attentive listening may have been as healing as the miracles He performed. By allowing them to speak, by honoring their words with His undivided attention, Jesus showed them that they were seen, heard, and valued. He recognized that their stories, their fears, and their dreams mattered.

Application in Sales: The DISCOVERING Stage

In the DISCOVERING stage of the IDEAS Sales System, embracing the same approach of patient, attentive listening can be transformative. It involves not only framing the right questions but also fostering an environment where the prospect feels comfortable sharing. Like Jesus, one must resist the impulse to interrupt, to jump in with solutions or opinions, and instead commit to genuine understanding.

By giving the prospect space to express themselves fully, salespeople can gain deeper insights into their needs and concerns. This patient listening can lead to a stronger connection, a more tailored solution, and ultimately, a more satisfying and successful sales experience.

The art of listening, as demonstrated by Jesus, is not merely a tool but a powerful expression of empathy and respect. In the world of sales, adopting this approach within the DISCOVERING stage can elevate the entire sales process, reflecting not just professional understanding but also a deeper, more human connection. The lesson from Jesus' patient listening extends an invitation not only to hear but also to truly understand those we seek to serve, thereby enriching our professional relationships and our lives.

From Inquiry to Integrity: The Role of Questions in Ethical Sales

Questions are powerful tools. They can illuminate, clarify, and guide. However, like any tool, they can be wielded for both constructive and destructive purposes. It's essential to approach the art of questioning with sensitivity and intention, ensuring that our inquiries are designed to assist rather than harm.

In the realm of sales, questions are often employed to uncover a potential customer's needs, desires, and pain points. However, distinguishing between revealing a pain point and causing pain is crucial. In sales terminology, a pain point refers to a specific problem or challenge a customer faces. Identifying these pain points allows salespeople to offer solutions that genuinely address the customer's needs. On the other hand, causing pain through a question is unnecessary and counterproductive. It can alienate the customer and damage the trust that's so vital in a sales relationship.

Crafting questions with care and empathy is not just a best practice; it's a moral imperative. Every question should be posed with the intention of understanding, assisting, and building a genuine connection. It should never be used as a weapon to corner, manipulate, or belittle.

The Impact of a Single Question

Let's take a moment to think about the power of a single question. It's not just a matter of asking the right thing at the right time. It's about the intention behind the question and the effect it can have on people's lives. This goes beyond sales techniques and gets to the core of who we are as people.

In the Bible, the very first question ever asked was by Satan to Eve: "Did God really say, 'You must not eat from any tree in the garden'?" This wasn't just a simple question. It was a trap, a way to create doubt and confusion. Satan knew what he was doing, and Eve was caught off guard.

Before this question, everything was perfect. People lived in harmony with God, and there was complete trust. But this one question changed everything. It was a lie, a trick to break humanity's most important relationship. It wasn't about understanding or helping; it was about causing harm.

This question led to the fall of humanity. It separated us from God and left a mark that we still feel today. It's a powerful reminder of what can happen when a question is used for the wrong reasons.

Now, think about this in the context of sales. People are often afraid of salespeople because they worry about being tricked or misled. They fear that someone might use a question to manipulate them, just like Satan did with Eve. This is why the sales profession sometimes lacks respect.

But it doesn't have to be this way. Sales can be about helping, not hurting. It can be about understanding what people need and finding ways to meet those needs. It's about asking the right questions for the right reasons.

Jesus, the greatest salesperson of all, never used tricks or lies. He showed us a better way, a way to build trust and help others. He offered something more valuable than anything else, and He did it with honesty and compassion.

Sales is essential to our economy, and good salespeople are vital. But it's not just about making a sale; it's about making a difference. It's about asking questions that help, not harm. It's about building relationships and making connections.

It's heartbreaking when people use manipulation in sales or any other part of life. It's wrong, and it's something we should all strive to avoid. If you find yourself going down this path, take a moment to reflect on your actions and ask for forgiveness. Remember the teachings of Jesus and strive to follow his example.

So, the next time you find yourself in a sales situation, consider the questions you're asking. Are they meant to help or to manipulate? Are they coming from a place of understanding or deceit? Choose your questions wisely, because they have the power to change lives.

Remember the lesson from history and strive to use your questions for good.

God's Pursuit: "Where Are You?" - A Call to Connection

After the first question in the Bible led to humanity's fall, a significant shift occurred. The second question, asked by God, was a heartfelt cry: "Where are you?" (Genesis 3:9). This question wasn't about finding Adam and Eve's physical location; God knew where they were. It was a plea, a call to reconnect. It was God saying, "Why are you hiding from me? Why have you pulled away?"

This question sets the stage for a pattern we see throughout the Bible: God's relentless pursuit of His people. It's a love story, where the Creator is always seeking His creation, no matter how far they've strayed or what they've done wrong.

When Jesus came, He continued this pursuit. His words and actions were a constant call to connection. When He said, "Come to me, all you who are weary and burdened, and I will give you rest" (Matthew 11:28), He was calling us out of hiding, inviting us to step out from our shame and guilt.

Think about the parable of the lost sheep (Luke 15:3-7). It shows a shepherd who will do anything to find one lost sheep. It's a reflection of God's never-ending search for us. Or consider Jesus' conversation with the Samaritan woman at the well (John 4). His questions reached into her soul, just like God's call to Adam and Eve.

Now, let's bring this back to the world of sales. A good salesperson seeks out opportunities to help, to fix things. They're not out to manipulate or deceive; they're there to make a genuine connection and provide real solutions.

The Allure of Manipulation in Sales

Sales is a challenging field, often driven by targets and results. Over time, some salespeople have been tempted to use manipulation as a tool to meet their goals. But why does this temptation exist in the first place?

Historically, many sales training programs have emphasized aggressive tactics. These tactics, rooted in older sales cultures, often prioritize making the sale over genuinely understanding and serving the customer. Such methods might involve diverting a customer's attention away from a product's flaws or exaggerating its benefits. This approach, unfortunately, became a standard for many, leading to the misconception that manipulation was just a part of sales.

The immense pressure to meet quotas and achieve targets can also push salespeople towards a short-term mindset. When the immediate goal is to close a deal, building a lasting relationship with the customer can sometimes take a backseat. This pressure, combined with the fear of losing a sale to competitors, can lead to tactics that aren't entirely transparent.

Additionally, if salespeople aren't fully confident in the product they're selling, they might feel the need to embellish its features. Instead of addressing a product's limitations, they might manipulate the conversation to avoid them. Moreover, the way sales incentives are often structured can unintentionally promote such behavior. If rewards focus solely on immediate sales without considering long-term customer satisfaction, it can further tempt salespeople to prioritize the sale over genuine customer service.

From Tactics to Transformation: Recognizing the Need for Change

While the sales industry is often believed to have leaned on manipulative tactics, there comes a moment of reckoning for many professionals. As they reflect on their careers, some salespeople realize that they've been mere pawns in a larger game, they themselves manipulated into manipulating others.

This realization can be a jarring wake-up call, leading to feelings of guilt and regret. Just as individuals grapple with the aftermath of being deceived, so too do salespeople who recognize that they've been led astray by their training and leadership. This introspection, though painful, can be the first step towards genuine change, paving the way for a more ethical and empathetic approach to sales.

Here's where the story of God's pursuit can bring comfort. Since the moment in the Garden, God has been seeking us. His call is not a judgment; it's an invitation. No matter how long you've been hiding or how far you've wandered, His response is always the same: grace and compassion.

The essence of Christianity, the heart of the Gospel, is a God who seeks, loves, and longs for a reunion with His children. Every message of hope, every call to repentance, every teaching of Christ is a way of asking that age-old question, hoping we'll step out and say, "Here I am."

So, whether you're a salesperson looking to make a positive impact or someone who's been hurt by manipulation, remember this profound truth: God is always seeking you. His embrace awaits, filled with understanding and love. It's a reminder that we can all strive to be more like Him, seeking to help and heal, rather than harm.

Empathy and Grace: Healing from Manipulation

We've all had moments when we feel vulnerable, misled, or even guilty. Whether you've been manipulated or have found yourself manipulating others, these feelings can weigh heavily on your conscience. This is especially true in the world of sales, where the pressure to meet quotas or the way you've been trained might lead you to act in ways that don't align with your core values.

Imagine how Adam and Eve felt after being deceived by the serpent. They were overwhelmed with shame and guilt, and their first instinct was to hide. You might feel the same way if you've been manipulated or have manipulated others. But it's essential to remember that God's response to Adam and Eve wasn't condemnation; it was a call to connection: "Where are you?"

God's capacity for understanding, empathy, and forgiveness is limitless. Jesus knew the unique burdens each heart carried, and He tailored His words of redemption and assurance to meet those individual needs. If you're grappling with the ethics of sales, questioning how to get appointments, overcome objections and close deals, know that your profession can be honorable and aligned with divine principles when approached with honesty, integrity, and a genuine intent to serve. Whether you feel like the manipulator or the manipulated, God's grace is always available. He's been seeking you since the very beginning, and His arms remain wide open.

This message is a powerful reminder for all of us. Whether we've been led astray or led others astray, healing and forgiveness are available. We can learn from our mistakes, grow in our understanding, and strive to act with integrity and compassion. God's grace is there for us, offering empathy and healing, no matter what we've done or how we've been hurt. It's a call to connection, a call to come out of hiding, and a call to embrace the love and forgiveness that's always available to us.

The Art of Discovery: A Path to Connection and Integrity

The journey through the section on DISCOVERING in the IDEAS Sales System has been a profound exploration of the power and potential of questions. We've delved into the heart of the sales process, uncovering the essence of the discovery through questions, and drawing inspiration from the masterful questioning of Jesus Christ.

Through various biblical instances, we've seen how Jesus used questions not merely as tools for gathering information but as instruments for connection, revelation, and transformation. His questions were not manipulative or self-serving; they were designed to guide individuals towards truth, self-realization, and a deeper relationship with the divine.

In the world of sales, the Discovery Stage is not just about identifying a customer's needs or finding opportunities to sell a product. It's about engaging with the customer on a human level, understanding their unique challenges, desires, and values, and guiding them towards solutions that genuinely serve them. It's about asking the right questions with the right intentions, fostering trust, and building meaningful connections.

We've also explored the darker side of questioning, recognizing the potential for manipulation and deceit. The cautionary tale of Satan's question to Eve serves as a stark reminder of the potential harm that can arise from malicious intentions. But we've also seen the grace and empathy of God, who seeks connection and offers forgiveness, even in the face of manipulation.

As salespeople, we are called to approach our profession with integrity, empathy, and a genuine desire to serve. We must be mindful of the weight our questions carry and the impact they can have on others. We must strive to be like Jesus, using our questions to enlighten, uplift, and guide, rather than mislead or harm.

The DISCOVERING Stage is not just a step in the sales process; it's a philosophy, a way of engaging with others that reflects our character, values, and commitment to service. It's about recognizing the dignity and worth of every individual and treating them with respect and compassion.

As we conclude this section, let us reflect on the lessons we've learned and the insights we've gained. Let us commit to being salespeople who seek to understand, who ask questions with care and intention, and who strive to make a positive difference in the lives of those we engage with. Let us be inspired by the example of Jesus, the best salesperson ever, and carry forward the principles of the DISCOVERING Stage with conviction and purpose, knowing that we have the power to bridge understanding and genuinely serve.

Ultimately, the art of discovery is about more than sales; it's about humanity, connection, and the pursuit of something greater. It's a path that leads us not just to success in our profession but to fulfillment, growth, and a deeper understanding of ourselves and others. It's a journey worth taking, guided by the wisdom of the past and the promise of a future filled with possibility and hope.

> **"He who has ears to hear, let him hear."**
> Matthew 11:15 (ESV)

CHAPTER ELEVEN

EVALUATION

BRIDGING UNDERSTANDING AND SOLUTIONS

As we delve deeper into the IDEAS Sales System, we transition from the Discovery stage to the crucial EVALUATION Stage.

The Discovery stage is akin to the Census Bureau's work: collecting raw data. It's about asking questions and gathering as much information as possible. Think of this stage as laying out all the pieces of a puzzle on a table.

The EVALUATION Stage, on the other hand, is where the real artistry comes into play. It's not just about having the puzzle pieces; it's about understanding how they fit together to create a clear picture. This stage is about interpreting the data, understanding its implications, and determining the best way to serve the customer based on the insights gained. It requires a deeper level of understanding and empathy, reminiscent of how Jesus of Nazareth approached those he interacted with.

In essence, while Discovery is about collecting the puzzle pieces, Evaluation is about assembling them to see the bigger picture. It's a transformative phase that demands both wisdom and compassion, ensuring that the sales approach is tailored to the unique needs and desires of each customer.

This stage is about more than superficial understanding. It's about delving into the core of the customer's experience, recognizing their fears, dreams, and unique circumstances. It's about adopting the mindset of Jesus of Nazareth, who saw beyond the surface and understood the deeper needs of the people He encountered.

The EVALUATION Stage is the bridge that connects understanding with action. It's where you translate the customer's words into a clear vision of what they need and how you can provide it. This stage is delicate and intricate, requiring time, attention, and a genuine commitment to serving the customer's best interests, just as Jesus did in His ministry.

As we delve into this vital stage, we will draw inspiration from Jesus, who exemplified the art of evaluation in His interactions. His approach to understanding was not just analytical; it was profoundly human. He recognized the patterns and connections that revealed people's true needs, reflecting His compassion, wisdom, and divine insight.

The EVALUATION Stage of the IDEAS Sales System is a deeply human endeavor that reflects our values, ethics, and commitment to service. It's a path that leads us not just to successful sales but to meaningful connections, lasting relationships, and a profound understanding of what it means to serve.

Together we will explore this rich and multifaceted stage, guided by the wisdom and compassion of Jesus of Nazareth. His approach to understanding offers timeless insights that can help us not just in our professional lives but in our personal journeys towards empathy, insight, and ethical engagement with the complex world of human needs and desires.

The Mastery of Evaluation: Jesus' Way of Understanding

The EVALUATION stage in the IDEAS Sales System echoes the timeless wisdom we can find in Jesus' interactions with the people around Him. His approach to understanding, internalizing, and acting upon the information received offers profound insights into how to excel in this vital phase of sales. Let's explore how Jesus exemplified this evaluative process in His ministry.

A Patient Listener

First, we must remember Jesus' ability to listen intently to those who sought Him out, a quality that every salesperson can cultivate to enhance their connection with clients. His patient and empathetic approach allowed people to open up, share their burdens, and express their needs. This was not a mere transactional interaction; it was a human connection founded on genuine interest and care.

One particularly illustrative example is His interaction with the woman at the well, as recounted in the Gospel of John. When Jesus encountered the Samaritan woman at the well, He initiated a conversation by simply asking for a drink (John 4:7). This seemingly ordinary question led to an extraordinary dialogue. The woman was surprised that a Jew would speak to a Samaritan, but Jesus continued to engage her, leading to deeper questions about living water (John 4:10).

Throughout this interaction, Jesus demonstrated attentive listening. He recognized her physical thirst for water but went further to discern her deeper spiritual thirst. He told her, "Everyone who drinks this water will be thirsty again, but whoever drinks the water I give them will never thirst. Indeed, the water I give them will become in them a spring of water welling up to eternal life" (John 4:13-14, NIV).

His words were not a prepared speech but a response that emerged from His deep understanding of her inner longing. He heard not just her words but the unspoken desires behind them. The conversation then shifted to her personal life, and Jesus' insights led her to exclaim, "Sir, I can see that you are a prophet" (John 4:19, NIV). Eventually, through His attentive listening and probing questions, the woman came to recognize Him as the Messiah (John 4:29).

For modern salespeople, this encounter offers invaluable lessons. Listening with empathy, asking thoughtful questions, and seeking to understand the underlying needs of clients can lead to more meaningful connections. This approach goes beyond merely selling a product or service; it's about understanding and addressing the deeper needs and desires of the customer. By emulating Jesus' patience and discernment, salespeople can foster trust and offer solutions that truly resonate with their clients.

Interpreting Needs: A Lesson in Empathy and Insight

One of the many profound skills that Jesus demonstrated throughout His ministry was the ability to not only hear the words of those who came to Him but to internalize and understand their underlying needs and emotions. This keen awareness allowed Him to respond with empathy and wisdom, meeting the multifaceted needs of those He encountered.

A striking example of this can be found in the story of Jairus, a synagogue leader who sought Jesus to heal his gravely ill daughter. As described in the Gospel of Mark, Jairus fell at Jesus' feet and pleaded with Him, saying, "My little daughter is dying. Please come and put your hands on her so that she will be healed and live" (Mark 5:23, NIV). Jesus' response to this desperate plea was immediate; He went with Jairus without hesitation.

But the story reveals much more than Jesus' willingness to perform a miracle. What's often overlooked is the profound expression of faith that Jairus displayed. In his time of crisis, he turned to Jesus, believing in His power to heal. Jesus recognized not just a plea for a miracle but also a profound expression of faith.

As they were on their way, messengers came with the news that Jairus's daughter had died. Yet, Jesus reassured Jairus, saying, "Don't be afraid; just believe" (Mark 5:36, NIV). When they arrived at the house, Jesus told the mourners, "The child is not dead but asleep" (Mark 5:39, NIV), and then proceeded to raise the girl to life, saying, "Little girl, I say to you, get up!" (Mark 5:41, NIV).

In this miraculous event, Jesus' response was tailored to meet both the physical need for healing and the emotional need for affirmation of faith. He addressed not only the urgent medical crisis but also reassured and strengthened Jairus's faith, encouraging him to believe even in the face of despair.

Jesus heard the plea, understood the situation, and then acted in a way that was unique to this person.

For modern salespeople, this story serves as a poignant reminder of the importance of truly understanding clients. It's not enough to hear their words; one must also recognize their underlying needs, concerns, and motivations. Whether it's a product or a service, the client is often seeking something more profound, and recognizing this deeper need allows for a more personalized and effective response.

By taking the time to understand the client's perspective, as Jesus did with Jairus, salespeople can create solutions that resonate on multiple levels, addressing both the practical requirements and the emotional connections. This comprehensive approach fosters trust, satisfaction, and often leads to long-term loyalty. It's a lesson in empathy, insight, and responsiveness that transcends mere transactional interactions and elevates the practice of selling into an art of human connection.

Going Beyond the Surface: Healing and Understanding the Whole Person

In sales, truly understanding a client's needs often means looking beyond the obvious to uncover hidden desires, fears, and aspirations. This principle is vividly demonstrated in Jesus of Nazareth's interaction with a paralytic man, as recorded in the Gospel of Mark.

The story unfolds in a crowded house where Jesus was teaching. A group of men, desperate to bring their paralyzed friend to Jesus for healing, removed the roof above Him and lowered the man on his mat. The effort was tremendous, the need apparent. But Jesus' response was unexpected. Instead of immediately addressing the physical ailment, He said to the paralytic, "Son, your sins are forgiven" (Mark 2:5, NIV).

This statement startled the onlookers, some of whom questioned Jesus' authority to forgive sins. Yet Jesus saw beyond the apparent physical need to the deeper spiritual need. He recognized that the man's greatest burden wasn't his inability to walk but the weight of his sins. By forgiving his sins first, Jesus addressed the core of the man's condition, healing him from the inside out.

But Jesus didn't stop there. To demonstrate His authority and to meet the physical need as well, He told the man, "I tell you, get up, take your mat and go home" (Mark 2:11, NIV). The man did just that, walking out in full view of them all.

This dual healing, both spiritual and physical, embodies the idea of diving deep to understand feelings, concerns, and dreams. It's a lesson in looking beyond the surface and recognizing the whole person, not just a set of problems to be solved.

For the modern salesperson, this story offers profound insight. Clients often come with apparent needs or specific requests for products or services. But beneath these requests may lie deeper desires or concerns. Perhaps it's not just about finding a cost-effective solution but also about feeling secure, valued, and understood. Maybe it's not only about the functionality of a product but the status, comfort, or fulfillment it may bring.

A salesperson who follows Jesus' example learns to ask probing questions, listen attentively, and discern underlying motivations and emotions. It's about understanding the whole person and responding to both the expressed and implicit needs. This approach leads to a more personalized, satisfying experience for the client, builds trust, and often results in a lasting relationship.

In a world where transactions can often feel impersonal and rushed, taking the time to see beyond the surface is not just good sales practice; it's a way of honoring the dignity and complexity of each individual. Just as Jesus did with the paralytic man, it involves seeing people not as problems to be solved but as unique individuals with distinct dreams, concerns, and needs.

The Bridge to Customized Solutions: Gaining Wisdom and Insight

In the multifaceted world of sales, the journey from understanding a client's needs to delivering the perfect solution can often feel like crossing a complex bridge. At the heart of this bridge is the EVALUATING stage of the IDEAS Sales System, where listening, interpretation, and deep understanding come into play. In this crucial phase, the biblical example of Jesus of Nazareth offers timeless wisdom and practical insights.

Jesus' interactions with people were marked by patience, empathy, discernment, and the ability to see beyond the surface. Whether healing the sick, forgiving sins, or teaching profound truths, He displayed a keen awareness of the multifaceted human condition. Jesus didn't just hear; He listened. He didn't merely see; He perceived. He understood.

This approach is beautifully encapsulated in the wise words of Solomon: "Counsel in the heart of man is like deep water; but a man of understanding will draw it out" (Proverbs 20:5, KJV). This proverb underscores the notion that true understanding requires effort, insight, and a willingness to delve beneath the surface.

For the modern salesperson, Jesus' method provides a clear, actionable blueprint. It's not just about identifying what the customer says they want; it's about discerning what they truly need. This, as demonstrated in the DISCOVERY Stage, involves probing questions, active listening, and a genuine desire to see the bigger picture. It's about creating a bridge between surface-level requests and deeper, more nuanced solutions.

Consider a customer who approaches a salesperson with a request for a specific product. Following Jesus' example, a wise salesperson would not just process the order but would take the time to understand why the customer needs that particular product. Are there underlying concerns or aspirations driving this choice? What are the long-term goals? By asking thoughtful questions and genuinely listening to the answers, the salesperson can uncover insights that lead to a more tailored, satisfying solution.

This approach not only enhances the customer experience but builds trust and loyalty. It elevates the sales process from a mere transaction to a meaningful relationship. Just as Jesus saw individuals, not crowds, and addressed specific needs, not generalities, the salesperson can cultivate a client-centric approach that resonates on a personal level.

In the EVALUATING stage, Jesus' example serves as a beacon, guiding us toward greater empathy, discernment, and wisdom. By internalizing His approach, we can forge the essential bridge between identifying customers' needs and crafting solutions that genuinely improve their lives. It's a path that leads not just to higher sales but to enriched connections, satisfied clients, and a deeper sense of fulfillment in our professional endeavors. It teaches us that in the art of selling, as in life, the path to success lies in understanding and compassion, in seeing beyond the immediate, and striving to touch the very core of human needs and desires.

Evaluating Through Reflection: Wisdom from Scripture for Modern Salesmanship

The EVALUATING stage of the IDEAS Sales System is intrinsically linked to the acts of thinking, contemplation, and reflection. This essential process bears a striking resemblance to the practices of some of the most revered characters in both the Old and New Testaments. Here's how some additional ancient lessons translate to modern-day salespeople seeking to enhance their approach:

Solomon's Judicious Contemplation: As King Solomon faced complex matters, his wisdom was his guide, most notably displayed in his discerning judgment between two women claiming to be the mother of the same child (1 Kings 3:16-28). Solomon's ability to see beyond the surface and ponder the deeper motivations of the women led him to the truth. Similarly, a salesperson must think deeply about the customer's words, seeking to understand not just what is being said but the underlying needs and desires.

David's Meditative Reflections: King David's profound connection between reflection and right action is beautifully illustrated in his own words: "But his delight is in the law of the Lord, and on His law he meditates day and night" (Psalm 1:2, ESV). Salespeople can emulate this practice by consistently contemplating customer interactions, absorbing insights, and working to understand them. Like David's meditations on the law, this continuous reflection can build a deeper understanding of one's craft, enriching their approach and enhancing their ability to connect with clients.

Daniel's Thoughtful Prayer: Daniel's wisdom and contemplative prayers (Daniel 9) were central to his understanding of his people's condition and his relationship with God. Salespeople can learn from Daniel's practice of setting aside regular time for contemplation, seeing it not as a mere pause but as an essential part of crafting solutions tailored to each customer's unique situation.

Jesus of Nazareth's Intentional Pauses for Reflection: Even Jesus often withdrew to solitary places to pray and reflect (Luke 5:16). His periods of contemplation were instrumental in His ministry. For salespeople, taking intentional time to evaluate the information gathered from a customer is not only valuable but essential. This reflective process allows for the crafting of responses that are not reactionary but carefully tailored to meet the individual needs of each client.

Elijah's Quiet Reflection: The still, small voice that Elijah encountered (1 Kings 19:12) teaches the value of quiet reflection. A salesperson, amid the noise of the marketplace, must also find that quiet space to evaluate and connect the dots, to understand patterns and connections within the customer's needs, wants, and emotions.

Seeing Through Different Lenses

The ability to shift one's perspective and view the world through the eyes of another is a remarkable and uncommon strength. It's akin to a muscle that requires constant exercise to develop. Many of us, instead, have focused on strengthening our self-centered muscles, such as self-preservation, self-promotion, or self-satisfaction. These muscles dominate our interactions, leaving our empathy and understanding underdeveloped and weak. The same holds true in sales situations, where these self-serving behaviors may override the ability to truly see things through the customer's eyes.

Allow me to illustrate this concept by drawing a parallel with the making of a movie.

In the movie of our lives, we all play the protagonist. The narrative revolves around our journey, struggles, and growth. The antagonists, changing from scene to scene, bring tension and conflict, driving us towards change. Supporting characters, friends, family, or even minor adversaries, add depth, assist, challenge, or guide us.

Consider this: in someone else's movie, your role might shift dramatically. Instead of the hero, you could be the antagonist, introducing challenges and obstacles. Or perhaps, you're just a fleeting character, momentarily crossing their path.

This cinematic analogy underscores the EVALUATING stage of the IDEAS Sales System, emphasizing the importance of understanding the customer's perspective. By recognizing that the same events can be seen so differently, we open ourselves to empathy, deepening our relationships and strengthening our approach to sales and life in general. It reminds us that the ability to see the world through another's eyes isn't just a skill to be admired; it's a vital aspect of human connection.

This stage encourages you to walk into their movie, sit in their seat, and watch the world through their lens. By doing so, you gain a more nuanced understanding of their needs, desires, and concerns. Recognizing that each individual's movie is unique enables you to adapt your approach and create a connection that goes beyond mere transactions.

In sales, as in life, shifting your perspective to see through another's eyes isn't just a skill to be admired; it's a critical aspect of building genuine relationships. By exercising this empathy muscle and developing the ability to switch lenses, you open doors to more meaningful interactions and successful connections. It's a step away from mere self-preservation and towards genuine understanding, and it's the core of the EVALUATING stage in the IDEAS Sales System.

Embracing the Challenge: The Transformative Power of the EVALUATION Stage

The EVALUATION stage of the IDEAS Sales System stands as perhaps the most challenging and transformative phase in the entire process. It's not merely a step; it's a paradigm shift. A paradigm, in this context, refers to a fundamental change in approach or underlying assumptions. It's a reorientation of how one sees the world, a shift in perspective that alters everything.

In the realm of sales, this shift is profound. It's not about asking a series of questions or reading from a pre-written script. It's not about following a routine or adhering to a rigid set of guidelines. The EVALUATION stage is, in fact, the exact opposite of that. It's about engaging every one of your senses, tapping into your empathic abilities, and thinking about things in ways you may never have considered before.

This stage requires you to THINK differently, to approach conversations and interactions with a fresh perspective and an open mind. It's about seeing beyond the surface, understanding the underlying needs, fears, and desires of the customer, and crafting solutions that are genuinely tailored to them.

But let's be clear: This is not easy. It's not a skill that will develop overnight or after one reading of this book. It's a skill that may require significant changes in how you approach every conversation, every interaction, every aspect of your life. It's a skill that demands continuous effort, practice, and growth.

This is hard. It's challenging. It's a journey that will push you to your limits and force you to confront your own assumptions, biases, and habits.

But here's the truth: This is also what separates great salespeople from the rest of the pack. This is what elevates the art of selling from a mere transaction to a meaningful connection. This is what transforms a salesperson into a trusted advisor, a partner, a guide.

Working your EVALUATION muscle is like any other form of exercise. It requires repeated efforts, carried out over a long period of time. It requires dedication, persistence, and a willingness to learn, adapt, and grow. And as you embark on this journey, as you commit to this path, you will get better and better. You will see things more clearly, understand people more deeply, and connect with customers more authentically.

The EVALUATION stage is more than a step in a process; it's a philosophy, a way of being, a way of seeing the world. It's a commitment to excellence, to empathy, to understanding. It's a challenge, but it's also an opportunity—an opportunity to transcend the ordinary, to rise above the crowd, to become not just a salesperson but a true professional, a true servant, a true partner in your customers' success.

Embrace this challenge. Embrace this opportunity. Embrace the power of EVALUATION, and watch as it transforms not just your sales but your entire life.

Your local church community may offer an unexpected but fertile ground for honing the skills required in the EVALUATION stage. Rooted in the teachings and examples of Jesus of Nazareth, many churches are devoted to caring for and supporting each other through life's challenges. Whether through prayer groups, life groups, or fellowship gatherings, these communities foster an environment of empathy, understanding, and compassion.

Joining these groups is not about selling or promoting anything; it's about immersing yourself in a setting where you can practice truly listening to others and empathizing with their feelings and experiences. It's an opportunity to shift your perspective, to see through another's lens, just as Jesus did in His interactions with people from all walks of life.

By engaging in these church activities, you can exercise your EVALUATION muscle in a supportive and ethical context. You'll find that this practice not only enriches your personal and spiritual life but also enhances your professional abilities, setting you on the path to becoming not just a great salesperson but a more compassionate and insightful human being

Strengthening the Evaluation Muscle: Techniques and Insights for a Deeper Understanding of the Customer's Perspective

The ability to truly understand a customer's needs, desires, and emotions is paramount. The EVALUATION stage of the IDEAS Sales System is not merely a step in the process but a transformative skill that requires a profound shift in thinking. In this chapter we delve into the skills of seeing through the customer's lens, offering practical exercises and biblical wisdom to hone this essential skill. As we explore various techniques to build this evaluation muscle, we'll uncover the path to more empathetic and effective salesmanship, aligning our approach with timeless principles exemplified by Jesus of Nazareth.

Empathetic Listening: A Transformative Exercise for Seeing Through the Customer's Lens

Empathetic Listening Practice is a vital exercise that can significantly enhance a salesperson's ability to evaluate a customer's needs, emotions, and perspectives. This practice goes beyond merely hearing words; it's about truly understanding the emotions and underlying thoughts that drive those words. It's a shift in perspective that requires the salesperson to put themselves in the customer's shoes, seeing the world through their eyes.

A salesperson can perform this exercise by engaging in one-on-one conversations with a colleague or friend, where the focus is on truly understanding the other person's feelings, concerns, and desires. The listener must resist the urge to interject, solve, or advise, instead concentrating solely on absorbing what is being said. They can ask open-ended questions that encourage the speaker to share more deeply, such as "How did that make you feel?" or "Can you tell me more about why that's important to you?" The listener's role is to reflect on what's being said, to nod, to show understanding through facial expressions, and to provide verbal affirmations like "I see" or "I understand."

In the context of scripture, we can find a parallel in the story of Job's friends in the Book of Job. When Job was in deep distress, his friends initially sat with him in silence for seven days and nights, showing their empathy and solidarity (Job 2:13). Though their later responses were flawed, this initial act of simply being present and listening is a powerful example of empathetic engagement.

For the modern salesperson, this practice of empathetic listening can be transformative. It's not about crafting the next sales pitch or finding the immediate solution; it's about truly understanding the customer's world. By practicing this skill with colleagues or within supportive community groups, a salesperson can cultivate the ability to see beyond the surface, to recognize patterns and connections that might otherwise be missed. This deeper understanding can lead to more personalized, satisfying solutions for the customer, building trust, and fostering a lasting relationship. It's a skill that requires patience, focus, and a genuine desire to understand, but its impact on the evaluation stage of the sales process can be profound.

Reflective Journaling: A Path to Deeper Understanding

Reflective journaling is a powerful tool that can significantly enhance the EVALUATION stage of the IDEAS Sales System. By taking the time to write about customer interactions, a salesperson can delve into the nuances of what was said, analyze the underlying needs and desires, and reflect on how to approach similar situations in the future. This practice encourages a thoughtful evaluation that leads to a deeper understanding of the customer's perspective.

Consider, for example, a salesperson who has just completed a meeting with a potential client. By journaling about the conversation, the salesperson can dissect the client's words, expressions, and body language, identifying patterns and connections that may not have been apparent during the interaction. This reflective process allows the salesperson to see beyond the surface and recognize the client's true needs and emotions.

In the scriptures, we find a parallel in the wisdom literature, where reflection and contemplation are highly valued. The Book of Proverbs is filled with insights gained through careful observation and thoughtful reflection. Proverbs 4:26 (NIV) advises, "Give careful thought to the paths for your feet and be steadfast in all your ways." This wisdom can be applied to the practice of reflective journaling, where careful thought and reflection guide the salesperson in understanding the paths and needs of their clients.

Reflective journaling is not a quick fix but a disciplined practice that requires time and commitment. It's about changing one's perspective and thinking differently, aligning oneself with the customer's viewpoint. By consistently engaging in this exercise, a salesperson can develop a more empathetic approach, crafting solutions that are genuinely tailored to the customer's unique situation. It's a practice that echoes the thoughtful contemplation found in scripture, leading to a more profound connection with others and a more successful and fulfilling sales experience.

Mindfulness Meditation: Cultivating Presence and Insight

Mindfulness meditation is a practice that has gained significant attention in various fields, including sales, for its ability to enhance focus, awareness, and presence. In the context of the EVALUATION stage of the IDEAS Sales System, mindfulness meditation can be a transformative exercise, allowing salespeople to be fully present during customer interactions and leading to more insightful evaluations.

The practice of mindfulness meditation involves sitting quietly and paying attention to the present moment without judgment. For a salesperson, this can be a daily practice where they spend a few minutes focusing on their breath, sensations in the body, or even visualizing a successful customer interaction. The goal is to cultivate a state of mind that is attentive, clear, and free from distraction.

This heightened awareness can translate into more effective customer interactions. By being fully present and attentive, a salesperson can pick up on subtle cues, understand underlying needs, and respond with empathy and insight. It's about seeing through the customer's lens, recognizing their unique perspective, and thinking differently about how to meet their needs.

While the practice of mindfulness meditation may not be explicitly mentioned in scripture, the principles align with biblical teachings on attentiveness, discernment, and wisdom. In Proverbs 8:34 (NIV), wisdom is personified, saying, "Blessed are those who listen to me, watching daily at my doors, waiting at my doorway." This attentiveness and watchfulness can be cultivated through mindfulness meditation, leading to a deeper understanding and connection with others.

In the fast-paced world of sales, where distractions are many and the pressure is high, mindfulness meditation offers a path to clarity and focus. It's a practice that requires dedication and consistency but can lead to significant improvements in the ability to evaluate and understand customers. By embracing this practice, a salesperson can develop a more empathetic and insightful approach, not only enhancing their sales success but also enriching their personal and professional lives. It's a practice that echoes the timeless wisdom found in scripture, guiding us toward a more mindful and compassionate way of engaging with the world.

Role-Playing Scenarios: Embracing Different Perspectives through Practice

Role-playing scenarios present a dynamic and engaging way to exercise the "Evaluation" muscle in the context of sales. By creating real-life sales scenarios with a colleague and practicing the evaluation stage, salespeople can immerse themselves in various customer perspectives, allowing them to think differently and adapt their approach accordingly.

Imagine a scenario where a salesperson and a colleague decide to role-play a complex sales situation. One takes on the role of a hesitant customer, concerned about budget constraints, while the other embodies the salesperson, tasked with evaluating these concerns and crafting a tailored solution. Through this exercise, the salesperson can explore different angles, ask probing questions, and practice empathy, all while receiving immediate feedback from their colleague.

This hands-on approach to learning resonates with the biblical principle of gaining wisdom through experience and counsel. In Proverbs 27:17 (NIV), it is stated, "As iron sharpens iron, so one person sharpens another." This metaphor illustrates the value of interaction, collaboration, and mutual growth, principles that are at the core of role-playing exercises.

Role-playing scenarios also align with the teachings of Jesus of Nazareth, who often used parables to illustrate complex spiritual truths. By engaging His listeners with relatable stories and characters, Jesus encouraged them to see things from different perspectives and to think more deeply about their beliefs and actions. Salespeople can apply this same principle by using role-playing to step into their customers' shoes, understanding their unique needs, fears, and desires.

In the world of sales, where every customer interaction is unique, role-playing scenarios offer a valuable tool for developing the flexibility and empathy required in the evaluation stage. It's a practice that encourages salespeople to think creatively, to challenge their assumptions, and to grow in their ability to connect with diverse customers. By embracing this method, salespeople can not only enhance their evaluation skills but also foster a more collaborative and supportive work environment, reflecting the timeless wisdom and compassion found in scripture.

Reading Literary Fiction: Enhancing Empathy through the Exploration of Complex Characters

Reading literary fiction is an unconventional yet highly effective way to exercise the "Evaluation" muscle in sales. By engaging with complex characters and intricate narratives, salespeople can develop a deeper understanding of human motivation, emotions, and behavior. This enhanced empathy and insight can be instrumental in the evaluation stage, where understanding a customer's underlying needs and desires is paramount.

Consider a salesperson who chooses to read a novel filled with multifaceted characters, each with their unique backgrounds, desires, and conflicts. As the salesperson delves into the story, they begin to see the world through the eyes of these characters, understanding their fears, hopes, and motivations. This practice of immersing oneself in another's perspective fosters empathy and a more nuanced understanding of human nature.

In the context of sales, this ability to empathize and understand can be applied to the evaluation stage, where a salesperson must discern the underlying needs and desires of a customer. By drawing on the insights gained from reading literary fiction, the salesperson can approach the evaluation process with greater sensitivity and insight, recognizing patterns and connections that may not be immediately apparent.

Jesus was a master storyteller, often using parables to convey profound spiritual truths. His stories were filled with relatable characters and situations, designed to engage the listener and encourage them to think more deeply about their own lives and beliefs.

In the same way, reading literary fiction invites readers to step into the shoes of others, to see the world from different angles, and to reflect on their own assumptions and biases. It's a practice that not only enriches the mind but also the heart, fostering compassion, curiosity, and a willingness to see beyond the surface.

For salespeople looking to strengthen their evaluation skills, reading literary fiction offers a unique and rewarding path. It's an exercise in empathy, a journey into the complexity of the human condition, and a valuable tool for those seeking to connect more authentically with their customers. By embracing this practice, salespeople can cultivate a more thoughtful and empathetic approach to evaluation, reflecting the timeless wisdom and compassion that are at the core of both effective salesmanship and spiritual growth.

Attending Empathy Workshops: Cultivating Emotional Intelligence for Deeper Connection

Empathy is a vital skill in the evaluation stage of the IDEAS Sales System, allowing a salesperson to discern the underlying needs, desires, and emotions of a customer. Attending workshops focused on empathy and emotional intelligence can be a powerful way to develop this skill.

Empathy workshops are designed to help participants explore and understand both their own emotions and those of others. Through various exercises, role-playing scenarios, and guided discussions, attendees learn to recognize and respond to emotional cues, build deeper connections, and communicate more effectively. For a salesperson, these skills are invaluable in the evaluation stage, where understanding a customer's perspective is key to crafting personalized solutions.

For example, an empathy workshop might include an exercise where participants are paired up and asked to share a personal story. The listener's task is not to respond or advise but simply to listen actively and reflect back what they've heard. This practice helps in honing the ability to truly hear what someone is saying, without judgment or preconceived notions. It's a skill that can be directly applied to customer interactions, where attentive listening leads to more insightful evaluations.

While the concept of empathy workshops may not be directly found in scripture, the underlying principles align closely with the teachings and example of Jesus of Nazareth. Throughout His ministry, Jesus displayed profound empathy and compassion. A notable example is Jesus' interaction with Zacchaeus, the tax collector (Luke 19:1-10). Despite Zacchaeus's unpopular profession and societal judgment, Jesus saw beyond the surface and recognized his longing for acceptance and redemption. By inviting Himself to Zacchaeus's home, Jesus offered not just companionship but also a transformative experience that led to Zacchaeus's repentance and generosity.

This story illustrates the power of empathy in understanding and connecting with others, a lesson that is highly relevant to the evaluation stage in sales. By looking beyond the surface and recognizing the whole person, salespeople can approach the evaluation stage with greater sensitivity, insight, and effectiveness.

Attending empathy workshops offers salespeople a structured and supportive environment to develop these essential skills. By learning to see through their customer's lens, salespeople can approach the evaluation stage with greater sensitivity, insight, and effectiveness. It's a practice that not only enhances professional success but also fosters personal growth and a more compassionate way of being in the world. In embracing empathy as a core value, salespeople align themselves with a timeless principle that resonates deeply with the teachings and example of Jesus of Nazareth, the master of empathy and connection.

Peer Review and Feedback: Collaborative Growth through Insightful Evaluation

In the complex and nuanced world of sales, the evaluation stage is pivotal. It's where a salesperson takes the information gathered during the discovery phase and analyzes it, seeking to understand the customer's needs and desires from various angles. This process can be greatly enhanced through peer review and feedback, where colleagues review the evaluation process and provide insights that might otherwise be missed.

Imagine a scenario where a salesperson has just completed a significant customer interaction. They've gathered information, asked probing questions, and feel they have a solid understanding of the customer's needs. By sharing this information with a trusted colleague and asking for their perspective, the salesperson opens the door to new insights. The colleague might see connections or patterns that the salesperson missed or offer a different interpretation of the customer's words and behavior. This collaborative approach can uncover blind spots, challenge assumptions, and lead to a more nuanced and effective evaluation.

The principle of seeking wisdom and counsel from others is well-supported in scripture. In the Book of Proverbs, a collection of wise sayings often attributed to King Solomon, we find the counsel: "Without counsel, plans go awry, but in the multitude of counselors they are established" (Proverbs 15:22, NKJV). This timeless wisdom underscores the value of seeking input from others, recognizing that multiple perspectives can lead to a more robust and well-rounded understanding.

In the context of sales, this scriptural insight translates into the practice of peer review and feedback. By inviting colleagues to review and comment on the evaluation process, a salesperson can gain new perspectives and insights that enhance their ability to see through the customer's lens. It's a practice that fosters collaboration, continuous learning, and professional growth.

Furthermore, this approach aligns with the broader principles of humility and teachability, qualities that were central to Jesus of Nazareth's teachings. By recognizing that we don't have all the answers and that others can provide valuable insights, we position ourselves to learn and grow in ways that would not be possible alone.

Peer review and feedback in the evaluation stage is not just a practical tool for improving sales skills; it's a practice that resonates with timeless wisdom and the teachings of Jesus of Nazareth. By embracing this collaborative approach, salespeople can enhance their ability to understand and serve their customers, building relationships that are not only profitable but also deeply satisfying and aligned with core values. It's a path that leads not just to professional success but to personal growth and a more compassionate and connected way of being in the world.

Visual Mapping: Illuminating Connections through Tangible Insights

In the intricate process of evaluation, salespeople are often tasked with deciphering complex information, discerning patterns, and understanding the multifaceted needs and desires of their customers. One powerful tool to aid in this process is visual mapping. By creating visual representations of customer needs, wants, and emotions, salespeople can see connections and patterns more clearly, making the evaluation process more tangible and insightful.

Visual mapping might involve drawing diagrams, flowcharts, or mind maps that represent the customer's statements, concerns, and desires. For example, a salesperson could create a mind map after a discovery session with a customer, placing the customer's primary need in the center and branching out to various related wants, concerns, and emotions. By visually connecting these elements, the salesperson can gain a holistic view of the customer's situation, uncovering insights that might be missed in a more linear or text-based analysis.

This practice of visualizing complex information can be related to the biblical concept of wisdom and understanding. In the Book of Proverbs, wisdom is often portrayed as something to be sought after, like hidden treasures, and understanding as something to be discerned and grasped (Proverbs 2:3-5). The act of creating visual maps to understand a customer's needs can be seen as a modern application of this ancient pursuit of wisdom and understanding.

A scriptural example that resonates with this practice is the vision of the prophet Ezekiel. In Ezekiel's vision of the dry bones (Ezekiel 37:1-14), he sees a valley filled with dry bones, and through God's guidance, these bones come together, take on flesh, and become a living army. This vivid, visual experience provided Ezekiel with a profound understanding of God's power and plan for Israel. While the context is vastly different, the principle of using visual imagery to gain deeper insight and understanding can be applied to the sales process.

In the realm of sales, visual mapping serves as a practical tool to help salespeople think differently and change their perspective. By translating words and ideas into visual forms, they can see connections and patterns that might otherwise be obscured. It's a practice that not only enhances the evaluation process but also aligns with timeless principles of wisdom and understanding found in scripture.

Visual mapping is more than just a creative exercise; it's a strategic approach to evaluation that can lead to more insightful and personalized solutions. By embracing this practice, salespeople can deepen their connection with their customers, offering products and services that truly resonate with their needs and desires. It's a path that leads not only to professional success but also to a more empathetic and thoughtful way of engaging with the world, reflecting principles that are as relevant today as they were in the time of the biblical prophets.

Practicing Socratic Questioning: A Philosophical Approach to Deep Understanding

The art of Socratic questioning, named after the ancient Greek philosopher Socrates, is a method of engaging in dialogues that probe deeper into thoughts and beliefs. Rather than accepting statements at face value, Socratic questioning encourages critical thinking, challenging assumptions, and seeking to understand underlying principles. For salespeople aiming to enhance their evaluation skills, this method can be a powerful tool to foster deeper understanding and change perspectives.

In the context of sales, practicing Socratic questioning means engaging with customers in a way that encourages them to think more deeply about their needs, wants, and motivations. Instead of simply asking what a customer wants, a salesperson might ask why they want it, what underlying needs or concerns are driving that desire, or how they envision the product or service improving their life. By asking these probing questions, the salesperson can uncover deeper insights that guide the evaluation process, leading to more personalized and effective solutions.

A scriptural example that aligns with this practice can be found in the interaction between Jesus and the Pharisees regarding the greatest commandment. When asked by a Pharisee, "Teacher, which is the greatest commandment in the Law?" Jesus responded with profound wisdom, summarizing the essence of the Law and the Prophets (Matthew 22:36-40). His response was not merely an answer but a profound insight that invited further reflection and understanding. Jesus' way of engaging with questions and providing answers that encouraged deeper thought reflects the essence of Socratic questioning.

For a salesperson, adopting this method means not only asking probing questions but also listening attentively to the customer's responses and asking follow-up questions that dig even deeper. It's a dynamic, interactive process that requires patience, empathy, and a genuine desire to understand. It's not about leading the customer to a predetermined conclusion but about exploring their thoughts and feelings together, discovering insights that might not be apparent at first glance.

Practicing Socratic questioning is more than a sales technique; it's a way of thinking and engaging with others that fosters mutual understanding and growth. It's a practice that aligns with the principles of empathy, compassion, and wisdom found in scripture, and it's a path that can lead to not only greater success in sales but also a more thoughtful and reflective way of living.

Socratic questioning is a valuable practice for salespeople seeking to strengthen their evaluation muscle. By engaging in dialogues that probe deeper into thoughts and beliefs, they can gain a richer understanding of their customers, offering solutions that truly resonate with their needs and desires. It's a practice that requires effort and intention, but the rewards are well worth it, reflecting timeless principles that are as relevant today as they were in the time of Socrates and Jesus.

Observing Non-Verbal Cues: The Silent Language of Understanding

In the complex dance of human communication, words are only part of the story. Non-verbal cues, such as body language, facial expressions, and tone of voice, often convey more about a person's true feelings and needs than their spoken words. For salespeople aiming to excel in the EVALUATION Stage of the IDEAS Sales System, the ability to observe and interpret these non-verbal cues can add a profound layer of understanding, enabling them to see through their customer's lens with greater clarity.

Observing non-verbal cues is about more than just watching how a customer moves or the expressions on their face. It's about tuning in to the subtleties of their communication, noticing the nuances that might reveal underlying emotions or concerns. For example, a customer might say they're interested in a product, but their crossed arms, averted gaze, or hesitant tone might suggest uncertainty or doubt. By picking up on these cues, a salesperson can ask more targeted questions, explore those doubts, and tailor their approach to address the customer's true needs.

Scripture offers a beautiful example of this kind of attentive observation in the story of Jesus and the woman who anointed His feet with perfume (Luke 7:36-50). Though the woman said nothing, her actions spoke volumes, and Jesus understood the depth of her repentance and love. He also observed the reactions of the Pharisee who had invited Him, discerning his judgmental thoughts without a word being spoken. Jesus' response to both the woman and the

Pharisee demonstrated His deep understanding of their hearts, an understanding that went beyond words.

In the realm of sales, mastering the art of observing non-verbal cues is invaluable. This skill isn't limited to direct sales interactions; it can be honed in various settings. For instance, one might observe a conversation between two individuals, focusing solely on deciphering the messages conveyed through body language. Consider the nuances: Does a person's stance reveal their unspoken feelings about a situation? Can their choice of attire or the subtle shifts in their facial expressions provide deeper insights? The positioning of their arms, hands, and even feet can offer a wealth of information.

Furthermore, reflecting on past sales interactions can be enlightening. By revisiting these encounters, salespeople can identify non-verbal signals they might have overlooked. Recognizing these missed cues can provide invaluable insights for future evaluations, ensuring a more comprehensive understanding of the customer's perspective.

This practice requires patience, focus, and a willingness to look beyond the surface. It's about learning to see with the eyes of empathy, recognizing that every gesture, expression, or tone of voice is a piece of the puzzle that makes up a person's experience. It's a skill that can deepen not only a salesperson's professional interactions but also enrich their personal relationships, fostering a greater connection with others.

Observing non-verbal cues is a vital practice for anyone seeking to strengthen their evaluation muscle. It's a skill that goes beyond the realm of sales, touching on the very essence of human communication and connection. By learning to see and understand the silent language of body language and non-verbal communication, salespeople can gain a richer, more nuanced understanding of their customers, offering solutions that truly resonate with their needs and desires. It's a path that requires effort and intention, but the rewards are profound, reflecting timeless principles of empathy and understanding that resonate deeply with the teachings of Jesus.

Studying Behavioral Psychology: Unveiling the Human Mind for Effective Evaluation

The field of behavioral psychology delves into the intricate workings of the human mind, exploring how people think, feel, and act. For salespeople striving to master the EVALUATION Stage of the IDEAS Sales System, studying behavioral psychology can provide invaluable insights into human behavior and motivation. This academic approach equips them with foundational knowledge that can transform their ability to see through their customer's lens and change their perspective in profound ways.

Behavioral psychology explores concepts such as conditioning, reinforcement, motivation, and cognition. By understanding these principles, salespeople can better interpret the needs, wants, and emotions of their customers. For example, learning about motivational theories can help a salesperson recognize what drives a customer's decisions, whether it's a desire for status, security, or personal growth. Understanding cognitive biases can help a salesperson identify potential obstacles in a customer's thinking and find ways to address them.

A salesperson might engage in this exercise by taking a course in behavioral psychology, reading books on the subject, or even seeking mentorship from a professional in the field. The goal is to build a solid understanding of human behavior that can be applied in the evaluation process, allowing for a more nuanced and empathetic approach.

A scriptural example that resonates with the study of behavioral psychology is the story of King Solomon's wisdom in judging between two women who claimed to be the mother of the same baby (1 Kings 3:16-28). Solomon's ability to understand human behavior and motivation led him to propose a shocking solution: dividing the baby in two. His keen insight into the true mother's love allowed him to discern her identity when she immediately offered to give up her claim to save the child's life. This story illustrates the power of deep understanding and clever evaluation in uncovering the truth.

For salespeople, the study of behavioral psychology is not just an academic exercise; it's a practical tool that can enhance their ability to evaluate and connect with customers. It's about recognizing the complex interplay of thoughts, emotions, and actions that shape human behavior and using that understanding to craft solutions that truly resonate with the customer's unique needs and desires.

Studying behavioral psychology is a powerful way for salespeople to exercise their "Evaluation" muscle. It's a journey into the human mind that offers practical insights and tools for effective evaluation. By embracing this academic approach, salespeople can deepen their understanding of what makes people tick, allowing them to see through their customer's lens with greater clarity and empathy. It's a path that requires commitment and curiosity, but the rewards are significant, reflecting timeless principles of human understanding that align with the teachings of Solomon and the core values of the sales profession.

Setting Aside Reflection Time: Cultivating Thoughtful Evaluation Through Intentional Contemplation

In the bustling world of sales, it's easy to get caught up in the constant flow of interactions, meetings, and transactions. However, the EVALUATION Stage of the IDEAS Sales System calls for a different approach, one that requires a salesperson to pause, reflect, and think differently. Setting aside regular time for contemplation and reflection on customer interactions is not just a valuable practice; it's essential for thoughtful evaluation and a deeper understanding of the customer's perspective.

Reflection time allows a salesperson to revisit conversations, analyze responses, and consider the underlying needs and desires expressed by the customer. It's an opportunity to step back and see the bigger picture, to connect the dots, and to recognize patterns that might not be apparent in the heat of the moment. This intentional practice encourages a salesperson to change their perspective, to see through the customer's lens, and to think differently about how to serve them best.

A salesperson might perform this exercise by scheduling a specific time each day or week to review notes from customer interactions, to meditate on the insights gained, and to consider how those insights might shape future engagements. It's a time to ask probing questions like, "What is the customer really seeking?" "How do their needs align with our products or services?" "What emotions are driving their decisions?" By engaging in this reflective practice, a salesperson can cultivate a more empathetic and nuanced approach to evaluation.

A scriptural example that aligns with the practice of setting aside reflection time is the story of the prophet Elijah's encounter with God in 1 Kings 19:11-13. After a powerful display of wind, earthquake, and fire, Elijah experiences the presence of God in a "gentle whisper." This profound moment of quiet reflection teaches the value of stillness and contemplation in discerning the voice of truth.

Similarly, salespeople can find wisdom and insight in the quiet moments of reflection, away from the noise and distractions of the marketplace. It's in these intentional pauses that they can truly hear the "gentle whispers" of their customers' needs and desires, allowing them to craft solutions that resonate on a deeper level.

Setting aside reflection time is a vital exercise for salespeople seeking to strengthen their Evaluation muscle. It's a practice that requires discipline and intentionality but offers rich rewards in terms of deeper understanding, empathy, and effectiveness in serving customers. By following the example of Elijah and embracing the power of quiet contemplation, salespeople can transform their approach to evaluation, seeing through their customer's lens with greater clarity and compassion. It's a path that leads not just to better sales but to a more fulfilling and meaningful connection with the people they serve.

Practicing Gratitude: Enhancing Empathy and Positive Thinking in Evaluation

The practice of gratitude is often associated with personal well-being and contentment, but it also has profound implications for the professional realm, particularly in the field of sales. In the EVALUATION Stage of the IDEAS Sales System, cultivating a habit of gratitude can be a transformative exercise, enhancing positive thinking, empathy, and a deeper understanding of the customer's perspective.

Gratitude is about recognizing and appreciating the positive aspects of life, both big and small. It's a mindset that focuses on what is good and valuable, rather than dwelling on problems or shortcomings. For a salesperson, practicing gratitude can shift the focus from merely selling a product to genuinely appreciating the opportunity to serve and make a difference in a customer's life. It fosters a positive attitude that can permeate the entire sales process, from the initial introduction to the final transaction.

A salesperson might perform this exercise by starting each day with a gratitude journal, listing things they are thankful for, including successful customer interactions, lessons learned, and even challenges that have led to growth. This daily practice can set a positive tone for the day, encouraging a more empathetic and thoughtful approach to evaluation. It's about seeing the customer not just as a potential sale but as a unique individual with specific needs, wants, and emotions.

The practice of gratitude can also be applied directly to customer interactions. By expressing genuine appreciation for the customer's time, insights, and business, a salesperson can create a more positive and trusting relationship. It's a way of acknowledging the value of the connection, not just the transaction.

A scriptural example that resonates with the practice of gratitude is found in the Apostle Paul's letter to the Philippians. In Philippians 4:8, Paul encourages the believers to focus on whatever is true, noble, right, pure, lovely, and admirable. This exhortation to dwell on positive and virtuous things aligns with the practice of gratitude, fostering a mindset that looks for the good and seeks to understand and appreciate others.

In the context of sales, this scriptural wisdom can inspire a salesperson to approach the evaluation process with a grateful heart, recognizing the inherent value in each customer interaction and seeking to understand and serve with integrity and compassion.

Practicing gratitude is more than just a personal growth exercise; it's a powerful tool for enhancing empathy and positive thinking in the evaluation stage of sales. By cultivating a habit of gratitude, salespeople can change their perspective, think differently, and enrich their approach to understanding and serving their customers. It's a practice that not only elevates the sales process but also contributes to a more fulfilling and meaningful professional life.

Building Diverse Relationships: Broadening Perspectives for Enhanced Evaluation

In the world of sales, and in life, understanding the diverse needs and perspectives of various people is paramount. One of the most enriching ways to develop this understanding is by building and cultivating relationships with people from different backgrounds, cultures, and walks of life. This practice not only broadens one's perspective but also enhances the ability to evaluate different customer needs effectively.

Building diverse relationships is about intentionally seeking connections with people who might have different viewpoints, experiences, or backgrounds than oneself. For a salesperson, this could mean joining community groups, attending cultural events, or engaging in social activities that expose them to a wide array of people. By interacting with individuals from various socio-economic, cultural, or age groups, a salesperson can gain insights into different ways of thinking, values, and needs.

These relationships can provide a salesperson with a more nuanced understanding of how different customers might perceive a product or service. It encourages empathy and the ability to see things from multiple angles, which is crucial in the EVALUATION Stage of the IDEAS Sales System. It's about recognizing that there's no one-size-fits-all approach and that each customer's needs and desires are shaped by their unique context.

A scriptural example that illustrates the value of diverse relationships can be found in the Acts of the Apostles. In Acts 10, Peter's vision of the unclean animals leads him to the house of Cornelius, a Gentile. This encounter challenged Peter's preconceived notions and opened his eyes to the universality of God's love and acceptance. Peter's willingness to step out of his comfort zone and engage with someone from a different background led to a profound revelation and a broader understanding of his mission.

Similarly, a salesperson's willingness to engage with diverse individuals can lead to revelations about how to approach the evaluation process. It can uncover hidden biases, challenge assumptions, and foster a more inclusive and empathetic approach to understanding customers.

In practical terms, a salesperson might make a concerted effort to attend networking events that cater to various industries, join social clubs that attract a diverse membership, or volunteer in community service projects that bring together people from different backgrounds. These experiences not only enrich personal growth but also provide valuable insights that can be applied to the evaluation process in sales.

Building diverse relationships is a powerful exercise for any salesperson seeking to strengthen their "Evaluation" muscle. By actively seeking connections with people from various backgrounds, a salesperson can broaden their perspective, enhance their empathy, and develop a more nuanced approach to evaluating customer needs. It's a practice that not only enriches professional skills but also contributes to personal growth and a more inclusive and compassionate worldview.

Cultivating the Evaluation Muscle: A Journey of Empathy, Care, and Perspective

Building strength in your evaluation muscle is a complex and nuanced process. It's not a skill that can be acquired overnight or mastered with a quick read of a book. It requires dedication, practice, and a willingness to step out of your comfort zone. It's a journey that demands a shift in thinking, a paradigm change that goes beyond mere transactional interactions.

Throughout this chapter, we've explored various exercises and practices that can help salespeople become more empathetic, caring, and aware of different perspectives. From engaging in reflective journaling to practicing Socratic questioning, from observing non-verbal cues to building diverse relationships, each exercise offers a unique pathway to enhance the evaluation process.

Empathetic Listening Practice: This involves truly hearing what the customer is saying, understanding their emotions, and seeing beyond surface-level responses. It's about connecting on a human level and recognizing the feelings and needs that lie beneath the words.

Mindfulness Meditation: By practicing mindfulness, salespeople can enhance their focus and awareness, being fully present during customer interactions, leading to more insightful evaluations.

Role-Playing Scenarios: Creating real-life sales scenarios with colleagues and practicing the evaluation stage helps in understanding different customer perspectives, making the process more tangible and relatable.

Studying Behavioral Psychology: Learning about human behavior and motivation provides foundational knowledge for effective evaluation, allowing salespeople to delve deeper into the human psyche.

Building Diverse Relationships: Cultivating friendships with people from various backgrounds broadens perspective and enhances the ability to evaluate different customer needs, fostering a more inclusive and empathetic approach.

These exercises, along with others discussed in this chapter, are not just theoretical concepts but practical tools that can be integrated into daily routines. They require repeated efforts, carried out over a long period of time, much like physical exercise. And just like physical exercise, the more you practice, the better you become.

But it's essential to recognize that this journey will be challenging. It will require significant changes in the way you approach every conversation, not just in your professional life but in all aspects of your interactions with others. It's about transforming the way you see the world, the way you relate to people, and the way you understand their needs and desires.

This is what separates great salespeople from the rest of the pack. It's what elevates the sales process from a mere transaction to a meaningful connection. It's what aligns the art of selling with the timeless wisdom exemplified by Jesus of Nazareth, who saw individuals, not crowds, and addressed specific needs, not generalities.

The journey to strengthen your evaluation muscle is a path filled with opportunities for growth, understanding, and connection. It's a path that leads not just to higher sales but to enriched relationships, satisfied clients, and a deeper sense of fulfillment in your professional endeavors. It's a path that invites you to see through your customer's lens, to change your perspective, and to think differently. It's a path worth pursuing, for it leads to the very heart of what it means to serve, to sell, and to succeed.

Conclusion: Embracing Evaluation in the IDEAS Sales System

The EVALUATION stage of the IDEAS Sales System represents a critical juncture where understanding deepens, insights emerge, and the path forward becomes clear. By examining the life and teachings of Jesus, we can recognize the profound impact of careful evaluation in all our interactions.

Jesus actively sought out those who needed Him, as evidenced in the INTRODUCING stage. He ventured into their world, met them where they were, and initiated connections. Moving into the DISCOVERY stage, He took the time to know them by asking thoughtful and sometimes challenging questions, allowing them to reveal their true selves. But He didn't stop there.

Jesus' ability to evaluate was built upon the foundation laid in these initial stages. He listened intently to the responses, internalized the emotions, recognized the underlying needs, and contemplated how best to meet them. This evaluation allowed Him to craft a message that was uniquely tailored to each individual, preparing Him to move into the ADAPTING stage where His teachings and actions would become highly relevant and resonant.

This practice is not confined to the ancient world but serves as a guiding model for the modern-day salesperson. Like Jesus, salespeople today must actively seek their prospects, engage in genuine discovery, and spend time in thoughtful evaluation. It is in this process that they not only gain a deeper understanding of their customer's needs but also build the essential bridge toward providing meaningful solutions.

These steps are not mere tactics or strategies; they form the links to selling with a service mindset. When embraced with sincerity and commitment, they elevate the art of sales beyond mere transactions, transforming it into a path of connection, empathy, and service.

By internalizing the lessons from Jesus and other scriptural examples, salespeople are empowered to approach their craft with a new depth and purpose. In the words of Solomon, "The purposes of a person's heart are deep waters, but one who has insight draws them out" (Proverbs 20:5, NIV). May the insights gained in the EVALUATION stage guide you toward a more compassionate, thoughtful, and successful journey in your sales endeavors.

"Do nothing out of selfish ambition or vain conceit. Rather, in humility value others above yourselves."

Philippians 2:3 (NIV)

CHAPTER TWELVE

ADAPTING

CRAFTING A UNIQUE MESSAGE

IN A WORLD WHERE automation and repetition often overshadow genuine interaction, the significance of personalization and sincerity in communication is paramount. The conventional approach to sales, often characterized by rehearsed scripts and one-size-fits-all presentations, may seem efficient on the surface. However, it lacks authenticity and can come across as insincere to the customer.

A salesperson driven by a genuine desire to help, solve problems, and enrich the lives of customers understands that each interaction must be as unique as the individual they are serving. This understanding forms the core of the ADAPTING stage of the IDEAS Sales System.

The preceding stages of the system have laid the foundation for this critical phase, guiding the salesperson in identifying prospects, introducing themselves, and discovering the unique experiences and needs of the customer. Through thoughtful questions and careful evaluation, a vivid mental picture is formed, allowing the salesperson to truly grasp the customer's perspective.

Now, the time has come to translate that understanding into action. The ADAPTING stage is where the salesperson crafts a message that resonates specifically with this customer. It's about using words, phrases, ideas, and suggestions that carry personal significance, connecting on a level that a generic presentation never could.

The model for this practice can be found in the teachings and parables of Jesus. He exhibited a remarkable ability to speak directly to the hearts and minds of those He encountered, choosing His words carefully to meet the distinct needs of each individual.

Jesus had a unique approach when it came to delivering his message; he always personalized it according to his audience's backgrounds, fears, hopes, and questions. He believed in adapting his words to suit their specific circumstances, which allowed him to connect with people on a profound and personal level, be it a single individual or a crowd.

Today, the ADAPTING stage encourages modern salespeople to follow a similar practice. Instead of relying on rote presentations, salespeople are encouraged to engage with each customer as a unique individual with unique needs. This shift focuses on providing solutions rather than merely selling products and building long-lasting relationships instead of just transactions.

This chapter will explore the principles and techniques that enable salespeople to make this shift successfully. Drawing on biblical examples and practical insights, we will delve into the art of personalized communication. By embracing the lessons of the ADAPTING stage, salespeople can transform their approach, building trust and understanding, and paving the way for genuine connections and lasting impact. It's not just about closing a deal; it's about opening a dialogue that can change lives.

The Key to Adaptation: Strengthening the EVALUATION Muscle

Adapting to the needs and perspectives of your customers is a critical aspect of a successful sales process. It's akin to entering their world and playing a role that's in harmony with their story. But how do you effectively adapt your approach? How do you ensure that your presentation resonates with them? The answer lies in strengthening a vital skill: the EVALUATION muscle.

As we explored in the previous chapter, the EVALUATION muscle is the ability to look through different lenses, to understand what drives your customer, and to adapt your role within their story accordingly. By strengthening this ability, you not only align yourself with their narrative but also facilitate a more positive and meaningful engagement. This strength is not developed overnight; it requires practice, reflection, and a commitment to seeing things through the customer's eyes. The exercises, examples, and insights provided in the preceding chapter offer a comprehensive guide to building this essential skill.

In the dynamic journey of the IDEAS Sales System, we've navigated the stages of identifying customers, discovering their needs through thoughtful questions, and evaluating everything they've said by working hard to see things through their own eyes. As we've just discussed, strengthening the EVALUATION muscle is key to this process, and the exercises and insights from the previous chapter provide a roadmap for this development.

Now, we arrive at a pivotal stage: ADAPTING the presentation to the uniqueness of the customers in ways that they will value. This is the ADAPTING stage, a crucial turning point that sets the stage for a meaningful connection and a successful sale.

The concept of adapting a presentation may seem straightforward, but it's often either overlooked or executed poorly. Many businesses train their salespeople to script out generic presentations that fail to demonstrate the unique ways a specific product can cater to individual needs. Such presentations leave customers with only a general understanding, lacking the personalized benefits that align with their unique situation and desires.

Part of the adapted presentation is also about you, the salesperson. You bring a level of service that nobody else can replicate. When the customer buys this product, they are investing in you and the personalized experience you offer. Your presentation must be unique, highlighting how you will enhance the value of the product through your service, commitment, and understanding of the customer's needs.

The more you have worked your evaluation muscle, the more you will be able to adapt your presentation to resonate with the customer on a personal level. Jesus exemplified this approach by tailoring His message to the specific needs and understanding of those He encountered, speaking to the hearts and minds of individuals.

In the world of sales, the ADAPTING stage is what separates a transaction from a transformation. It's what turns a product pitch into a personalized solution, building trust, fostering loyalty, and creating lasting relationships. It's a stage that demands attention, effort, and a willingness to see beyond the obvious, recognizing the unique value in every customer.

As we delve deeper into this stage, we will explore various strategies, exercises, and insights that can help you master the adapted presentation. It's a journey that will not only enhance your sales skills but enrich your understanding of human connection, empathy, and the power of personalized service. It's a journey that invites you to be not just a salesperson but a servant, a guide, and a partner in your customer's success.

Adapting the Message: Lessons from Jesus on Tailoring Our Approach

In the realm of sales, the ability to adapt and tailor presentations to individual clients is paramount. It's a skill that transcends mere customization; it's about understanding, empathy, and connection. Few have demonstrated this ability with more mastery and grace than Jesus of Nazareth. His teachings, interactions, and parables were never generic or one-size-fits-all; they were carefully crafted to resonate with the unique circumstances, backgrounds, and needs of those He encountered. Whether speaking to a fisherman, a Pharisee, a sinful woman, or a crowd of diverse listeners, Jesus' words were chosen with precision and compassion. In this section, we will explore some of these remarkable examples, drawing insights and lessons that modern salespeople can apply in the ADAPTING stage of the IDEAS Sales System. Through these timeless examples, we'll uncover the art of truly personalized communication, turning ordinary sales presentations into transformative connections.

Jesus' Adaptive Approach with Peter: Fishing for Understanding

When Jesus encountered Peter, a fisherman, His approach was uniquely tailored to Peter's life and needs. Peter's livelihood and identity were tied to the sea, and after a fruitless night of fishing, he was feeling disheartened. Jesus recognized Peter's context and need, so He spoke to him in a way that resonated with his specific experience.

In the Gospel of Luke, Jesus instructed Peter, "Put out into deep water, and let down the nets for a catch" (Luke 5:4). Peter obeyed, albeit with some initial hesitation, and his boat was filled to overflowing with fish. This miraculous catch wasn't just about the abundance of fish; it was a personal invitation to Peter, an example of Jesus' generosity and power that was profoundly significant to him. It was a direct encouragement that spoke to Peter's heart and experience. As Jesus told him, "Don't be afraid; from now on you will fish for people" (Luke 5:10).

Through this experience, tailored to Peter's personal context, Jesus invited him to a higher calling and demonstrated His ability to provide and guide in a way that was both tangible and deeply meaningful. The story of Jesus and Peter illustrates the power of understanding and adapting to the unique context of an individual.

Just as Jesus recognized Peter's connection to fishing and used it to convey a deeper message, salespeople must strive to understand their customers' unique needs, interests, and experiences. By crafting a presentation that resonates with the specific context of the customer, salespeople can create a connection that is not only relevant but deeply meaningful. It's about moving beyond generic pitches and finding the personal touch that speaks directly to the customer's heart and situation. In doing so, salespeople can transform a simple transaction into a relationship that carries lasting impact and value.

Adapting the Message for Paul's Transformation: A Road to New Perspectives

Contrast Jesus' interaction with Peter to His encounter with Paul on the road to Damascus. At that time, Paul was known as Saul and was a zealous persecutor of Christians. A presentation akin to

Peter's miraculous catch of fish would have been incongruent and meaningless to Saul. Instead, Jesus chose a way that would resonate with him. He appeared in a blinding light and confronted Saul with the question, "Saul, Saul, why do you persecute me?" (Acts 9:4).

This dramatic encounter wasn't just a spectacle; it was a direct challenge to Saul's actions and beliefs. It was a tailored approach that spoke directly to his particular situation and mindset. The effect was profound, leading to his immediate blindness and a subsequent transformation. Ananias, following Jesus' instructions, restored Saul's sight, and Saul became Paul, a dedicated apostle of Christ (Acts 9:17-18).

Jesus' interaction with Paul demonstrated a thoughtfully adapted approach that opened Paul's eyes to a new perspective, leading him from persecution to proclamation of the faith. This story underscores the importance of recognizing the unique beliefs, attitudes, and circumstances of each individual. In sales, a one-size-fits-all approach may not only be ineffective but also counterproductive. By understanding the specific needs and mindset of the customer, salespeople can craft a message that challenges, resonates, and transforms. It's about recognizing where the customer is coming from and adapting the presentation to lead them to a new understanding.

By fostering meaningful dialogue and building strong connections with customers, salespeople can improve their effectiveness and also enhance customer satisfaction. By taking the time to understand your customers and their preferences, you can create a more comprehensive and engaging customer experience that fosters loyalty and repeat business. By learning to ADAPT your presentations to demonstrate the value that your customer perceives will almost guarantee you long-term success and growth.

Adapting the Approach for the Blind: A Vision of Personalized Healing

Consider how Jesus healed the blind; His approach varied with each person. When healing a blind man in Bethsaida, He took the man by the hand, led him out of the village, and after spitting on his eyes and laying hands on him, the man regained his sight "And he took the blind man by the hand and led him out of the village, and when he had spit on his eyes and laid his hands on him, he asked him, 'Do you see anything?' And he looked up and said, 'I see people, but they look like trees, walking.' Then Jesus laid his hands on his eyes again; and he opened his eyes, his sight was restored, and he saw everything clearly." (Mark 8:22-25).

On another occasion, Jesus used mud made from His saliva and applied it to the eyes of a man blind from birth, instructing him to wash in the Pool of Siloam "And when he had said these things, he spat on the ground and made mud with the saliva. Then he anointed the man's eyes with the mud and said to him, "Go, wash in the pool of Siloam" (which means Sent). So he went and washed and came back seeing." (John 9:6-7).

In Jericho, He simply spoke a word to blind Bartimaeus, whose faith healed him "And Jesus said to him, "Go your way; your faith has made you well." And immediately he recovered his sight and followed him on the way." (Mark 10:52, ESV)

These diverse methods of healing demonstrate Jesus' ability to adapt His approach to the unique needs and circumstances of each individual. He didn't rely on a single method but chose the one that would resonate most profoundly with the person in need. This adaptability in approach is a powerful lesson for salespeople. It emphasizes the importance of not relying on a single, standardized presentation but being flexible and creative in crafting a message that speaks directly to the customer's unique situation and needs.

By being attentive to the customer's specific context and adapting the approach accordingly, salespeople can create a more meaningful connection and offer solutions that are not only relevant but deeply resonant. It's a practice that goes beyond mere selling and enters the realm of understanding, empathy, and personalized service, reflecting a genuine desire to meet the customer where they are and guide them toward a solution that truly fits their needs.

Adapting the Approach for the Criminal on the Cross

Jesus' interaction with one of the criminals crucified alongside Him is a poignant example of adaptability. While one criminal hurled insults, the other recognized Jesus' innocence and asked, "Jesus, remember me when you come into your kingdom" (Luke 23:42). Jesus' response was immediate and compassionate: "Truly I tell you, today you will be with me in paradise" (Luke 23:43). Jesus adapted His message to the desperate plea of a dying man, offering hope and assurance in a moment of profound need.

The lesson is that salespeople must possess the ability to recognize urgent needs and respond to them with empathy and assurance. This entails being able to identify when a customer is in a pressing situation and needs urgent attention and then approaching the situation with sensitivity and understanding. By doing so, salespeople can build trust and loyalty with their customers, which can ultimately lead to increased sales and business success.

Sometimes, customers may be in a situation where they the salesperson to take immediate action. Adapting the approach to meet those urgent needs with compassion and responsiveness can make a significant difference in the relationship and the outcome of the interaction.

Jesus' Adaptation with Children

Jesus' interaction with children offers a beautiful example of adaptability. When the disciples tried to prevent children from coming to Him, Jesus rebuked them and said, "Let the little children come to me, and do not hinder them, for the kingdom of heaven belongs to such as these" (Matthew 19:14). Jesus adapted His approach to connect with the innocence and simplicity of children, embracing them and blessing them. He didn't engage them with complex theology but met them with love and acceptance.

The takeaway for salespeople is the importance of simplicity and genuine care in communication. Sometimes, the most profound connections are made through simple, heartfelt interactions. Adapting to the needs and understanding of the audience, even if it means simplifying the message, can create a more meaningful and authentic connection.

Jesus' Conversational Adaptation with Nicodemus

The Gospels highlight Jesus' interaction with Nicodemus, a Pharisee and member of the Jewish ruling council. In John 3:1-21, Jesus engaged Nicodemus in a profound theological discourse about being born again, using complex spiritual metaphors and challenging Nicodemus's existing religious understanding.

The takeaway here is the ability to engage with individuals at their level of understanding and interest. In sales, this means recognizing when a customer is open to a more in-depth exploration of a product or service and adapting the presentation to meet that level of interest and comprehension.

Jesus' Adaptation with the Samaritan Woman

Contrast Jesus' conversation with Nicodemus to His interaction with the Samaritan woman at the well, as recounted in John 4:4-26. With her, Jesus started with the simple context of water, a daily necessity she could relate to, to lead her into a deeper spiritual understanding about the living water that only He could provide. He didn't burden her with theological complexities; instead, He connected with her on a personal and practical level.

The takeaway for salespeople is the importance of meeting customers where they are and guiding them to where they need to be. This adaptability translates into recognizing the customer's current understanding and needs and crafting a message that resonates specifically with them, much like Jesus did with those He encountered.

These examples collectively illustrate the wide range of conversational techniques Jesus employed, adapting His approach to suit the unique needs, backgrounds, and situations of those He encountered. They provide rich insights for modern-day salespeople, emphasizing the importance of empathy, adaptability, and personalized communication.

Compassion and Insight: Jesus' Forgiving Encounters

In the Gospels, Jesus' encounters with those in need of forgiveness are marked by compassion and insight, always tailored to the unique circumstances and needs of the individuals he met.

Consider the case of the woman caught in adultery (John 8:1-11). Jesus' response was gentle and insightful, challenging her accusers with the profound statement, "He that is without sin among you, let him first cast a stone at her." Then, with compassion, he told the woman, "Neither do I condemn you; go, and sin no more." His forgiveness was not a blanket approval but a personal and specific response to her situation, reflecting a deep understanding of her heart and her needs.

Similarly, when a sinful woman washed Jesus' feet with her tears (Luke 7:36-50), he recognized her act as one of genuine repentance and love. While others in the room judged her, Jesus offered forgiveness and encouragement, saying, "Your faith has saved you; go in peace." His response was not a generic absolution but a deeply personal acknowledgment of her faith and remorse, adapted to her unique experience.

These examples demonstrate Jesus' profound ability to adapt his interactions to the individual's heart and situation. He was not content with surface-level judgments or generic platitudes. His words were carefully chosen to heal, uplift, and inspire.

The takeaway for salespeople lies in the importance of a meticulous Discovery phase. It's not enough to understand the client's needs superficially. A salesperson must delve deeper, empathizing with the client's unique challenges and aspirations. This approach lays the groundwork for a presentation that resonates on a personal level, offering solutions that not only solve problems but also inspire trust and loyalty. Like Jesus' compassionate encounters, a salesperson's proposal can be a source of upliftment, encouragement, and genuine connection when adapted to the individual client's story. By truly understanding and adapting to the client's unique situation, a salesperson can create a connection that goes beyond mere transaction and becomes a transformative experience.

Parabolic Wisdom: Jesus' Tailored Teachings

Jesus' parables stand as an exemplary demonstration of His ability to craft narratives that resonate with diverse audiences. These stories were not mere allegories but carefully chosen illustrations that aligned with the understanding, culture, and daily life of the people He was speaking to.

Consider the Parable of the Sower (Matthew 13:1-23). Jesus used the familiar context of farming to describe how different types of soil (or hearts) respond to the seed (or Word of God). To an agricultural society, this comparison was immediate and profound, illustrating the varying degrees of receptivity in human hearts.

In the Parable of the Prodigal Son (Luke 15:11-32), the story of a wayward son who squanders his inheritance only to return and find forgiveness from his father was a poignant illustration of God's boundless grace and mercy. In a culture that held family honor in high regard, this narrative struck a deep chord.

The Parable of the Good Samaritan (Luke 10:25-37) challenged the prejudices of Jesus' audience by casting a despised Samaritan as the hero who showed compassion to a wounded Jew. This lesson about neighborly love transcended racial and cultural barriers, speaking directly to the hearts of those who heard it.

Using the metaphor of a master entrusting his servants with different amounts of money in the Parable of the Talents (Matthew 25:14-30), Jesus conveyed the importance of faithfulness and stewardship. This spoke to the economic practices of the time and urged listeners to use their God-given abilities wisely.

Finally, the Parable of the Mustard Seed (Mark 4:30-32) emphasized the potential of small beginnings and the expansive growth of God's Kingdom by referencing one of the smallest seeds known to His listeners. This was a concept that even the simplest farmer could grasp.

Jesus, in His teachings, utilized parables that were specifically designed to resonate with the cultural, social, and economic backgrounds of His audience. This exhibits His profound comprehension of the human psyche and His adeptness at tailoring His message to effectively reach His listeners. His ability to adapt His teachings to the unique circumstances of His audience highlights His significance as a teacher and leader.

Modern salespeople must recognize the importance of contextual understanding and the ability to craft messages that resonate with the unique backgrounds and needs of their customers. Just as Jesus used parables to connect with His audience on a personal and cultural level, salespeople must adapt their presentations to reflect the values, interests, and concerns of their clients. By doing so, they can create a connection that is not only engaging but also deeply meaningful, transforming a standard sales pitch into a personalized conversation that speaks directly to the heart of the customer.

The adaptability demonstrated by Jesus in His words, actions, and miracles serves as a timeless model for sales professionals. By emulating His empathy, customization, and effective communication, and aligning these principles with the IDEAS Sales System's stages of Introduction, Discovery, Evaluation, and Adaptation, salespeople can craft presentations that are not merely tailored but truly transformative.

Just as Jesus met people where they were, offering precisely what they needed for spiritual growth, sales professionals have the opportunity to connect with clients on a deeper level, providing solutions that resonate with their unique needs and aspirations. This approach transcends the mere act of selling; it elevates the entire relationship, turning transactions into meaningful, lasting connections that can change lives.

The Sales Lesson from Jesus' Adaptive Approach

Building on the diverse and personalized ways Jesus interacted with those around Him, we find a profound lesson for today's sales professionals. Too often, salespeople fall into the trap of peppering their customers with pre-scripted questions, pulling them down a path that only benefits the salesperson. They offer a one-size-fits-all presentation that fails to resonate with the customer's unique situation and needs. In essence, they fill their customer's chariot with fish, rather than opening their eyes to a new perspective.

The instances of Jesus' interactions serve as a reminder of the significance and potency of comprehending our audience and customizing our approach to connect with them on a personal level. It entails perceiving their perspective, acknowledging their requirements, and presenting something that is truly significant to them.

As salespeople, we must strive to move beyond a one-size-fits-all approach. We must learn to adapt our presentations to our customers' unique situations, opening their eyes to new perspectives, rather than merely filling their chariots with fish. By doing so, we can create more impactful, sincere, and successful engagements.

By extending invitations, granting forgiveness, promoting healing, and providing encouragement, we can create deeper, more genuine connections with those we serve. This approach not only improves our sales strategy but also enhances our relationships with others, teaching us the importance of compassion and empathy.

The Art of ADAPTING - A Path to Genuine Connection

The journey through the ADAPTING stage of the IDEAS Sales System has been an exploration of empathy, creativity, and the profound ability to see through the eyes of others. Drawing inspiration from the teachings and examples of Jesus, we have uncovered the essence of crafting a unique message that resonates with each individual customer.

Adaptation is not merely a technique; it's an art form that requires a deep understanding of human nature, a willingness to engage with others on a personal level, and the flexibility to tailor our approach to their unique needs and desires. It's about moving beyond rehearsed scripts and generic presentations to create a dialogue that is meaningful, authentic, and transformative.

In this chapter, we have seen how Jesus' interactions with various individuals, from fishermen to Pharisees, from the blind to the sinful, were characterized by an uncanny ability to adapt His message to their specific context. His words were not only wise but also compassionate, insightful, and perfectly attuned to the hearts and minds of those He encountered.

We have learned that the key to successful adaptation lies in strengthening our EVALUATION muscle, a skill that enables us to truly understand our customers and to craft presentations that align with their unique stories. We've explored various strategies, exercises, and insights that can help us master this art of personalized communication.

The lessons drawn from Jesus' parables, His compassionate encounters, and His forgiving and healing interactions have illuminated the path to a sales approach that is not just about closing deals but about opening hearts. It's an approach that transcends transactions and builds relationships, that turns products into solutions and customers into partners.

As we conclude this chapter, let us reflect on the transformative power of adaptation. Let us recognize that our ability to connect with others on a profound and personal level is not just a skill to be learned but a calling to be embraced. It's a calling that invites us to be not just salespeople but servants, guides, and partners in our customers' success.

The ADAPTING stage is a celebration of our shared humanity, a reminder that every interaction is an opportunity to enrich lives, to solve problems, and to make a lasting impact. It's a stage that challenges us to be more thoughtful, more creative, and more compassionate. It's a stage that inspires us to be not just better salespeople but better human beings.

In the world of sales, as in life, adaptation is not a destination but a journey. It's a journey that requires continuous growth, learning, and reflection. It's a journey that invites us to see the world through others' eyes and to walk in their shoes. It's a journey that leads us to a place of genuine connection, trust, and understanding. It's a journey that, when embraced with sincerity and commitment, can change not only our approach to sales but also our approach to life.

> **"The heart of the discerning acquires knowledge,**
> **for the ears of the wise seek it out."**
> Proverbs 18:15 (NIV)

Chapter Thirteen

SERVING

A Commitment Beyond Transactions

In the intricate tapestry of human relationships, the act of serving stands as a timeless testament to empathy, compassion, and genuine connection. It transcends the boundaries of mere transactions and elevates the experience into a partnership, a shared journey towards fulfillment and growth. This profound understanding of service is the cornerstone of the SERVING stage in the IDEAS Sales System, a stage that encapsulates the essence of what it means to be not just a salesperson but a servant, a guide, and a partner.

The concept of serving is deeply rooted in the teachings and life of Jesus of Nazareth. His ministry was marked by a relentless pursuit of service, a selfless dedication to the needs, hopes, and aspirations of those He encountered. Whether healing the sick, feeding the hungry, or offering forgiveness and redemption, Jesus' actions were guided by a profound understanding of service as a calling, a mission that goes beyond mere duty and becomes a way of life.

In the sales world, this service-first approach finds its expression in the IDEAS Sales System. It's a philosophy that recognizes the inherent dignity and worth of every customer, treating them not as mere consumers but as individuals with unique needs, desires, and dreams. It's an approach that seeks to understand, to empathize, and to offer solutions that resonate on a deeply personal level.

The SERVING stage begins with the very first act of reaching out, an intention to help rather than just to sell. It's a mindset that permeates every interaction, every decision, and every presentation. From the discovery phase, where we delve into the customer's unique challenges and needs, to the evaluation phase, where we tailor our solutions to their specific situation, the act of serving guides our path.

Therefore the SERVING stage is not confined to the process leading up to the sale. It's a continuous commitment that extends beyond the transaction, a promise to be there, to support, to guide, and to enhance the customer's experience. It's about proactive engagement, anticipating needs, and offering solutions before they become problems. It's about building trust, fostering loyalty, and creating lasting relationships.

Jesus' example teaches us that serving is not a task to be completed but a journey to be embraced. It's a journey that invites us to walk alongside our customers, to share in their struggles and triumphs, and to offer our expertise, our compassion, and our commitment as we guide them towards their goals.

In the following pages, we will explore the principles, strategies, and techniques that define the SERVING stage of the IDEAS Sales System. Drawing on biblical insights, practical wisdom, and real-world examples, we will delve into the art and science of serving. We will learn how to transform our approach to sales, moving beyond transactions to create genuine connections, meaningful partnerships, and lasting impact.

The SERVING stage is not just the conclusion of a sales process; it's the beginning of a relationship. It's a mindset that challenges us to see beyond the sale, to recognize the human being behind the customer, and to commit ourselves to their success, satisfaction, and growth. It's a stage that invites us to be more than salespeople; it invites us to be servants, guides, and partners in a journey that can change lives.

In the words of Jesus, "The greatest among you will be your servant" (Matthew 23:11). As we embark on this exploration of the SERVING stage, let us embrace this timeless wisdom, recognizing that our ability to serve, to connect, and to enrich the lives of others is not just a skill to be mastered but a calling to be fulfilled. It's a calling that can transform our approach to sales, our relationships with customers, and our understanding of success. It's a calling that can lead us to a place of genuine connection, trust, and fulfillment. It's a calling that invites us to be not just salespeople but true servants in the noblest sense of the word.

A Continuous Commitment in the IDEAS Sales System

In the IDEAS Sales System, the act of serving is not confined to a single stage; it's a continuous thread that weaves through every interaction, every decision, and every presentation. It's more than just a method; it's a commitment to fulfilling the genuine needs of the customer, a commitment that begins with the very first step and expands throughout the entire process.

The service journey begins with the intention to help, not merely to sell. From the first act of introducing ourselves and our offerings, we extend a hand not just to transact but to assist. This primary intention sets the tone for a relationship based on empathy, care, and understanding, mirroring the compassionate approach exemplified by Jesus.

Our next phase of discovery focuses on truly knowing the customer's needs. Here, we grant our full attention, not just to sell but to serve. By understanding their problems, we prepare ourselves to provide precise and meaningful solutions, aligning with their unique situation and desires.

As we proceed into evaluation, our service deepens, and a sense of obligation emerges. If we have identified that our product or service will indeed solve the customer's problem, it becomes not just an option but a duty to provide them with that solution. The act of presenting a tailor-made answer is an extension of our desire to serve, now guided by a responsibility to help the customer move one step closer to their goals.

With the invitation to purchase, our opportunity to serve expands even further. The official serving stage begins with asking for the sale, an invitation into a partnership where we can help solve their problem. It's not merely a request for a transaction; it's an extension of the service they need.

This service continues far beyond the sale. From ensuring promises are kept to offering help when questions arise, our proactive approach builds trust and proves we are a reliable source of assistance. It's a reflection of the ongoing commitment to service that defines the IDEAS Sales System, a commitment that transforms transactions into meaningful connections and sales into lasting relationships. It's a commitment that invites us to be not just salespeople but true servants, guided by the timeless wisdom and compassionate example of Jesus.

Emulating Jesus' Way

In every interaction, whether suggesting timely upgrades or providing support for a new product, the act of service amplifies the customer's experience. These ongoing acts of service foster loyal customers and a brand reputation that genuinely cares about its clients.

The serving stage in the IDEAS Sales System is not merely a final step but an expanding mindset present throughout every interaction. This concept of service is the core of the sales process, forging and strengthening the relationship with the customer.

When we approach sales with the primary motivation of serving, we align ourselves with a philosophy that sees success not just as a goal but as a natural outcome. By transforming the act of selling into a continuous journey of service, we create a sales system that isn't just about transactions but about fulfilling obligations, building lasting relationships, and turning customers into lifelong allies.

In essence, the SERVING stage brings the IDEAS Sales System to its culmination. It's more than a method or a final phase; it's an ever-expanding commitment to service that doesn't stop with a sale but continues to evolve. By putting service at the forefront of our sales approach, we foster customer satisfaction, loyalty, and consistent business growth, turning the act of selling into a profound connection and mutual success.

The parallels between the IDEAS Sales System's approach to service and Jesus' way of serving are both profound and instructive. Just as the IDEAS Sales System emphasizes a deep and ongoing commitment to serving the customer's needs, Jesus' interactions with individuals demonstrate an unparalleled dedication to understanding, empathy, and personal connection.

Jesus' ministry was never about fleeting or superficial engagements; it was about meeting people where they were and serving their unique needs and situations. He adapted his approach, his words, his miracles to resonate with those he sought to reach, always putting service at the forefront of his mission.

Consider Jesus' interaction with the two disciples on the road to Emmaus. They were disheartened, struggling to understand recent events. Jesus approached them, listened to their concerns, and then, using the scriptures, explained everything concerning himself. By the end of their journey, their hearts were aflame with understanding and hope. Here, Jesus didn't merely "sell" a belief system; he offered clarity, understanding, and hope.

Similarly, in the IDEAS Sales System, the act of selling is transformed into a process of service that recognizes the individual, seeks to understand their specific needs, and offers tailored solutions. It's not about a one-size-fits-all sales pitch but about developing a relationship founded on empathy, trust, and a genuine desire to help.

As we progress through this chapter, we will delve deeper into how Jesus served his "customers" and explore how his approach to service can be a guide for modern sales techniques. The lessons from Jesus' way of serving offer timeless insights into how genuine service can transcend mere transactions, forging connections that are both meaningful and enduring. It's a testament to how the principles of service, when rooted in sincerity and compassion, can create relationships that not only satisfy immediate needs but nourish the soul.

Closing the Sale: A Commitment to Continuous Service

Closing the sale is often perceived as the final act in a transaction, a mere conclusion to a business deal. However, when viewed through the lens of the IDEAS Sales System, it takes on a more profound meaning. It becomes a pivotal moment of service, a responsibility we hold towards our customers, and an opportunity to unlock the true value of what we offer.

The stages of Introduction, Discovery, Evaluation, and Adapted Presentation are not mere steps in a process; they are building blocks that lead us to a comprehensive understanding of how we can genuinely assist our customers. Whether it's about saving them money, enhancing their lives, boosting their confidence, or fulfilling a specific need, our product or service is designed to be a solution. Failing to close the sale is akin to turning away from a problem we have the means to solve.

Imagine witnessing someone drop their wallet. You have the ability to help them retrieve something valuable. Withholding that assistance would be ignoring a clear opportunity to serve. The moral obligation to act, similar to preventing a child from stepping into the street, is the same underlying principle that drives our duty to close the sale.

The IDEAS Sales System equips us with the insight and tools to recognize and address our customers' problems. If we believe in our industry, trust in our product's quality, and understand how our solution meets the customer's needs, then closing the sale becomes more than an opportunity; it becomes a moral imperative. We must guide our customers to a decision that allows our product or service to fulfill its intended purpose.

Closing the sale transcends persuasion; it's an act of service. It's not about finalizing a deal but about initiating a relationship. It's about recognizing the opportunity to provide genuine assistance and embracing our role in delivering it.

The act of closing is not the end but a new beginning, marking the start of various ways we continue to serve the customer. This profound understanding of closing as an ongoing commitment forms the foundation for what we will explore in the following sections, where we will delve into the multifaceted dimensions of serving beyond the sale. The art of closing is, in essence, a pledge to a journey of continuous service, where each sale is a promise to assist, empower, and enrich our customers' lives. It's a testament to the transformative power of service, turning transactions into lasting connections and customers into lifelong partners.

Assumptive Closing: A Lesson from Jesus in Genuine Service and Connection

The sales process is a complex interplay of understanding, empathy, conviction, and timing. Within this intricate dance lies the pivotal moment - the close. How do we navigate this essential yet nuanced part? By turning our attention to one of history's most impactful communicators and 'salesmen,' Jesus Christ, we can unearth powerful lessons in the art of the assumptive close.

Jesus' approach to spreading His message and bringing followers into the fold was never marked by pushiness or blatant selling techniques. Instead, He exemplified the "Triad of Belief": belief in His industry (the Kingdom of God), belief in His product (Salvation), and unwavering belief in Himself. This solid foundation allowed Him to transfer that conviction to those He spoke with, engaging them in a relationship rather than a mere transaction.

Consider His interaction with Matthew, a tax collector, a profession considered undesirable in those times. Jesus didn't propose a sales pitch or offer arguments. He simply said, "Follow Me" (Matthew 9:9). In that brief but potent invitation, Jesus acknowledged Matthew's needs, offered His solution, and assumed that Matthew recognized the truth and value of what was being offered. Matthew's immediate response to leave his tax booth and follow Jesus demonstrated the power of this approach.

Similarly, when Jesus encountered Peter, He recognized Peter's potential and the depth of his faith. He invited Peter to come with Him, promising to make him a "fisher of men" (Matthew 4:19). It wasn't a request but a profound understanding that Peter was ready to embrace the truth. Peter's quick acceptance was a testament to the effectiveness of Jesus' approach.

The interaction with Zacchaeus, a chief tax collector, further illustrates Jesus' mastery of the assumptive close. Jesus didn't plead or bargain. He simply told Zacchaeus, "Zacchaeus, come down immediately. I must stay at your house today" (Luke 19:5). Jesus knew what Zacchaeus needed, and He offered Himself as the solution, assuming that Zacchaeus would accept. The result? Zacchaeus's life was transformed.

From healing a paralyzed man at the pool of Bethesda to resurrecting Lazarus from the tomb, Jesus' interactions showcase His absolute confidence in His ability to provide the necessary solution and His skill in recognizing when that solution fits the needs of the individual before Him.

These examples underscore the essence of the assumptive close, where both the salesperson and the customer recognize the solution being offered as the right one. There's no hedging or uncertainty, just a confident, "ok, let's start." It is an approach steeped in deep understanding, empathy, belief, and service.

Jesus' way of closing the sale wasn't about manipulation or coercion; it was about recognizing the right moment, having absolute belief in what He was offering, and understanding the needs and desires of the person in front of Him. It was, at its core, a form of service, offering the keys to the Kingdom of God in a manner that resonated with each individual.

For salespeople seeking to master the art of closing, Jesus' approach offers timeless wisdom. By genuinely understanding and believing in your industry, product, and yourself, and by recognizing when the customer shares that belief, the assumptive close becomes a natural, effective, and deeply satisfying part of the sales process. It transcends selling, transforming transactions into meaningful connections, and customers into followers. Just as Jesus did, so can we all.

Embracing the Assumptive Close: The Art of Seamless Commitment

The assumptive close is more than just obtaining a commitment to purchase; it's about guiding the customer to envision how they will start using the product or service. This delicate and confident transition is rooted in a profound understanding of the customer's needs and a shared belief in the solution. Here's how the IDEAS Sales System helps modern-day salespeople transition to this close with artful precision:

Understanding Needs: "Based on our conversation, I've tailored this solution perfectly for you. We can start implementing it this week, or if you prefer, next Monday."

Presenting a Customized Solution: "Given our alignment, I've prepared the contract. We can finalize it today, or would tomorrow morning be more convenient?"

Demonstrating the Product: "I can have our team begin installation by the end of next week, or should we get started sooner?"

Addressing Objections: "Since everything is in line with your expectations, let's move forward. I'll send the paperwork right after our meeting."

Assessing the Budget: "This package fits within your budget. Would you like to set up delivery and installation for next Monday, or a different day?"

Reviewing Benefits: "With all the benefits we've discussed, I'll arrange for onboarding next week. Is there a specific day that you prefer?"

Aligning with Long-term Goals: "I propose we initiate our partnership with the first project starting next month, or we could align it with your next strategic meeting."

Building Trust and Relationship: "I feel confident that we're ready to proceed. We can schedule the kickoff meeting for next Tuesday, or adjust based on your calendar."

Confirming Value Proposition: "Since our solution delivers the value you've been looking for, I'll coordinate the transition. Would you like a status update on Friday or earlier?"

In each instance, the assumptive close gracefully nudges the customer to think about the immediate next steps rather than whether or not to make the purchase. The question is not if but how they want to begin benefiting from the product or service.

The IDEAS Sales System emphasizes this type of close as an integral part of a sales approach grounded in service, empathy, and collaboration. It's not about closing a transaction but opening a partnership that continues to flourish. This philosophy resonates deeply with principles found in the teachings of great figures like Jesus, who mastered the art of inviting others into a relationship through understanding and purposeful direction.

Jesus' Earthly Service: A Timeless Model for Sales Professionals

Jesus' acts of service, ranging from miraculous healings to profound teachings, were always rooted in empathy, compassion, and love. His concern for physical well-being was matched by a deep commitment to spiritual growth, providing a timeless model for sales professionals today.

Consider his teachings in the house of Martha and Mary, where he emphasized that service to others, combined with spiritual devotion, leads to true fulfillment (Luke 10:38-42). Or his healing of a paralyzed man, where he offered not only physical restoration but also forgiveness and spiritual healing (Mark 2:5). These acts demonstrated Jesus' compassionate service, transcending his immediate community.

His miracles, such as calming a storm (Mark 4:39) or feeding thousands with limited resources (Matthew 15:32-39), reflected his mastery over nature and his desire to meet immediate needs. But his service extended beyond miraculous interventions. He broke social barriers by spending time with those considered outcasts, teaching humility by washing his disciples' feet (John 13:14), and providing spiritual nourishment through teachings like the Sermon on the Mount (Matthew 5-7).

Whether embracing children (Mark 10:14), healing the Woman with an Issue of Blood (Mark 5:34), or raising Lazarus from the dead (John 11:1-44), Jesus' actions were clear demonstrations of inclusive, tender service to all, irrespective of societal norms or traditional boundaries.

His life was a consistent portrayal of compassion, humility, and unwavering dedication to improving the lives of those he encountered. Whether through miraculous deeds or simple human kindness, Jesus' service on earth stands as a timeless example of love in action.

These lessons from Jesus' earthly service resonate deeply with modern life and, notably, in the context of sales. Salespeople can look to Jesus' life as a model, recognizing that genuine service goes beyond transactions or personal gain. They can transform service into a powerful tool for building trust, fostering relationships, and genuinely improving the lives of customers.

Drawing from Jesus' service, salespeople can take actionable steps to serve their customers meaningfully:

Empathy: Just as Jesus listened and provided healing, salespeople must understand the unique needs of their customers, tailoring solutions that exceed expectations.

Humility and Willingness: Embodying Jesus' lesson of washing his disciples' feet, salespeople can provide exceptional support and continuous assistance, even in roles outside the typical sales process.

Inclusivity and Non-Judgment: Jesus broke social barriers, and salespeople should treat every customer with respect and consideration, regardless of their purchasing power or background.

Guidance and Education: Sales representatives can offer valuable insights and information, helping customers make informed decisions, just as Jesus' teachings provided new ways of understanding.

Integrity and Honesty: Salespeople must represent their products faithfully, building trust through transparency and accountability, reflecting Jesus' embodiment of truth.

By embodying these principles, salespeople can transform the buying process into a meaningful act of service, creating relationships that extend beyond a single transaction. They can reflect a commitment to the well-being and success of their customers, akin to the compassionate and selfless service Jesus demonstrated throughout his life.

Jesus' Ultimate Sacrifice

A Profound Act of Service

The cross. A symbol that has transcended time, culture, and geography. For many, it represents the very essence of love, sacrifice, and redemption. But for Jesus, it was more than a symbol; it was His destiny, His calling, His ultimate act of service to humanity.

Jesus' death on the cross is not merely a historical event; it's a profound statement about the depth of His belief in His industry, His product, and Himself. His industry was the Kingdom of God, a realm where love reigns supreme, justice prevails, and eternal life awaits. His product was Salvation, an offer of redemption that transcends our earthly existence. And His belief in Himself was unshakable, for He knew He was the only pathway to this salvation.

The cross was not a tragedy; it was a triumph. Jesus knew the cost, yet He willingly accepted it, not out of obligation but out of love. He was offering a transformation, a new way of life that could only be attained through His sacrifice.

Consider the profound significance of Jesus' sacrifice. The very Creator of the universe chose to become human, enduring suffering and death, even when faced with rejection from those He came to save. This act wasn't just about sacrifice; it was about bridging the vast divide between divine perfection and flawed humanity. It was an answer to the poignant question posed in the Garden of Eden: "Where are you?" This act wasn't just a demonstration of service; it was an unparalleled expression of love that challenges our understanding.

As stated earlier in this book, the followers of Christianity far outnumber the users of the world's most popular products. This staggering growth, even after His death, is a testament to the power of Jesus' message and His method of service. His disciples were not just followers; they were transformed individuals, advocates of a belief that had reshaped their very existence.

For the modern-day salesperson, Jesus' example serves as more than a guide; it's a calling. It's a reminder that service is not about transactions or quotas; it's about understanding the transformative potential of what you're offering and being willing to go to extraordinary lengths to ensure that your customers can access it.

The parallel between sales and Jesus' method may not initially seem apparent, but the correlation is both profound and instructive. While His sacrifice stands alone in its incomparable nature, the underlying principles of belief, empathy, commitment, and service are directly applicable to the sales profession.

As salespeople, we are invited to a path of selflessness, integrity, and genuine concern for the needs and well-being of our customers. By embracing this call, we not only honor the legacy of Jesus but also elevate our profession to a level that transcends mere transactions and enters the realm of transformation.

Jesus knew this. He lived it. His example continues to inspire and challenge us to approach sales, not as a job but as a calling, a mission to serve others with the same passion, dedication, and love that He demonstrated throughout His life and in His ultimate sacrifice.

In the shadow of the cross, we find our purpose, our inspiration, and our true success. It's a path that leads us not just to sales but to service, not just to success but to significance. It's a journey that echoes the footsteps of the greatest servant of all, inviting us to follow, to learn, and to love.

Jesus' Commitment to Salvation: A Model for Belief and Service

While Jesus' ultimate sacrifice on the cross is a profound act of love and redemption, it also represents His unwavering belief in His mission: Salvation. This belief was not merely an intellectual assent but a deep, abiding conviction that drove every aspect of His life and ministry.

In the world of sales, belief in a product is often seen as essential for success. Salespeople must understand, advocate for, and stand behind what they are offering. But Jesus' belief in Salvation went beyond mere endorsement; it was a commitment that led to the ultimate sacrifice.

His death was not an unfortunate conclusion but a deliberate decision, a strategic move in a divine plan. He knew that the barrier of sin between humanity and God required a perfect sacrifice, a payment that only He could provide.

This understanding led to an act of service on an unimaginable scale. By giving Himself on the cross, Jesus offered Salvation as a free gift, demonstrating a love that transcends human comprehension.

For modern salespeople, this sacred act may seem distant, but the underlying principles are strikingly relevant. Belief in a product is not just about recognizing its value; it's about understanding its transformative potential for those you serve. It's about being willing to go beyond the expected, to invest yourself fully in the success and well-being of your customers.

Jesus' sacrifice is a timeless reminder of the profound connection between belief and service. His willingness to give completely of Himself challenges us to reflect on our own commitments, our own beliefs, and our own willingness to serve.

In embracing these principles, we find a path not just to success but to significance. Jesus' life, teachings, and ultimate sacrifice guide us to a deeper, more meaningful approach to sales and life itself. They challenge us to consider what we are willing to give for the products, the people, and the purpose we believe in.

The Essence of Service: A Comprehensive Reflection on the IDEAS Sales System

The SERVICE stage of the IDEAS Sales System is not merely a final step in a transaction but a philosophy that permeates the entire sales process. It's a commitment that begins with the initial introduction and continues to evolve, even after the sale is made. This expansive understanding of service is deeply rooted in empathy, care, understanding, and a genuine desire to help.

A Continuous Commitment to Serve: Service in the IDEAS Sales System is an ongoing journey. It's about recognizing the customer's needs and providing precise and meaningful solutions. From the initial act of introducing ourselves to the continuous acts of serving beyond the sale, the focus remains on fulfilling the genuine needs of the customer. This commitment to service is not confined to a single stage but resonates throughout every interaction, turning customers into lifelong allies.

Closing the Sale: An Act of Service: The act of closing the sale is transformed from a mere transaction into an obligation to help. It's a moral duty, akin to assisting someone in immediate need. The closing becomes a new beginning, ushering in various ways to continue serving the customer. It's about recognizing an opportunity to provide genuine help and fulfilling our role in delivering it. This profound understanding of closing as service forms the foundation for a journey of continuous service.

Jesus' Earthly Service: A Model for Salespeople: The life and teachings of Jesus provide a timeless example of love in action.

His acts of service, whether miraculous or simple human kindness, were grounded in empathy, humility, and an unwavering dedication to improving the lives of those he encountered. Salespeople can draw from Jesus' principles of empathy, humility, inclusivity, guidance, and integrity to transform the buying process into a meaningful act of service.

A Commitment to Salvation: A Model for Belief and Service: Jesus' unwavering belief in His mission of Salvation led to the ultimate sacrifice. His death was a deliberate decision, a strategic move in a divine plan. For modern salespeople, this sacred act is a timeless reminder of the profound connection between belief and service. It challenges us to reflect on our own commitments and our willingness to serve.

The SERVICE stage of the IDEAS Sales System is a multifaceted concept that transcends the traditional understanding of sales. It's about building lasting relationships, fostering trust, and genuinely improving the lives of customers. By embracing this call to service, we not only honor the legacy of Jesus but also elevate our profession to a level that goes beyond mere transaction and into the realm of transformation. It's in this space that true success is found, not just in numbers but in lives touched, problems solved, and relationships built. The principles of service, when rooted in sincerity and compassion, create a sales system that is not just about transactions but about fulfilling obligations, building lasting relationships, and turning customers into lifelong allies.

> **"For even the Son of Man did not come to be served, but to serve, and to give his life as a ransom for many."**
>
> Mark 10:45 (NIV)

CHAPTER FOURTEEN

NAVIGATING ETHICAL CROSSROADS

PROFIT, HONESTY, DIVERSITY, AND BALANCE IN SALES

IN THE WORLD OF sales, the path to success is often fraught with ethical dilemmas and complex decisions. The pursuit of profit, the fine line between business engagement and dishonesty, the challenge of selling to diverse audiences, and the quest for work-life balance are all integral aspects of a salesperson's journey. These are not mere theoretical concerns; they are real-world challenges that every sales professional must navigate.

The IDEAS Sales System, rooted in principles of empathy, understanding, and service, provides a robust framework for addressing these challenges. But even within this system, there are areas that require careful consideration and thoughtful reflection. How do we define a fair profit, and when does profit-seeking become exploitation? Where is the line between persuasive communication and dishonesty? How do we approach selling to those who may not share our faith or cultural background? And how do we balance the demanding nature of sales with our personal lives and well-being?

This chapter delves into these critical questions, exploring the ethical crossroads that salespeople often encounter. Drawing on the teachings of Jesus and the principles of the IDEAS Sales System, we will provide insights and guidance to help you navigate these complex issues with integrity, compassion, and wisdom. Whether you are a seasoned sales professional or just starting your career, these reflections will equip you to approach your work with a deeper understanding of the ethical dimensions of sales and a renewed commitment to serving your customers and honoring your own values.

Trials, Triumphs & Tough Topics: Navigating the Complex Landscape of Sales

The life of a salesperson is a complex tapestry woven with challenges, opportunities, ethical dilemmas, and personal growth. It's a journey that demands not only professional acumen but also a profound understanding of human nature, societal dynamics, and one's own values and beliefs. In this chapter, we will delve into the multifaceted struggles that salespeople often encounter, struggles that resonate with the timeless challenges faced by prophets, leaders, and even Jesus himself.

From the intricate balance between profit and integrity to the ethical considerations surrounding truthfulness in sales, we will explore the fine line that salespeople must walk. We'll examine the rich diversity of customers and the unique approaches required to connect across cultural and personal divides. The resistance from customers, a universal challenge in sales, will be dissected to understand its roots and how to navigate it with grace and effectiveness.

Work-life balance, a concern that transcends professions, will be addressed with insights into maintaining harmony, focus, and well-being. These topics are not isolated; they intertwine and interact, reflecting the complex reality of modern sales.

Drawing from the wisdom of the Triad Of Belief and the IDEAS Sales System, along with lessons from Jesus' ministry, this chapter will provide guidance, encouragement, and practical strategies. It's about equipping salespeople to face these struggles not as insurmountable obstacles but as opportunities for growth, learning, and transformation.

As we embark on this exploration, remember that the struggles are not mere hindrances; they are the crucibles in which character is forged, skills are honed, and true success is defined. In the words of Jesus, "In the world you will have tribulation. But take heart; I have overcome the world." (John 16:33, ESV). Let this chapter be a roadmap to overcoming the challenges, guided by principles that have stood the test of time and shaped by a philosophy that views selling as a noble act of service.

Navigating Profit with Ethical Integrity: A Biblical Perspective

In the dynamic world of sales, profit often emerges as the primary metric of success. It's the driving force behind business growth and personal achievement. Yet, the pursuit of profit, while essential for sustainability, can sometimes lead to ethical dilemmas. The Bible, a timeless source of wisdom, offers profound guidance on this matter, emphasizing the virtues of honesty, integrity, and fairness in business dealings.

The book of Proverbs, known for its wisdom literature, states, "A false balance is an abomination to the Lord, but a just weight is His delight" (Proverbs 11:1). This scripture accentuates the significance of fairness and honesty in profit-making, cautioning against deceptive practices that might lead to unjust gains. In today's context, this could be likened to businesses that charge one group of customers differently for the same product or service than another, without transparent justification. Such differential pricing, if not rooted in clear reasons, might be perceived as discriminatory or exploitative.

The Old Testament provides further insights into ethical dealings. The Israelites received divine instructions on treating those in their employ with fairness and compassion. "Six days you shall labor, but on the seventh day you shall rest; even during the plowing season and harvest you must rest" (Exodus 34:21). This directive ensures that everyone, including those in subservient roles, was granted the same rights to rest and worship as their employers.

From these scriptural insights, salespeople are reminded that the essence of a sale isn't just in its achievement, but in the manner it's accomplished. It's about recognizing and understanding the customer's needs, offering genuine solutions, and ensuring that the value provided is consistent and fair for all. This approach embodies principles of empathy, humility, and integrity. It's not only about balancing the pursuit of profit with ethical considerations but also about stewardship, reflecting a deep commitment to both the company and the customer's well-being and success.

The IDEAS Sales System, with its emphasis on INTRODUCING, DISCOVERING, EVALUATING ADAPTING, and SERVING, aligns seamlessly with these biblical principles. It's a system that views selling not just as a transaction but as an act of service. By approaching profit with this mindset, salespeople can achieve success that's not only financial but also ethical, meaningful, and enduring.

The Bible doesn't portray profit as inherently bad or unethical. In fact, fair profit, when achieved for scripturally sound reasons, is encouraged by God for the sustainability, growth, and improvement of His people. God desires success for us; He wants us to enjoy and utilize the resources He created. In the Garden of Eden, God intended for mankind to have unlimited access to all that He created, making Adam and Eve incredibly "wealthy" in the sense that they had control over everything in creation. This abundance was God's original plan. Achieving financial success, even extreme wealth, is not sinful in itself, provided that the method through which it was achieved did not come at the detriment of someone else.

The Bible is replete with instances that underscore God's desire for His people to prosper and enjoy the blessings He bestows upon them. For instance, Deuteronomy 8:18 reminds us that it is God who empowers us to gain wealth, fulfilling His promises. Proverbs 10:22 emphasizes that wealth from God's blessing is pure and devoid of sorrow. Jesus, in His sermon in Matthew 6:31-33, emphasizes the importance of prioritizing God's kingdom, assuring that when we do, our material needs will be taken care of.

Throughout the scriptures, there's a recurring theme: God's desire for His people to prosper. Whether it's through the direct blessings He bestows, the abilities He grants, or the opportunities He presents, God's generosity is evident. However, it's essential to understand that this prosperity is not an end in itself. It's a means to fulfill God's purposes, to bless others, and to further His kingdom. The Bible encourages trust in God's provision, emphasizing that when we prioritize Him and His righteousness, our needs – both material and spiritual – will be abundantly met.

The Parable of the Talents and Fiduciary Responsibility

In the Parable of the Talents (Matthew 25:14-30), Jesus illustrates the importance of profit as a stewardship responsibility. The master praises the servants who have invested wisely and made a profit, while condemning the one who made no profit at all.

This parable offers a lesson for salespeople and entrepreneurs, emphasizing the fiduciary responsibility to the owner of the company, oneself, and one's family to earn a profit. It's about wisely investing time, effort, and resources to create value for both the company and the customer, recognizing the trust placed in the salesperson, and honoring that trust by seeking a fair and just profit.

Profit, when pursued with integrity, honesty, and a focus on value, aligns with the teachings of Jesus and the principles of the IDEAS Sales System. It's not merely a financial goal but a reflection of stewardship, trust, and responsibility. By approaching profit-making with care and a commitment to ethical considerations, salespeople can find success not just in financial terms but in the deeper, more meaningful dimensions of service, value, and faith.

The challenge lies in balancing the pursuit of profit with a genuine desire to serve, understanding the unique needs and problems of customers, and offering solutions that not only meet but exceed expectations. By embodying principles of empathy, humility, inclusivity, guidance, and integrity, salespeople can transform the buying process into a meaningful act of service, reflecting a commitment to the well-being and success of their customers, akin to the compassionate and selfless service Jesus demonstrated throughout his life.

Understanding Value in Sales

In the realm of sales, a foundational principle emerges that goes beyond the mere transactional aspects: the price of a product or service isn't always directly tied to its production cost. Instead, it's anchored more deeply in its perceived value to the potential buyer. This concept of "value" is pivotal, and understanding it is essential for every sales professional.

Take, for instance, the construction of a home. The price of a newly built house isn't just a reflection of the raw materials—the lumber, bricks, or tiles—or even the labor that went into its construction. It encompasses the design aesthetics, the ambiance of the neighborhood, the convenience of its location, and the promise of memories to be made within its walls. This is the essence of value.

Another illustrative example is brand-name footwear. A pair of high-end sneakers might cost a fraction of its retail price to produce. However, consumers are often willing to pay a premium for the brand's reputation, the design, the comfort, or even the status associated with wearing them. The sneakers' value isn't just in the materials and labor; it's in the intangible elements that resonate with the buyer.

For a salesperson to effectively convey this value, they must be deeply rooted in the Triad of Belief: a steadfast belief in their industry, their specific product or service, and, most importantly, in themselves. When a salesperson embodies these beliefs, they can adeptly highlight the inherent value of their offering to the customer. And in many cases, this illuminated value can justify a premium price.

Consider a company that offers a premium service tier, guaranteeing round-the-clock customer support. Customers might willingly pay more for this, not necessarily because they anticipate frequent issues, but for the peace of mind that comes with knowing assistance is always at hand. The actual cost to the company for maintaining this service might be minimal, especially if few customers use it. Yet, the perceived value for the customer—the assurance of having a safety net—can warrant the elevated price.

In essence, the art of sales is more than just transactional exchanges. It's about discerning and articulating value, ensuring that customers not only understand but also appreciate the worth of what's being offered. When executed with finesse, this approach doesn't just result in a sale—it builds trust and highlights a salesperson's commitment to understanding and prioritizing the customer's perspective.

Lying & Business Engagement: Navigating Ethical Dilemmas in Sales

Early in my sales career, I faced a seemingly simple yet morally complex question from a customer: "Isn't there any more room on the price?" Though there was room to move, I was torn between the need for profit and the ethical consideration of honesty. This question has continued to leave me reflecting on whether my answer was appropriate.

The Bible's stance on lying is clear, as Ephesians 4:25 instructs, "Therefore, having put away falsehood, let each one of you speak the truth with his neighbor, for we are members one of another." But how does this apply in the nuanced world of sales? In business, negotiations often involve strategic decisions and a certain level of gamesmanship. The question of "more room on the price" is not merely about the numerical value but about perceived value, customer relationships, and overall business strategy.

While my dilemma was relatively minor, there are far more condemnable areas of dishonesty in sales that must be addressed. Making false claims about a product or service, known as false advertising, is a clear violation of ethical principles. It not only damages trust with customers but can lead to legal consequences. Deliberately omitting critical information about a product or service can mislead customers and is tantamount to lying. Transparency is key to maintaining integrity. Using manipulative or coercive tactics to pressure customers into a purchase is unethical and can harm long-term relationships. While promoting a product, it's natural to highlight its best features. However, exaggerating or embellishing the truth crosses the line into dishonesty. Salespeople must be careful to represent their products accurately and honestly.

The challenge for salespeople is to promote their products effectively while maintaining integrity. Clear communication about the product's features, benefits, and limitations builds trust with customers. Emphasizing the genuine value the product offers, rather than exaggerating its capabilities, fosters an honest relationship. Respecting the customer's autonomy and avoiding high-pressure tactics helps maintain ethical boundaries. Reflecting on the teachings of Colossians 3:9, which states, "Do not lie to each other, since you have taken off your old self with its practices," emphasizes the importance of honesty and integrity in all dealings.

Lying and business engagement present a complex interplay of ethical considerations in sales. From the seemingly minor dilemma I faced to more serious breaches of trust, the principles of integrity, empathy, and clear communication must guide salespeople. By adhering to these principles and aligning with the timeless teachings of Jesus and the core values of the IDEAS Sales System, salespeople can navigate these challenges with confidence. They can transform not only their sales approach but their entire professional ethos, recognizing the inherent worth of their products, the importance of profit, and the ethical responsibility to engage with customers honestly and respectfully.

Selling to a Diverse: Universal Principles in Sales

Navigating the intricate realm of sales, professionals often find themselves engaging with a diverse clientele, each distinguished by their unique backgrounds, cultures, belief systems, races, ancestries, and societal statuses. For a Christian salesperson, this presents a multifaceted challenge: How can one effectively sell to such a diverse audience, ensuring that each interaction is respectful and understanding of these differences?

The teachings of Jesus and the apostles consistently emphasize love, respect, and unwavering integrity. One of the most profound teachings from Jesus, the Sermon on the Mount, encapsulates this ethos: "So in everything, do to others what you would have them do to you, for this sums up the Law and the Prophets" (Matthew 7:12). This Golden Rule, revered across many cultures and religions, establishes a foundational ethic for engaging ethically with all, transcending religious, racial, and societal boundaries.

Central to the sales process is the Triad of Belief, which accentuates belief in one's industry, unwavering faith in the company and its offerings, and a deep-rooted belief in oneself. The culmination of this triad is the transfer of this belief to the prospect. This principle resonates harmoniously with the teachings of Jesus and the apostles, underscoring the paramount importance of genuine belief and integrity in every interaction.

The writings of Apostle Paul provide further illumination on this subject. In 1 Corinthians 9:19-23, he articulates, "Though I am free and belong to no one, I have made myself a slave to everyone, to win as many as possible." Paul's methodology was rooted in forging common ground with individuals from diverse backgrounds, all while steadfastly upholding his core beliefs. This approach underscores the importance of understanding and valuing the unique needs, values, and perspectives of each customer, irrespective of their religious, racial, or cultural affiliations.

The Bible also offers glimpses into the interactions of figures like Solomon, renowned for his wisdom. Solomon's extensive trade agreements and interactions with various foreign nations are well-documented. A particularly notable instance is his celebrated encounter with the Queen of Sheba. Their exchange, as described in 1 Kings 10:1-2, was emblematic of mutual respect: "When the queen of Sheba heard about the fame of Solomon and his relationship to the Lord, she came to test Solomon with hard questions. Arriving at Jerusalem with a very great caravan—with camels carrying spices, large quantities of gold, and precious stones—she came to Solomon and talked with him about all that she had on her mind." Their dialogue facilitated the exchange of goods, services, and knowledge. Such interactions, characterized by mutual respect and understanding, serve as timeless examples for salespeople navigating the diverse terrains of their clientele.

In essence, when addressing the challenge of selling to a diverse audience, it's about anchoring oneself in the universal human values that underpin ethical sales. The IDEAS Sales System, with its holistic focus on INTRODUCING, DISCOVERING, EVALUATING, ADAPTING, and SERVING, seamlessly dovetails with these biblical principles and the Triad of Belief. These guiding principles, rooted in respect and understanding, are universally relevant, ensuring that every interaction is both meaningful and respectful.

Navigating Dishonesty in Sales: Biblical Insights

In the dynamic world of sales, professionals often encounter a myriad of challenges. One of the more intricate situations arises when customers employ deceptive tactics during negotiations. How should a salesperson, especially one rooted in Christian values, navigate such murky waters?

The Bible, a foundational source of wisdom and guidance, offers invaluable insights on this topic. Proverbs 26:4 provides a clear directive: "Do not answer a fool according to his folly, or you yourself will be just like him." This verse underscores the importance of not getting entangled in another's deceptive tactics. Jesus further amplifies this sentiment in Matthew 10:16, advising His followers to be "wise as serpents and innocent as doves." This counsel encourages salespeople to approach situations with discernment and wisdom, ensuring they maintain their integrity even when faced with deceit.

For sales professionals, these scriptural insights offer a roadmap. When faced with potential deception, it's essential to remain grounded in one's values, recognizing the situation and choosing not to mirror the deceptive tactics. Instead, wisdom, tact, and sometimes even a graceful exit from the negotiation might be the best course of action.

But what if the deception is more subtle? Should the salesperson address the customer's dishonesty? The Bible does touch upon the importance of Christians holding each other accountable. In Colossians 3:16, Paul writes, "Let the message of Christ dwell among you richly as you teach and admonish one another with all wisdom." This verse suggests that there's value in gentle correction, but it should be done wisely.

Being prepared for such scenarios is crucial. The DISCOVERING phase of the IDEAS Sales System can be particularly helpful here. By asking open-ended questions, a salesperson can encourage the customer to share more, potentially revealing their true intentions or concerns. For instance, if a customer seems to be downplaying the wear and tear on equipment they're trading in, a salesperson might say, "Your equipment seems well-maintained. Given its age, what kind of maintenance or refurbishments do you think it might need before the next owner uses it?" This approach allows the customer an opportunity to be more transparent, avoiding the discomfort of a direct confrontation.

Another scriptural reference that emphasizes the importance of correction within the Christian community is Ephesians 4:15, which encourages believers to "speak the truth in love." This principle can be applied in sales by addressing concerns or inconsistencies in a caring, non-confrontational manner.

Moreover, 2 Timothy 3:16-17 states, "All Scripture is God-breathed and is useful for teaching, rebuking, correcting, and training in righteousness, so that the servant of God may be thoroughly equipped for every good work." This passage reinforces the idea that scripture provides guidance not just for spiritual matters but for everyday challenges, including those in the realm of business and sales.

In conclusion, the world of sales is complex, and professionals will undoubtedly face challenges, including dealing with deceptive tactics. However, by grounding oneself in biblical principles and the IDEAS Sales System, salespeople can navigate these challenges with integrity, wisdom, and grace. The goal is not just to make a sale, but to do so in a manner that aligns with one's values and faith.

From Sales Targets to Sabbath: A Christian's Guide to Work-Life Equilibrium

The sales profession is unique in its demands and challenges. It can be an all-encompassing career that requires a deep emotional investment and often extends into personal time. The reality of sales goals, commission-based pay structures, and the potential financial and professional repercussions of not meeting targets can create immense pressure. This pressure can lead to a work-life imbalance, cutting into family time, damaging relationships, a disconnect from Jesus, and even causing emotional harm to oneself.

The Bible offers wisdom that can guide salespeople in navigating this ethical crossroad. In the pursuit of success, it's essential to recognize the value of relationships, personal well-being, and spiritual health. The Scriptures remind us that "What good will it be for someone to gain the whole world, yet forfeit their soul?" (Matthew 16:26). This profound question challenges us to consider the true cost of success and the importance of maintaining a balanced life.

The IDEAS Sales System, with its emphasis on serving the customer, also calls for a recognition of the importance of serving oneself and one's family. The principles of INTRODUCING, DISCOVERING, EVALUATING, ADAPTING, and SERVING can be applied not only to customer interactions but also to personal life. By evaluating priorities, adapting schedules, and serving the needs of family and self, a salesperson can strive for a harmonious balance.

Recognizing the importance of relationships is vital. Family, friends, and personal well-being should not be sacrificed at the altar of professional success. Building and maintaining healthy relationships is vital for emotional and spiritual health. The Bible emphasizes the importance of loving and caring for one's family and encourages us to bear one another's burdens.

Establishing clear boundaries between work and personal life can help prevent burnout and protect valuable family time. This might include setting specific work hours, limiting work-related activities during family time, and communicating openly with both customers and family about these boundaries.

Understanding what truly matters and making conscious choices to prioritize those values can lead to a more fulfilling and balanced life. This may involve reassessing sales targets, considering the real impact of not meeting certain goals, and weighing that against the potential harm to relationships and personal well-being.

Engaging with mentors, colleagues, coaches or workshops that understand the unique challenges of the Christian sales profession can provide encouragement and accountability. Sharing struggles and seeking wisdom from others can lead to practical solutions and emotional support.

The biblical principle of Sabbath, a time of rest and reflection, offers a model for maintaining balance. Regularly taking time to rest, reflect, and rejuvenate can lead to increased productivity and a healthier perspective on work and life.

Trusting in God's provision can alleviate some of the stress related to sales targets and financial pressures, allowing for a more balanced approach to work and life. The Bible teaches that God provides for our needs, and this trust can guide a balanced approach to the profession.

In conclusion, the ethical crossroad of work-life balance and sales targets is a complex and deeply personal challenge. The principles found in the Bible, along with the IDEAS Sales System, offer guidance and practical solutions. The pursuit of success need not come at the expense of personal well-being and relationships. By embracing a balanced approach, salespeople can find fulfillment in their profession while honoring their responsibilities to themselves and their loved ones.

> **"But seek first his kingdom and his righteousness, and all these things will be given to you as well."**
>
> Matthew 6:33 (NIV)

CHAPTER FIFTEEN

EMBRACING THE IDEAS SALES SYSTEM

RESISTANCE FROM CUSTOMERS: OVERCOMING DOUBTS AND EMBRACING SERVICE

THE WORLD OF SALES is a challenging landscape, marked by the peaks of success and valleys of resistance. Every salesperson, at some point, encounters customers who are hesitant, skeptical, or even outright resistant. This resistance often stems from past experiences with sales representatives who lacked the genuine "sell to serve" mentality. Such encounters can be disheartening, leading many to question their approach and even their career choice.

However, for those who view their profession through the lens of faith, there's a rich reservoir of wisdom and guidance available in the Bible. The scriptures are replete with lessons on facing adversity, standing firm in the face of challenges, and navigating resistance with grace and integrity.

Consider the uphill battle Jesus faced in bringing His product, salvation, to the world. He encountered skepticism, doubt, and even hostility. Yet, He remained unwavering in His mission, driven by genuine love and a desire to serve. This same spirit can guide salespeople in their interactions, helping them see resistance not as a barrier but as an opportunity to demonstrate authenticity and commitment.

The Apostle Paul, in his letter to the Ephesians, provides a vivid metaphor that can be applied to the sales profession. He writes, "Therefore put on the full armor of God, so that when the day of evil comes, you may be able to stand your ground, and after you have done everything, to stand. Stand firm then, with the belt of truth buckled around your waist, with the breastplate of righteousness in place" (Ephesians 6:13-14). This armor, symbolic of truth, righteousness, and faith, can serve as a protective shield for salespeople, enabling them to approach challenges with integrity and honesty.

Similarly, the words spoken to Joshua as he prepared to lead the Israelites resonate with encouragement and assurance. "Have I not commanded you? Be strong and courageous. Do not be afraid; do not be discouraged, for the LORD your God will be with you wherever you go" (Joshua 1:9). This divine assurance is a beacon for salespeople, reminding them that they are not alone in their endeavors. With faith and courage, they can navigate the complexities of their profession.

Paul's exhortation to the Corinthians further underscores this sentiment. "Be on your guard; stand firm in the faith; be courageous; be strong" (1 Corinthians 16:13). This is more than just advice; it's a clarion call to remain vigilant, to uphold one's values, and to face challenges head-on.

The Israelites' exodus from Egypt offers another poignant lesson. Trapped between the Red Sea and the advancing Egyptian army, they were consumed by fear. Yet, Moses, with unwavering faith, declared, "Do not be afraid. Stand firm and you will see the deliverance the LORD will bring you today. The Egyptians you see today you will never see again" (Exodus 14:13). For salespeople, this narrative serves as a powerful reminder that challenges, no matter how daunting, can be overcome with faith and perseverance.

In the face of resistance, it's essential to remember the core principles of the IDEAS Sales System and the Triad of Belief. These principles, rooted in service, empathy, and respect, align perfectly with the teachings of the Bible. By integrating these principles with biblical wisdom, salespeople can transform resistance into opportunities for genuine connection and trust.

In conclusion, the journey of sales, with its myriad challenges, is also a journey of growth, learning, and deepening of faith. The resistance encountered along the way is but a stepping stone, an opportunity to refine one's approach and deepen one's commitment. With the Bible as a guiding light, salespeople can navigate this journey with confidence, integrity, and a heart that truly seeks to serve.

A Journey of Transformation

The world of sales is a complex and multifaceted field, filled with challenges, opportunities, and ethical dilemmas. It's a profession that requires not only skill and strategy but also a deep understanding of human nature, empathy, and integrity. Throughout this book, we have explored the IDEAS Sales System, a method that transcends mere transactional interactions and leads us toward transformative relationships with our customers.

We've delved into the principles of INTRODUCING, DISCOVERING, EVALUATING, ADAPTING, and SERVING, and how they align with the teachings of Jesus Christ, the greatest salesperson ever known. We've examined the Triad of Belief, emphasizing the belief in your industry, your product or service, and yourself, and how this belief can be transferred to your prospects.

We've also navigated the ethical crossroads that salespeople often face, from understanding profit and value to maintaining integrity in the face of deception, from engaging with a diverse clientele to finding a work-life balance that honors both professional responsibilities and personal well-being.

As we draw this journey to a close, it's time to reflect on the profound impact that these principles can have on the sales profession and on our lives. The IDEAS Sales System is not just a method; it's a philosophy, a way of approaching sales that elevates it from a job to a calling, a mission to serve others with the same passion, dedication, and love that Jesus demonstrated throughout His life.

In this concluding chapter, we will summarize the key insights, reflect on the practical applications, and consider the transformative potential of embracing the IDEAS Sales System. It's an invitation to a new way of thinking about sales, a path that leads to success not just in numbers but in lives touched, problems solved, and relationships built. It's a call to a higher standard, a challenge to approach sales with a heart of service, guided by timeless truths that resonate with anyone who seeks to impact the lives of others through their work.

The IDEAS Sales System is a comprehensive approach to sales that transcends mere transactional interactions and focuses on building transformative relationships with customers. It's a method that aligns with timeless principles and ethical considerations, guiding salespeople to approach their profession with integrity, empathy, and a genuine desire to serve. Let's take a moment to summarize each stage of the IDEAS Sales System and highlight the key insights that have been explored throughout this book.

INTRODUCING: Identifying a Customer and Making an Intentional Introduction

The process begins with the intentional act of identifying potential customers and making a thoughtful introduction. This stage is about more than just a first impression; it's about establishing a connection and laying the groundwork for a meaningful relationship. Key insight: The introduction sets the tone for the entire sales process, and a thoughtful, intentional approach can create a foundation of trust and openness.

DISCOVERING: Extreme Active Listening

The DISCOVERY Stage emphasizes the importance of extreme active listening. It's about truly understanding the customer's needs, desires, and concerns. By actively engaging and asking insightful questions, salespeople can uncover the underlying motivations that drive a customer's decisions. Key insight: Active listening is not just about hearing; it's about understanding, empathizing, and connecting on a deeper level.

EVALUATING: Taking Time to Really Understand What the Customer Is Saying

Evaluation is the process of carefully considering what the customer has shared and assessing how the product or service can meet their specific needs. It's a reflective stage that requires critical thinking and a genuine desire to provide value. Key insight: Taking the time to evaluate ensures that the salesperson fully understands the customer's needs and can tailor the presentation accordingly.

ADAPTING: Adapting the Presentation so It Is Most Valuable to the Person

Adaptation is about personalizing the presentation to resonate with the individual customer. It's about recognizing their unique perspective, values, and concerns, and presenting the product or service in a way that speaks to them. Key insight: A one-size-fits-all approach is rarely effective; adapting the presentation creates a more personalized, engaging experience.

SERVING: Selling Is Serving, We Sell to Help the Customer

The final stage, serving, encapsulates the core philosophy of the IDEAS Sales System. Selling is not about persuading or manipulating; it's about serving the customer, providing solutions, and adding value to their lives. Key insight: Approaching sales as an act of service transforms the process from a transaction to a relationship, reflecting a commitment to the well-being and success of the customer.

A Summary of IDEAS

The IDEAS Sales System is a holistic approach that recognizes the complexity and humanity of the sales process. It's grounded in principles that resonate with the teachings of Jesus Christ and the Triad of Belief, emphasizing belief in the industry, the product or service, and oneself. By embracing this method, salespeople can elevate their profession, build meaningful connections, and find true success in the lives they touch and the relationships they build. It's a path that leads to not just sales success but personal growth, ethical engagement, and a fulfilling career.

The Timeless Sales Model

Drawing Wisdom from Jesus' Ministry

In the annals of history, no figure has been as transformative, influential, and enduring as Jesus of Nazareth. While His teachings and miracles have been the subject of theological study and spiritual reflection, there is another dimension to Jesus' ministry that resonates with the world of sales. Jesus, in His role as a communicator, a persuader, and a servant, can be seen as the ultimate salesperson.

Introducing Himself to the Lost

Jesus' mission was to introduce himself, bringing us salvation from the Kingdom of God. His approach was intentional and targeted, identifying those who were ready to hear His message. He began His ministry with a clear call to action: "Repent, for the kingdom of heaven is at hand." (Matthew 4:17, ESV). This was not a casual invitation but a profound proposition that required a response.

The Art of Discovery

Jesus' method of discovery was marked by extreme active listening. He engaged with people from all walks of life, understanding their needs, fears, and desires. When a rich young ruler approached Him with a question about eternal life, Jesus probed deeper, uncovering the man's attachment to wealth (Mark 10:17-22). His ability to discern the underlying issues allowed Him to tailor His message effectively.

Evaluating Needs and Desires

Jesus' ministry was characterized by a deep understanding of human nature. He evaluated the needs and desires of those He encountered, offering solutions that were both spiritual and practical. When He fed the five thousand, He recognized both their physical hunger and their spiritual longing (John 6:1-14). His ability to see beyond the surface set Him apart as a communicator and a healer.

Adapting the Message

Jesus was a master at adapting His message to different audiences. He spoke in parables to convey complex truths in simple terms, such as the Parable of the Sower (Matthew 13:3-9). He challenged the religious leaders with profound insights into the law (Matthew 22:34-40). His ability to adapt His presentation made His message accessible and compelling to diverse audiences.

Serving with Compassion

At the core of Jesus' approach was the principle of serving. He came "not to be served, but to serve, and to give His life as a ransom for many" (Mark 10:45, ESV). His miracles, teachings, and ultimate sacrifice on the cross were all expressions of His commitment to serving humanity. This selfless attitude is a model for salespeople who seek to help their customers genuinely.

Facing Rejection

Even Jesus, the best salesperson ever, faced rejection from those closest to Him, including His family. In His hometown of Nazareth, people dismissed Him, saying, "Is not this the carpenter's son?" (Matthew 13:55, ESV). This rejection extended to the religious authorities of the time, who felt threatened by His teachings. The Pharisees and Sadducees saw Jesus' message as a challenge to their authority, leading them to conspire against Him. Their opposition culminated in a plot that resulted in His arrest, false accusations, and ultimately, His crucifixion.

This profound example of facing rejection, both personal and institutional, serves as a powerful lesson for salespeople. It illustrates that rejection is a part of the process and can be faced with grace and resilience. The rejection Jesus faced did not deter Him from His mission, and His unwavering belief in Himself and His purpose offers a timeless model for those in the sales profession.

A Timeless Model

Jesus' approach to introducing Himself to humanity, discovering people's needs, evaluating their desires, adapting His message, and serving with compassion offers a timeless model for salespeople. His unwavering belief in His mission, His ability to connect with diverse audiences, and His commitment to serving others set Him apart as the ultimate salesperson.

The lessons drawn from Jesus' ministry are not merely historical or theological insights; they are practical principles that can guide modern sales professionals. By aligning with His approach, salespeople can transform their practice, moving beyond transactional interactions to build meaningful, lasting relationships.

In embracing the path laid out by Jesus, the best salesperson ever, whose industry was the Kingdom of God, and whose product was Salvation, salespeople are not only enhancing their skills but aligning themselves with principles that have proven effective across time and cultures. It's a call to a higher standard, a challenge to approach sales with a heart of service, guided by timeless truths that resonate with anyone who seeks to impact the lives of others through their work.

More about Service

Enriching Relationships, Engaging Community, Redefining Success

The concept of service, deeply embedded in the IDEAS Sales System and the teachings of Jesus, is not confined to the realm of sales. It's a philosophy that transcends professional boundaries and becomes a way of life, a guiding principle that can reshape our interactions, relationships, and understanding of success.

A Philosophy for Life

Service is not merely about fulfilling a need or closing a deal; it's about recognizing the inherent value in others and seeking to enhance their lives. This perspective shifts the focus from self-interest to self-giving, from what we gain to what we give. It's a way of living that reflects the true essence of what it means to serve, mirroring the life of Jesus, who demonstrated a life of selfless service.

Transforming Personal Relationships

In personal relationships, a service-first approach fosters empathy, humility, and genuine care. It's about listening more than speaking, understanding more than judging, and giving more than taking. This approach can deepen friendships, strengthen family bonds, and create a sense of community that enriches our lives.

Enhancing Community Engagement

Service extends to our broader community, where it becomes a catalyst for positive change. Volunteering, mentoring, or simply being there for a neighbor in need are manifestations of this philosophy. It's about contributing to the well-being of others, not for recognition or reward but for the intrinsic joy of making a difference.

Aligning with the Triad of Belief

The service-first approach also aligns with the Triad of Belief, emphasizing belief in the industry, the product or service, and oneself. It's about recognizing the potential value in what you offer and being committed to delivering it in a way that honors the dignity and worth of each person you engage with, whether in sales or in life.

Redefining Success

The transformative power of service redefines success. It's not just about numbers, accolades, or material gains. Success becomes about the lives touched, problems solved, and relationships built. It's a success that resonates with our deepest values and provides a sense of purpose and fulfillment that transcends conventional measures.

A Pathway to Transformation

Embracing a service-first approach is a pathway to transformation. It's a call to a higher standard, a challenge to approach all aspects of life with a heart of service, guided by timeless truths. By adopting this philosophy, we not only honor the legacy of Jesus but elevate our lives to a level that goes beyond mere transaction and into the realm of transformation.

In the end, the service-first philosophy is not just a method for sales; it's a blueprint for living. It's an invitation to a life that values others, seeks to give, and finds joy in the act of serving. It's a way of living that can transform not just our professional lives but our personal lives, our communities, and our world.

> **"Each of you should use whatever gift you have received to serve others, as faithful stewards of God's grace in its various forms."**
>
> 1 Peter 4:10 (NIV)

Chapter Sixteen

Embracing Change

A Call To Action

As we draw this journey to a close, I extend to you a heartfelt invitation to embrace the principles and insights laid out in this book. The path we've explored is not merely a set of techniques or strategies for sales success; it's a calling to a higher purpose, a mission to serve others with the same passion, dedication, and love that Jesus demonstrated throughout His life.

Sales, when approached with the mindset of service, becomes more than a profession; it becomes a vocation, a way to impact the lives of others positively. It's an opportunity to reflect the values of empathy, integrity, and selflessness that resonate with the very core of our human experience.

The IDEAS Sales System, the Triad of Belief, and the profound lessons drawn from Jesus' teachings offer a roadmap to a fulfilling and meaningful career in sales. They guide us beyond mere transactional interactions, leading us toward transformative relationships with our customers.

But this transformation begins with you. It begins with a choice to see sales not just as a job but as a calling, a chance to make a difference in the lives of those you serve. It's a commitment to continuous growth, learning, and adaptation, always striving to understand and meet the needs of your customers.

I encourage you to take these principles to heart, to reflect on them, and to apply them in your daily interactions. Let them inspire you to approach your work with renewed vigor, enthusiasm, and a genuine desire to serve.

Remember, the path may be challenging, filled with doubts and obstacles, but the rewards are immeasurable. By embracing this call to action, you not only honor the legacy of Jesus but also elevate your profession to a level that goes beyond mere transaction and into the realm of transformation.

In the words of the Apostle Paul, "Do not conform to the pattern of this world, but be transformed by the renewing of your mind" (Romans 12:2). Let this book be a catalyst for that transformation, guiding you to a deeper, more meaningful approach to sales and life itself.

The choice is yours. The opportunity is before you. Will you answer the call? Will you embrace the mission to sell with a service mindset, to reflect the love, compassion, and integrity that Jesus exemplified? The journey awaits, and the path to success, fulfillment, and a life of service is yours to walk.

> **"Let your light shine before others, that they may see your good deeds and glorify your Father in heaven."**
>
> Matthew 5:16 (NIV)

AFTERWORD

WHERE ARE YOU?

Bridging Faith and Sales: A Response To God's Question

In the beginning, humanity enjoyed a perfect relationship with God, walking with Him in the Garden of Eden. But with the fall of man, that relationship was severed, and a chasm opened between the Creator and His creation. The first question God asked after Adam's disobedience was not one of condemnation but of longing and concern. He called out, "Where are you?" (Genesis 3:9, ESV).

This question, echoing through the ages, is not a question about physical location but a profound expression of God's desire to restore the broken relationship. It's a question that resonates with each one of us, a call to recognize our need for reconciliation and to respond to God's relentless pursuit of our hearts.

One transformative morning, as I was reflecting on the IDEAS Sales System for another book, an epiphany struck me with the force of revelation: Jesus was a salesperson. In that flash of insight, everything suddenly aligned, and I felt a connection between my faith and my profession. More than that, I realized that I had finally heard God's voice calling out to me, asking, "Where are you?"

I have spent my entire adult life immersed in sales, marketing, advertising, and promotions. Like many, I've grappled with the challenge of carrying the "Sunday Morning" version of myself into the world for the rest of the week. But that morning, I felt God's presence in my work, and I understood that He had been looking for me all along, guiding me toward a deeper connection between my faith and my career.

My personal library is filled with books about business and sales by renowned authors. They have shaped my methods of selling, training, and coaching. Yet, nothing tied it all together quite like that moment of clarity, when I realized that the IDEAS Sales System was not just a framework for sales but a reflection of Jesus' approach to service.

This realization brought congruity between who I was on Sunday morning and who I was for the rest of the week. It allowed me to see sales not just as a job but as a calling, a mission to serve others in the way that Jesus served.

Approaching sales with the mindset of Jesus transformed my perspective. Preparing for a sales meeting with the understanding that the customer might be in need of my help, and that my goal was to discover if I could provide that help, changed the entire dynamic of the interaction.

The voice I heard that morning, God's voice asking, "Where are you?" was a call to align my professional life with the principles of faith. It was a call to see sales as a way to honor Jesus, reflecting His love, compassion, and integrity in every interaction.

I hope that this book, and the insights shared within, will lead you to hear God's call in your own life. May you find the congruity between your faith and your profession, and may you become the kind of salesperson that God wants you to be—the kind of salesperson that His Son was.

In embracing this mindset, you not only elevate your career but also answer a higher calling, one that transcends the ordinary and leads to a fulfilling, meaningful life of service.

May this journey inspire you, guide you, and transform you, as it has me. May you hear God's voice, as I did, calling you to a path of love, integrity, and service, and may you answer with a resounding "Here I am."

"Here I am! Send me."

Isaiah 6:8 (ESV)

ABOUT THE AUTHOR

GLEN PAVLOVICH

Glen Pavlovich's journey through the sales world is a tale of transformation and faith; his adaptability and resilience have been the cornerstones of his career.

In the initial stages, Glen admits he was far from the ideal salesperson. Sales were an uphill battle for him. Hindered by inadequate training and a perceived lack of innate skills, he often shied away from customer interactions, fearful of his own shortcomings and convinced he wasn't a natural-born salesperson.

Despite these setbacks, his fervor for sales grew. His initial lack of natural skills drove him to seek knowledge, igniting a passion for the art and psychology of selling. This led to the inception of Closer Classes, his platform to transform the perception of salespeople and address common misconceptions head-on.

This personal experience makes his dedication to uplifting salespeople all the more impactful. He understands the struggles and challenges budding salespeople face, having been in their shoes. This empathy and firsthand experience uniquely position him to guide sales professionals, offering insights that only someone who's walked the path can provide.

Inspired by the maxim of Thomas Watson Sr., "Nothing happens until a sale is made," he stands firm in his belief in the pivotal role salespeople play in the global economy. At Closer Classes, Glen not only challenges the stereotype that salesmanship is innate but also emphasizes the importance of effective training and mentorship. Through resources like Workshops, Mastermind Group Training, One-On-One Sales Training, and Abundance Coaching, he fosters an environment where salespeople can evolve from mere transactional roles to building genuine, enduring relationships with customers.

His journey isn't solely about sales; it's deeply intertwined with his walk of faith. Like many, he grapples with faith, sin, and the challenge of becoming the person he aspires to be. Trusting in God's provision has been a journey of its own. Writing about God and exploring ways to integrate faith into daily life has become a meaningful avenue for him to focus on the restoration of our relationship with God. Through his writings and teachings, Glen hopes to inspire others to find their path, both in sales and in faith.

His personal mantra, which also serves as the Closer Classes tagline, is "The customer is ready to buy. He needs you to help him believe." Glen is more than just a sales trainer; he embodies the belief that with the right guidance, dedication, and faith, anyone can master the art of selling.

> **"I can do all things through him who strengthens me."**
>
> Philippians 4:13 (ESV)

www.ingramcontent.com/pod-product-compliance
Lightning Source LLC
LaVergne TN
LVHW051037080426
835508LV00019B/1574